REBUILDING AMERICA

ALSO BY GAR ALPEROVITZ

Atomic Diplomacy
Cold War Essays
Strategy and Program (with Staughton Lynd)

ALSO BY JEFF FAUX

The Star-Spangled Hustle (with Arthur Blaustein)
New Hope for the Inner City

REBUILDING AMERICA

Gar Alperovitz
& Jeff Faux

PANTHEON BOOKS
New York

Library of Congress Cataloging in Publication Data

Alperovitz, Gar.
   Rebuilding America.

   Includes index.
   1. United States—Economic policy—1981-
I. Faux, Jeff. II. Title.
HC106.8.A42 1983   338.973   83-4206
ISBN 0-394-53200-7
ISBN 0-394-71619-1 (pbk.)

Manufactured in the United States of America

First Edition

G. A.—For Sharon
J. F.—For my parents, Polly and George

Contents

A man has only one life and if during it he has no great environment, no community, he has been irreparably robbed of a human right.

—PAUL GOODMAN,
from *Growing Up Absurd*

Preface

This book is one of many products of ten years of collaboration in which the authors explored alternative ways to manage the American economy. Our enterprise had a number of dimensions. We wrote articles and pamphlets, gave speeches, and testified before Congress. We organized, performed, and published research studies on a wide variety of topics, including the banking system, inflation, cooperatives, small business, natural-resource planning, economic policies in Europe, public enterprise, food production, and the waste of unemployment. We attempted to help a group of citizens and steelworkers in Youngstown, Ohio, rehabilitate a shut-down steel mill. We helped organize a coalition of organizations representing millions of Americans to promote a solution to inflation that did not require massive unemployment. And we became involved in a variety of political campaigns that we hoped would create the space for a more open and responsible national dialogue on America's future.

Some of the efforts can be said to have succeeded; some—relative to our hopes—did not. But all contributed to this book, and the combination of research and action projects established the context for the development of our ideas. Moreover, they all belong to the larger work of building an economy that serves human growth and development, of which this book too is but a part.

Reflecting on these experiences, we concluded that the major problem facing the American political economy was not a lack of detailed proposals but the lack of fit between the way the world actually is and *perceptions* of the way the world is. We concluded that there is no solution to the dilemmas that beset us, e.g., the apparent incompatibility between full employment and price stability, the challenge of foreign competition, the waste of military spending, the tensions between conservation and economic growth, without a recognition of the importance of ideology in American economic life.

To ignore prevailing ideology is to be utopian. But to recognize it does not mean to accept it. This book tries to address a central question: What kind of economic policies meet the needs of the new economic era *while reinforcing certain values—especially community and fairness—essential to support the kind of economic policies we need?* A value-free economics is impossible; and only if we are clear about our values can we make informed decisions about them.

We need to move beyond traditional policies. We have proposed specific economic strategies to address new economic and political problems as well as encourage the process of changing institutions. And since individual behavior is in part a product of institutional environment, such policies will ultimately effect how we—and those who come after us—think and act. Of prime importance is whether we take conscious responsibility for the impact of our economic policies —conservative or liberal—or maintain the illusion that planning ahead is a practical necessity for every element in society but not for society itself.

We have also concluded that the new economic era is already cracking the old ideology of dog-eat-dog individualism. The failure of Reaganomics to deliver on its promises has destroyed the credibility of those who at the beginning of the 1980s were hailing the arrival of a neoconservative millennium. Whatever happens to this or any specific presidency, the historic metamorphosis of the economy toward more explicit economic planning will continue. The emerging debate over industrial policy, which despite the protests of its advocates *is* planning, is only the most recent case in point.

Part I of the book describes how the economic system is breaking down and examines the implications of the disjuncture between an obsolete ideology and the new economic era. Parts II and III propose an integrated series of solutions for the so-called trade-off between full employment and stable prices. Part IV considers some of the institutional and political requirements for democratic planning. Our perspective in each of the areas we address is the dual one of solving the immediate economic crisis in such a way as to contribute to the longer-term task of building a community whose democracy and fairness is reflected at the level of both the nation and the neighborhood. A new stress on locality is an important aspect of this approach. The effort to show how building community ought to and can be a major focus of economic policy is the central theme of this book. We think the absence of community is the central problem of our economy. Only in the context of a community-sustaining economics can the major specific threats to our survival—military, environmental, and political —be dealt with effectively.

Many people have greatly contributed to the ten years of work that informed this book.

David Hunter and Arch Gillies were, throughout, sources of encouragement, organizers of financial support, and partners. We could not have done it without them.

Mary Saville, who specializes in hard work and good cheer, was indispensable in this effort. As was Evelyn Goodavage, who was a patient and efficient administrator. Russell Libby pulled together much of the research and performed an heroic task with the footnotes. Roger Hickey helped in many ways, not the least of which was his continual reminder of the importance of our collective work. David Carley gave particularly significant encouragement and help at a difficult moment.

Others who helped in a major way over the years were Tom Dougherty, Karl Frieden, Bob Lightfoot, Michael Mazerov, Leslie Nulty, Michael Schaaf, and Amy Schectman. We wish we had space to thank individually the many other members of the staff, consultants, and friends who contributed to the effort. For their help in reviewing parts or all of the manuscript, we wish to acknowledge and thank Nancy Barrett, Cushing Dolbeare, Tom Dougherty, Christopher Jencks, Tom Joe, Nick Kotz, Phillip Lee, E. Phillip LeVeen, Harry Magdoff, W. Michael McCabe, Michael F. Mohr, Edward Rothschild, William G. Shepherd, Victor Sidel, Tom Smith, James Stone, and Phillip Webre.

Part of the initial work that went into this book was financed by Guggenheim and Phi Beta Kappa Bicentennial fellowships. We also wish to express our thanks to the many individuals and foundations that gave support to the larger research and action effort out of which this essay grew.

Part I

The ideas of economists and political philosophers, both when they are right and when they are wrong, are more powerful than is commonly understood. . . . Indeed the world is ruled by little else. Practical men, who believe themselves to be quite exempt from any intellectual influence, are usually the slaves of some defunct economist.

—JOHN MAYNARD KEYNES,
The General Theory of Employment,
Interest and Money

INTRODUCTION

If you were to examine the American economy from the outside, without preconceptions, like some economist from outer space, you would be struck first of all by the country's extraordinary natural resources. America produces enough food to feed its own population and to be the earth's largest food exporter. We have the climate, the soil, the thousands of miles of abundant fishing grounds, and the agricultural technology to increase substantially our already abundant food production. You would note that we have more of the raw ingredients necessary for industrial production than any of our major trade competitors. Our coal, natural gas, sunlight, and even oil taken together could make us energy self-sufficient in a few short years. We have the stone, lumber, clay, steel, and other materials necessary to house all our people comfortably and to build all of the stores, factories, schools, hospitals, roads, bridges, water systems, and other structures we will need for as far as we can see into the future.

You would also note our educated work force and a tradition of work. We have a vast network of teachers and schools that can be organized to produce the trained people to support a vigorous economy. We have sufficient military power to protect ourselves, Western Europe, Japan, Israel, and every other ally that has the support of its people, from military attack. Finally, you would see that we are in command of extraordinary new technologies. There would be little doubt in your mind that America possesses the intelligence to develop integrated circuitry, semiconductors, fiber optics, lasers, and other modern technologies to provide an opportunity for every citizen to secure the material basis for a fulfilling and balanced life.

You would also see some 10 to 12 million Americans willing and able to work who do not have a job. You would see the American Dream of owning one's own home disappearing rapidly. You would see millions of Americans not able to afford three square meals a day. You would see pessimism widespread in a country built on optimism and hope. You would examine the polls, a chorus of electronic intro-spection, reporting that Americans feel "things are not going to get any better in the future," that the "rich get richer and the poor get poorer," that a majority of the people feel "alienated and powerless."[1]

You might then turn to the country's leadership—in government, business, organized labor, the universities. And you would hear a cacophony of theories about why the economy isn't performing, few of which seem to be taken very seriously for any sustained period of time. When the Republicans were out of power they claimed that the federal deficit was the cause of all our troubles. But once in office, they tripled the deficit. Then the Democrats—who had invented the deficit as a way of putting people to work—attacked the Republicans for running the government into red ink in the midst of a recession. You would observe that big business had complained that high taxes were stifling their incentive to invest, but when corporate taxes were drasti-cally cut, corporations turned around and bought government bonds and each other's stock with their tax cut money, rather than build new factories. At the universities you would find professors proclaiming that inflation was caused by a high growth in the money supply. When the money supply slowed down and prices kept rising, they pro-claimed that the problem was in the *definition* of the money supply. And when the money supply had been redefined a dozen times, some of these professors said we should abandon paper money and switch to gold. You would find theories piled upon theories —conservative and liberal—declaring that fundamental laws of the universe required that large numbers of people had to be unemployed in order to avoid ruinous inflation.

So you would come upon a contradiction. The country was sup-posed to be a democracy, with ultimate authority in the hands of its citizens. Its citizens seemed to agree that the economy should provide certain minimal things—a useful job for everyone willing and able to work, stable prices for life's necessities, clean air and water, a comforta-ble old age, a stable neighborhood—that were perfectly compatible with the country's resources. Yet the country's leaders and their expert advisors spent their time telling the people that these things were not achievable. They explained that it was not the way the world "worked." Said the chairman of the country's central bank: "The standard of living of the average American has to decline."[2] And politicians, businessmen, professors, and editorial writers nodded their heads at his wisdom.

·   ·   ·

By now it is clear to everyone who can read or watch television that the American economy has entered a new era—one fundamentally different from the first two and a half decades following World War II. The cumulative effect of external shocks and internal breakdowns over the past ten years has replaced the old certainty that America could grow big enough and fast enough to solve not only its own problems but most of the world's as well. The decade of the 1970s produced a list of such shocks and breakdowns that is by now depressingly familiar. They include:

- The worldwide politicization of the oil market, creating dramatic price swings that have destabilized industries, sparked inflation, aggravated recessions, and pushed the world banking system to the brink of disaster.
- A huge military budget (and the inflationary spending of much of that budget in Vietnam) that absorbed huge amounts of the nation's capital and its best brains and technological organizations, while others overtook our supremacy in world commercial markets.
- The transformation of American companies into multinational corporations for whom the United States means little more than any other place on the globe and whose plants can be closed and communities abandoned at the flicker of a digit on a corporate computer terminal.
- An enormous increase in competition from foreign companies, often powerfully assisted by their governments.
- The growth of monopolies and quasimonopolies in markets for commodities, labor, professional services, and finance, each with its network of political alliances and protections.
- The reemergence of massive unemployment as a long-term condition of American life, and as a result the collapse of hope that chronic problems of poverty, race hatred, and sexual inequality can be resolved.
- A government, regardless of party, that appears unable to lead and that regularly treats the public treasury not as a capital to be invested for the public good but as a slush fund for the appeasement of powerful, organized interest groups.

The list goes on and on. Pundits argue and will continue to argue over the precise importance of one or another element, much as historians dispute the exact cause of the Great Depression or the Panic of 1893. But there is little argument that the effect has been to create a level of uncertainty in America unknown since the end of the Depression. Capital hides—avoiding long-term commitments. Labor is testy —fearful and militant at the same time. The public is wary—wanting to believe but trusting no one, choosing and discarding politicians like a cranky child in a toy store.

Especially for those who came to maturity during postwar decades, to be an American and to be uncertain about the economic future is a new experience. We were "number one and growing" for so long that we are tempted to think that the 1970s were an anomaly, a temporary detour from the major highway toward unlimited prosperity. Some "thing" must have gone wrong, some part must have fallen out. We look for a quick-fix repair job. Get the government off our backs. Get rid of welfare cheaters. Lower taxes. Anything to get us back to the seeming economic paradise of the 1950s and 1960s.

There will be no return to paradise. The economic currents of the new era have swept us beyond yesterday's safe moorings. These are new waters. They require not only new sailing strategies but also new theories of economic navigation. The heart of our problem is that the world has changed, but we remain caught in our old ideologies. Our political forums, *the only places for us to solve the problems of the new era,* are taken up with the incessant skirmishing for power between conservatives and liberals, both of whom are repeatedly forced to sell out their principles because they are not useful in addressing the problems of the new economic era.

Since trust in the future is essential for the process of sustained economic growth in any modern industrial economy, the resulting uncertainty is the first challenge we face in rebuilding America. It is not simply a matter of boosterism or patriotism or lack of leadership. The crisis of confidence is rooted in the lack of fit between our economic ideologies and the new economic reality we face.

In a democracy, political institutions cannot act without some set of ideas that explain reality. Yet as Professor George Lodge of the Harvard Business School has pointed out, we Americans like to think of ideology as alien European baggage, from which sensible, practical Americans are free. Indeed, American political tradition holds that the successful politician must portray him or herself as nonideological— just a "problem-solver." This is nonsense. The behavior of even such self-proclaimed pragmatists as American business executives is dominated by deeply held preconceptions about the world. Whether in business, politics, science, or wherever, a "problem-solver" must first define the problem. The decision about which problem to solve is inevitably ideological; it is defined by one's basic views about the world. To be human *is* to hold views, and there is no escape.

Resistance to change in ideology is fierce. Thomas Kuhn in his *Structure of Scientific Revolutions* points out that every scientific paradigm makes a distinction between relevant and irrelevant data. In the modern world, careers are built on mastering data. Paradigms are slower to change than reality itself, because when data become irrelevant, careers are jeopardized. A crisis pervades the professions, both because the prevailing theory cannot solve the puzzles of the new reality and because one's place in a new intellectual hierarchy is suddenly insecure. Perhaps most important, any theory rationalizes someone's present power. To threaten the paradigm is to threaten the power.

To challenge the conservative and liberal paradigms that dominate our ideology does not require us to abandon the values they reflect. The conservative concern with economic freedom and the liberal concern with economic justice remain fundamental perspectives from which we measure our economic performance. There are tensions between these two values, but we have demonstrated in the past that they are reconcilable, and any new approach must accommodate both. Given this reality, a productive American economy without freedom and excitement and risk-taking in the marketplace is not acceptable. A productive America without fairness and equality is not possible.

George Lodge has identified the issue:

> The vital tasks for this society are to recognize the ideological meaning of the changes that have already occurred in the real world; to understand precisely how far we have come from the traditional notions to which we have so ardently adhered; to work toward the formulation of a new, coherent, and generally acceptable ideology to take the place of the old; and to restructure and rearrange our institutions accordingly. This is a revolutionary task, but one that cannot be avoided.[3]

Chapter 2

THE BROKER STATE

America's prevailing political wisdom is that our economic problems are primarily a result of the overbearing weight of the public sector on private business. "We must get the government off our back!" cries Ronald Reagan. And most Democrats have in recent years answered, "Amen!"

There is little argument that the government's role in the economic system expanded after World War II: Starting with the mid-1950s we find that over a twenty-five-year period the importance of the public sector in the U.S. economy (as measured by tax receipts as a percentage of GNP) rose from about 24 percent to 31 percent in 1980. Most of this growth occurred in state and local government, which grew six times faster than the federal government.[1] As government grew, the proportions going for the various purposes shifted. Military spending, for instance, rose in absolute terms in the 1970s but shrank relative to other parts of the federal budget. But the argument against big government has been preoccupied with the non-military side of government —programs such as Social Security, Medicare, low-income housing, aid to education, and so forth. At the end of the Carter administration, military spending rose in relative terms as well, and of course accelerated under Reagan.

Government grows, runs the theory, because people have lost their spirit of self-reliance and want the government to take care of them. Government programs expand because the lazy and shiftless vote in politicians who then tax hardworking producers to provide for the lazy and shiftless.

In democratic societies, it is both politically and intellectually dangerous to blame fundamental flaws on the people themselves. Yet to follow some of the most likely causes for any decline in the work ethic—for example, television, which extols pleasure as the highest virtue—leads eventually to the boardrooms of corporate America, an uncomfortable prospect for conventional minds. So neoconservatism —the ideology that swept into power with Ronald Reagan—has supplied a villain. It is a "new class" of intellectuals and bureaucrats who have lured large numbers of otherwise honest and hardworking Americans down to the welfare office to pick up their checks.

Says ex-Treasury Secretary William Simon in a best-selling book:

[The United States] is now ruled, almost exclusively, by a political-social-intellectual elite that is committed to the belief that government can control our complex marketplace by fiat better than the people can by individual choice and that is ideologically committed to social democracy or democratic socialism.[2]

Says neoconservative guru Irving Kristol:

This "new class" . . . consists of a goodly proportion of these college-educated people whose skills and vocations proliferate in a "post-industrial society" . . . Members of the "new class" do not "control" the media, they *are* the media—just as they *are* our educational system, our public health and welfare system and much else. . . .[3]

The "new class" theory has found a receptive audience among business leaders. David Vogel of the School of Business Administration at the University of California observes, "Not since Herbert Spencer propounded the principles of Social Darwinism at Delmonico's in the late 1800s have American corporate executives proved so receptive to a new social theory."[4] Its acceptance has drawn a large increase in corporate support for conservative ideas through advertising in literary and intellectual magazines, endowing Chairs of Free Enterprise at universities, subsidizing students in Free Enterprise Clubs, and sponsoring a wide variety of corporation-university seminars and conferences.

As Kristol's comment suggests, the "new class" is seen as being motivated by power rather than economics. It is ideologically committed to taxing the wealth made by the "winners" in the marketplace struggle and distributing it to the less successful "losers." Since conservative theory tells us that the marketplace is the sole test of economic efficiency, this means transferring income from the "productive" to the "unproductive"—with appropriate images of welfare mothers on the dole, lazy teenagers ripping off unemployment insurance, bureaucrats who couldn't get a job anywhere else pulling down fat salaries in the government, etc.

The point is elaborated by a number of neoconservative writers.

Jude Wanniski tells us that high taxes are responsible for just about every calamity in the history of mankind, including pornography, Soviet collective farms, the decline of Rome, and World War II. George Gilder, who wrote *Wealth and Poverty*, which Jack Kemp and David Stockman claim is the most comprehensive argument for the supply-side ideology, maintains that America's economic problems stem from the new class's "war against wealth." Gilder, a protégé of David Rockefeller and author of several books attacking feminism, provides a fascinating glimpse into the protection of class privilege and male supremacy that ties together some of the disparate elements in the Reagan coalition.[5] According to Gilder, the basic weapon in the war on wealth—which also motivated the Nazis' extermination of Jews and the slaughter of the Ibo tribes in Nigeria—is the tax system, which undermines the incentives of rich people to invest in productive enterprises. Compounding the problem are welfare programs for the poor and antidiscrimination laws, both of which undermine the masculinity of young, poor, and minority men. Since not only economic growth but also all of civilized society depend on "male confidence and authority, which determines sexual potency, respect from the wife and children, and motivation to face the tedium and frustration of daily labor," the result is economic and moral decay.[6]

Leaving aside Gilder's preoccupation with the sexual, there is a grain of truth to the neoconservative theory. There *are* kids who don't want to work. There *are* welfare chiselers. There *are* lazy bureaucrats who are overpaid. There *are* intellectuals who want power. And there has certainly developed over the past three decades an expanded class of managers to run our expanded government. But as a description of the rise of the public sector in modern capitalism, the convenient "new class conspiracy" explanation is not plausible.

First, despite forty years of growing government, there is little evidence of a serious effort by the bureaucratic class to change the conservative public ideology of the American people. In fact, denouncing government is the single most popular theme in American politics. Republicans *and* Democrats, incumbents *and* challengers, conservatives *and* liberals, from Town Hall to the White House, regularly fill the political debate with pictures of a government that is incompetent, arrogant, and—most of all—a tax parasite draining the substance of hardworking workers and businesspeople.

Second, it is observable that the seats of power in America—the Pentagon, the congressional committees, the Presidency and Cabinet, the State Houses, the boards of major corporations, and the large labor unions—contain a relatively small percentage of people who would qualify as members of a new intellectual-liberal class. Universities, of course, and to a lesser degree the media, do harbor intellectuals, many of whom are liberal. It is probably no accident that the proponents of the new class theory tend to be neoconservative professors . . . in liberal universities. But in Washington, business interests typically dominate economic decision-making.

Most important, the theory that the growth of government represents a war on wealth flies in the face of the fact that the distribution of income and wealth in America has remained substantially unchanged for thirty-five years. Unemployment compensation, Social Security, and other income-transfer programs have put a floor under the lives of most Americans who work for a living. But these programs have decidedly *not* resulted in a redistribution of income and wealth in America. In 1947, the poorest 20 percent of American families received 5 percent of the nation's income; in 1982, they received 4.7 percent. On the other end of the scale, the nation's richest 20 percent received 43 percent of the income in 1947 and 42.7 in 1982. From 1949 to 1972, the latest year available, the percentage of wealth owned by the wealthiest *1* percent of the population dropped a statistically insignificant .1 percent, to 20.7 percent.[7] With the exception of France, the United States has the most unequal distribution of income among developed nations.[8] At best, three decades of government expansion have managed to keep the distribution of income and wealth stable— hardly much of an accomplishment for a sinister and powerful new class.

A more commonsense political explanation of government expansion might begin with the simple observation that with few exceptions people are against spending for everyone else's program but *theirs*. Polls, for example, consistently report that although people are against government spending in general, they tend to favor the specific programs that make up the bulk of government spending and that they see as benefiting *them*. Writing in *Fortune* magazine, poll expert Professor Everett C. Ladd summarized the contradictions: "The people are enraged over big government and their tax burden—and they want a lot more of the services they think government should provide." While 82 percent of Americans feel the federal government is "spending too much," 90 percent feel that there is not enough spending on improving and protecting the environment; 93 percent want more spending on improving national health; 89 percent want more spending to improve the nation's educational system; 78 percent feel that there should be more aid for big cities; 73 percent think more should be done to improve the conditions of black Americans. In addition, large majorities support wage-price controls (61–39 percent), national health insurance (67–33 percent), and the notion of government-guaranteed jobs (77–23 percent). Only in the area of welfare do a majority support cuts, and according to Ladd, only because "welfare" connotes an unwillingness to work. Other polls have reinforced this. When the question, "Do you support government aid for the 'needy'?" is asked, a majority answer "Yes."[9]

Political scientists Lloyd Free and Hadley Cantril conclude that the evidence reveals a personal and collective conflict in the American psyche between what they call "ideological" attitudes and "operational" ones.[10] Ideologically, Americans seem to believe in the principles of an eighteenth-century agrarian society of small, independent farms and businesses, an economy regulated by the self-correcting laws of the marketplace tempered by an assumed spirit of community and goodwill. There also are genuine populist elements in their distrust of centralized power and their support for decision-making close to home. Those who cannot compete in the market—the handicapped, the unlucky—are helped by the charity of their neighbors. The essential need for government is for protection from the outside—military attack and pestilence—and to keep the civil peace. "Operationally," however, Americans live in the twentieth century. They favor the whole panoply of modern government services and interventions that make their lives better and more comfortable—from Social Security to consumer protection. They don't think that the market "self-corrects" for adulterated food or water pollution, and they would rather have their old-age security a matter of right than depend on their children's luck in the marketplace or the charity of their neighbors. A major part of the growth of government is thus the result of democratic decision, pure and simple.

Nowhere is the contrast between the ideological and the operational views of government action more vivid than in the timeworn spectacle of conservative businessmen who rail against big-government handouts beating a path to Washington to be first at the trough for their own juicy subsidies. It is such a common sight that even the most fervent boosters of capitalism are forced into painful acknowledgment of the crude hypocrisy. Dr. Richard Landry, an economist for the U.S. Chamber of Commerce, for instance, told *The New York Times* that "the Chamber is a cathedral where we support our principles. One of those principles is the freest possible amount of competition in a free market." Yet he admitted that the Chamber does not take positions on individual subsidies because its members have vested interests in many of them. "I would not wish to particularize, it gets us into membership problems," he explained.[11]

The stark contrast between this reality and the public-relations rhetoric of the free market troubles even William Simon, whose heart and tongue blaze with passion for economic competition. In his book *A Time for Truth,* he says:

> During my tenure at Treasury I watched with incredulity as businessmen ran to the government in every crisis, whining for handouts or protection from the very competition that has made this system so productive. I saw Texas ranchers, hit by drought, demanding government-guaranteed loans; giant milk cooperatives lobbying for higher price supports; major airlines fighting deregulation to preserve their monopoly status; giant companies like Lockheed seeking federal assistance to rescue them from sheer inefficiency; bankers, like David Rockefeller, demanding government bailouts to protect them from their ill-conceived investments; network executives, like William Paley of CBS, fighting to preserve regulatory restrictions and to block the emergence of competitive cable and pay TV. And always, such gentlemen proclaimed their devotion to free enterprise and their opposition to the arbitrary intervention into our economic life by the state. Except, of course, for their own case, which was always unique and which we justified by their immense concern for the public interest. . . .[12]
>
> This practice totally destroys their credibility as spokesmen for a principled cause.[13]

If we take his statement at face value, Simon's "incredulity" makes him the most naïve Treasury Secretary in history. It is hard to imagine any reasonably intelligent businessman being "incredulous" at the effort of the businessmen to use government—or anything else—to further their own profits and growth. People are not in business for the abstract purpose of competing in free markets. As Simon's own Social Darwinist philosophy asserts, people are in business to make money and to secure their own status and power. Thus they will take advantage of every opportunity; whether from a government subsidy, a tax credit, or a sale in the marketplace, a dollar is a dollar. Simon's entire book is a paean to a social theory that maximum public good comes from permitting everyone to attempt to satisfy private greed. Exhorting businessmen to forgo their own interests in favor of a "principled cause" that holds that above all, businesspeople should not under any circumstances forgo their own interests, makes psychological hash out of neoconservatism.

The cardinal rule of business is, in the phrase immortalized by bank robber Willie Sutton, "to go where the money is." And increasingly, the money is in government, an arrangement generated in large part by big business itself. Moreover, despite their reverence for the free market, businesspeople have, since the beginning, used government power to further commercial interests. The history of nineteenth-century government in America is as much as anything a chronicle of government building canals and highways, subsidizing railroads, selling public lands, investing in banks, and so forth, to further this or that commercial interest. Like farmland, timber, gold, and other natural resources, the government has always been there to be mined by the aggressive entrepreneur. Herman E. Krooss, professor at the Graduate School of Business Administration, New York University, comments:

> Laissez-faire never existed in the United States despite the widely held illusion to the contrary. American governments on one level or another have always intervened in the economy. . . .
>
> Whether on the federal or local level, it was clear that in the general give-and-take of political economy, business, or more accurately, groups of businessmen were first in the business-government enterprise. This was what an interested or disinterested observer would have expected, for to quote Adam Smith, "Civil government is established by property owners to safeguard their property; property and birth give those who benefit from both the major sway in the operations of government."[14]

The point is not that businesspeople are greedier for public dollars than the elderly, the disabled, or the poor, but that the mythology of private enterprise tends to dismiss their dependence on government as marginal or aberrant, when in fact it is a major, ongoing element of the business system.

Still, for most of our history except for wartime, the size of government remained small. When the Great Depression hit in 1929, the federal government's share of the economy was a little more than 3 percent.[15] The Keynesian idea that government spending is necessary to stabilize the business cycle widened everyone's horizons about what government could do. Bureaucrats in the 1960s and 1970s were *inherently* no more interested in bigger staffs and larger budgets than the bureaucrats of the 1920s. Businessmen were no greedier for tax and other government benefits than they were fifty years before. Farmers did not *want* any more protection from falling farm prices in the 1970s than they did in the 1920s. What changed was the dominant set of ideas —the prevailing ideology.

Much of government spending was, and is, a sensible response to the growing problems of an interdependent and urban society. As Americans moved from the security of a small town or extended family to an atomistic, mobile, and consumer-oriented life-style, they required more public services. And there was no intrinsic reason why a prosperous society could not provide them. Home mortgage assistance, the War on Poverty, highway building, urban renewal, aid to education, environmental protection, and Medicare met with the approval of the overwhelming majority of the population when they were proposed. In each case, specific interest groups also benefited. But the general environment for government expansion—the *big* postwar change— was the result of a sensible if implicit agreement by the nation's business, government, and labor leaders that government must spend money *both* to solve specific problems *and* to avoid another depression. At the heart of the postwar social contract was the Keynesian pump,* whose fiscal flows these and other groups could claim for themselves. Since the idea was accepted that the government had to spend anyway, why not spend it on them?

THE BROKER STATE

Even before Reagan's massive tax giveaways to the wealthy and the corporations, the social contract had resulted not so much in a traditional "welfare state" as in a "broker state"—a term coined in the 1940s by conservative columnist John Chamberlain to describe a more haphazard arrangement in which spending programs are awarded to those groups that develop sufficient political clout to get a favored space at the Keynesian spigot. The postwar political battleground in America has not been some pure titanic struggle between the nation's haves and have-nots (although it has prevented the distribution of income and wealth from becoming more unequal); the battle is more like a free-for-all between a growing number of organized constituencies and shifting interest groups.[16]

Ronald Reagan, for instance, followed the established tradition of the broker state in heaping more public dollars on the military and its corporate allies. The military budget already dwarfed most other programs of the federal government. By 1981, over $2 trillion of citizen tax monies had been spent on military and related activities since the start of 1946—a sum exceeding the value of *all* the residential structures in the United States. Payments for past, current, and future military operations equaled almost half the 1980 "federal funds" bud-

*See Chapter Three, pp. 30–33.

get (the budget over which the President and Congress have direct discretion but that excludes permanent, self-financing trust funds such as Social Security and unemployment compensation). The budget for U.S. military agencies in fiscal year 1980 alone—$157 billion—was greater than the Gross National Product in all but eleven other countries of the world. And by 1984 the military budget was $245 billion.[17]

The broker state partnership between government and business in the military industries is carefully protected by a network of subsidies, uncompetitive practices, and special economic arrangements. More than 50 percent of all defense procurement is negotiated with an exclusive single contractor; less than 12 percent goes through a formal advertised competition. According to one little-known but often-used law passed during the Cold War in the 1950s, the Department of Defense is empowered to declare firms on the edge of bankruptcy "essential to the national defense" and provide them with overgenerous contracts and outright cash grants. From 1958 to 1980, this law was invoked 5,644 times.[18] But this is only the icing on the cake. Almost every category of military spending not directly paid out to servicepeople subsidizes a commercial interest. When the revolutionary government of Iran canceled its purchases of undelivered arms in 1979, the military budget was used to compensate private arms suppliers with hundreds of millions of dollars in termination payments. Many large contractors have been spared the necessity of capital investment. For example, LTV Aerospace, one of America's largest military manufacturers, at one point owned only 1 percent of the 6.7 million square feet of offices, plants, and laboratories it used; the rest was leased from the Department of Defense.[19] The typical defense contractor is little more than a very high-priced manager; it takes few risks and enjoys the large rewards for the government's organizing effort.

Whole industries have been built on the broad back of the war economy. During World War II, the U.S. government built 50 aluminum mills that it sold off to the private sector after the war, in the process creating the huge aluminum empires of the Kaiser and Reynolds corporations. It built fifty-one synthetic rubber plants at a government cost of $700 million, which it sold to the wartime operating companies without competitive bidding at prices less than 50 percent of the original government investment. By the end of 1946, 70 percent of disposed government plants were held by the country's 250 largest corporations. The top three steel firms—U.S. Steel, Bethlehem, and Republic—profited the most. For example, the Geneva Steel Mill, which cost $202.4 million of tax monies to build, was sold to U.S. Steel

for only $47.5 million. This pattern of government subsidy and invest-
ment, representing two thirds of all additions to the nation's industrial
capacity between 1938 and 1945, was instrumental in setting the stage
for American domination of world markets during the boom years.[20]

The nurturing of the defense industry has gone so far that the
Pentagon finances military contractors to tell it what it needs to have
and then, of course, to be first in line to sell the product. For example,
through the Pentagon's Independent Research and Development
(IR&D) and Bid and Proposal (B&P) programs, defense contractors
are reimbursed to the tune of over a billion dollars per year for military-
related research and development projects undertaken *on their own
initiative.* These are projects neither authorized nor directly reviewed
by Congress. Political scientist Gordon Adams and journalist Christopher Paine report that military contractors "in their efforts to get an
inside track on new military business, routinely peddle the results of
their IR&D programs to the military officials in charge of identifying
new military 'requirements,' and succeed in inducing them to invent
a requirement to fit a new weapon instead of the other way around."[21]

The pressure for more defense spending is largely concerned with
the purchase of new, more sophisticated and exotic military equipment
because this is where the big money is. At the same time, existing
military operational capabilities have been eroding for years because of
long-term neglect of spending for maintenance, symbolized by the
fatal breakdown of the helicopters in the Iranian hostage escape attempt. Equipment is in disrepair, aircraft are grounded, maintenance
crews are inadequately trained, taxiways are crumbling, and at one
Strategic Air Command base the hangars are uninsulated and "so cold
in winter that mechanics must repair America's most advanced strategic weapons with numbed hands."[22]

The commander of the Atlantic Fleet Naval Air Force admitted that
47 percent of its first-line F-14 fighters were not certified to fly peacetime missions because they were awaiting repairs. Even the head of the
Joint Chiefs of Staff had complained that there is no "constituency"
for maintenance programs.[23] The military lobbyists of Lockheed, General Dynamics, and similar firms have little interest in Congress appro-
priating more money for decent salaries for enlisted people, training
repair technicians, or ordering spare parts for the exotic equipment
they make.

"A culture of procurement has been created in the Pentagon," says
reporter James Fallows, "that draws the military toward new weapons
because of their great cost, not in spite of it. . . ."[24] Fallows describes
the massive "gold plating" of the new generation of ultrasophisticated

weaponry, which cannot perform without a huge support system of sensitive, air-conditioned computers that themselves need complex and extensive support systems. Such weapons are designed for maximum performance under ideal peacetime conditions but are sitting ducks in the exigencies of war. In this "market," costs rise at 30 and 40 percent per year as contractors design weapons systems, lobby Congress for appropriations, and then pile overrun on top of overrun to the point where the military ends up with fewer weapons than it needs because it simply can't afford their price tag.

The effect of the military industry on the spirit and purpose of the armed forces has been devastating—a lesson exposed but not learned in Vietnam. An increasingly important path to career advancement among Pentagon officers is to manage contractors. Literally thousands of senior officers (generals, admirals, colonels, and Navy captains) now represent procurement contractors with their old military comrades. Says the director of one U.S. Naval Weapons Center, a veteran of nineteen years in the system:

> If a retired general representing a client goes in to see an old classmate still on active duty, he will get a very attentive hearing. The officers on active duty are also thinking ahead. Fighting the system gets one blackballed, and then future employment prospects are bleak. In this way the industry has come to control DOD even more than its political appointees. This control is acquired with relatively little money and, to add insult to injury, the industry uses government money to get control of the government.[25]

Richard Nixon's then Treasury Secretary John Connally, discussing the Lockheed loan in 1971, said: "What do we care if they perform? We are guaranteeing them basically a $250 million loan. What for? ... So they can provide employment for 31,000 people throughout the country at a time when we desperately need that type of employment."[26]

The other major element in Reagan's program, the "tax cut," was also within the established interest-group jockeying of broker state politics. Actually, the phrase "tax cut" is a misnomer. By cutting the taxes of certain taxpayers and not others, Reagan's program increased the real net income of some people and decreased the income of others. For example, according to his Council of Economic Advisors, Reagan's initial cuts created an effective tax rate on new depreciable assets of 21 percent in electric utility and food industries, and *minus* 11 and *minus* 3 percent in autos and mining.[27]

This type of "tax expenditure" has been a favorite way to spend money for the last decade and a half. The tax expenditure budget, *not including the Reagan tax program,* rose to almost $200 billion in 1981, 40 percent faster than *direct* federal outlays. Some of the largest tax expenditures over the fifteen-year period were through the lowered tax rates on capital gains and property tax deductions, of which the wealthiest 12 percent of the population received, respectively, 92 and 62 percent of the benefits.[28]

For the corporate and upper-income clients of the broker state, there are many dimensions to the beauty of tax expenditures. First, because they are seen as a tax *decrease* for someone, they do not generate the political resistance that a direct spending program would, even though they might cost the taxpayers the same amount of money. For example, the tax benefits to Chrysler by virtue of its being an automobile company outweigh the value of the special loan guarantee it received from the government in 1980. Because the latter was a direct "expenditure," however, it was much more visible and therefore subject to widespread criticism.[29] Second, once enacted, tax expenditures do not have to be reauthorized or reviewed, and neither does money have to be reappropriated; funds simply continue to flow out to the favored group through the Treasury's "back door." Third, by their very nature, the value of tax deductions and credits is usually directly related to the beneficiary's income; the richer and bigger the beneficiary, the greater the tax expenditure. Finally, being hidden and permanent, they leave the beneficiary free to indulge in hypocritical opposition to other people's more visible subsidy. In 1978 Senator Russell Long, then chairman of the Senate Finance Committee and one of the chief architects of the tax-expenditure welfare program, made no bones about it: "I've always known that what we are doing is giving government money away," he says. It is the perfect handout.[30]

The hidden character of the tax expenditure system in broker state politics was revealed in a study of the hearings and floor debates on tax bills considered by Congress between 1971 and 1976. During this period, Congress approved $161 billion in tax expenditures *without a single public vote either in committee or on the floor of the House and Senate.* Of the total of eighty-six different tax-expenditure programs, thirty-six went through the Senate Finance Committee and twenty-five through the House Ways and Means Committee without a single witness appearing.[31]

Tax expenditures come in all shapes and sizes, and almost every income level gets something. There are tax credits for low-income people who need day care for their children in order to work, home mortgage interest deductions for middle-class homeowners, and special treatment of capital gains for the wealthy. But over the past decade and a half, the major beneficiaries of tax expenditures have been large corporations. Lobbyists for timber, oil, steel, auto, chemical, banking, agribusiness, and a long, exhausting list of other industries have steadily sliced away at their tax liabilities under both Democratic and Republican administrations, supported by both parties in Congress. As a result, the effective tax rate on large corporations dropped rapidly throughout the 1970s,[32] and it became common for large companies to escape paying income taxes altogether. A study of corporate income-tax returns showed that even before the Reagan tax cuts, such giants as Chase Manhattan, Squibb, and Monsanto paid no federal income taxes in 1980 despite domestic earnings totaling almost $500 million. Exxon paid 1.3 percent on domestic earnings of $2.5 billion, Bank of America paid 3.1 percent on $1 billion, and AT&T paid 8 percent on $7.7 billion. The study noted that the nation's largest ten banks paid 2.2 percent of their income in federal income taxes that year, while a typical couple earning $20,000 and with two children paid about 10 percent.[33]

The 1982 tax revisions forced on the President by a Congress feeling the heat from outraged constituents closed some of the most egregious loopholes that had been opened the year before. But the U.S. Tax Code remains a major source of benefits for those with the power and influence to participate in the broker state. Tax expenditures in the 1984 budget were estimated to total $388.4 billion.[34]

Beneficiaries of special features in the federal budget include America's most venerable industries—steelmakers and automakers, dairy farmers and wheat growers, sugar planters and tobacco companies, shipbuilders and papermakers, highway builders and home builders, chemical producers and airlines. With the rhetorical protection of laissez-faire and aided by a frightened labor movement, they have pressured the government for more and more subsidies as the new era squeezes their markets. When the dust settled on the first years of the Reagan revolution, it was possible to assess the overall impact of its assault on at least one key measure of "big government." The federal budget had amounted to 22.4 percent of the GNP in 1980 when the Republicans took office; in 1982, it was 24.6 percent, and by late 1983 it was growing higher.[35] Those who gained and lost had altered as spending on social programs went down and the military budget went up. Much had been written about the indifference and elitism of the Reagan program. But a larger point had been lost: The basic financial power of the broker state in the American economy had not changed.

METAMORPHOSIS

It is not surprising that American corporations would make a special effort to gain more tax subsidies for themselves, to bolster the parts of the military budget they have a stake in, or to transfer the burden of taxation onto consumers and workers in the face of a slowdown in growth and profit expectations. And it is not surprising that both major parties are instruments of these corporate strategies. But the assault on the public sector has not stopped there. Reducing taxes on profits is irrelevant if there are no profits. The broker state has had to come to the direct aid of a growing number of corporations and industries whose failure threatens to destabilize the whole financial system.

It began with the Penn Central Railroad. Having been milked of revenue by the parent holding company, which shifted investments from railroads to real estate, hotels, pipelines, and amusement parks, the railroad faced bankruptcy in 1970. The company chairman went to the Nixon administration for help. Attorney General John Mitchell, who had previously worked for Penn Central's law firm (as had Richard Nixon), and Under Secretary of the Treasury Paul Volcker (who had previously worked for Chase Manhattan, the second largest Penn Central creditor), arranged a $200 million loan under the Defense Production Act. But a Democratic Congress had to be persuaded, and before the lobbyists could get their work done, the company declared bankruptcy. Wall Street Republicans were not so concerned with the plight of the railroad as they were with the plight of the railroad's creditors. So the government came to *their* rescue, providing nearly $150 million in direct grants and $100 million in loan guarantees. In order to get political support the Republicans had to agree to save the railroads in the Northeast Corridor, so it set up Amtrak to buy out Penn Central's unprofitable passenger trains. In the words of historian Robert Sobel:

> What the assassination of Franz Ferdinand was to World War I and the stock market collapse of October 1929 was to the Great Depression, the bankruptcy of the Penn Central may prove to be for the accelerating evolution of American capitalism in the last quarter of the century.[36]

Lockheed Aircraft was next. Sloppy management led to massive cost overruns on military contracts that were generous in the first place. By

1971, the company was $400 million in debt to a consortium of twenty-four banks, and it needed another $250 million to meet its commitments to complete the L-1011 Tristar project. The banks agreed to provide the extra money on the condition that the government guarantee the loans. The loan was too risky for the private sector.

Having learned from the Penn Central experience, the Nixon administration moved quickly. Lockheed's bankers and its workers' unions trooped to Capitol Hill and persuaded Congress that a loan to Lockheed was in the public interest. Before the Senate Banking Committee, Treasury Secretary John Connally showed the new face of free enterprise:

> I think, as a matter of fact, that we have a pretty regulated society. We sometimes kid ourselves it is a free enterprise system but it is not all that free. . . . I am not sure that some of our corporations have now reached a size in volume of business that at least defies the ability of the traditional lending institutions to meet their demands.[37]

Connally later publicized the idea of a "new partnership," which gave the public sector the job of risk-taking and the private sector the job of profit-taking. And in the Lockheed case, it worked. In large part because the military contracts kept coming, the company was able to pay back the loan by 1977.

Then the bankers' own turn came. Franklin National Bank, the twentieth-largest bank in America, with total deposits of almost $4 billion, began to run up heavy losses from speculation in foreign currency. Most deposits by individuals were, of course, insured by the federal government, but the bankers in charge of the Treasury Department and the Federal Reserve Board responded to the plight of one of their own, pouring in $1.75 billion to support Franklin National. When the dust had cleared, four of the bank's officers were convicted of illegal financial practices during their tenure at the bank, and several were sentenced to jail.[38]

The chairman of the Federal Reserve at the time was Arthur Burns, another conservative Republican champion of an unfettered, free market. Again, reality ruled the day. Burns and the Federal Reserve acted "responsibly" in bailing out the Franklin National; its collapse would have set off frantic waves of liquidation throughout the country's vast and intricate financial network. Given the additional debt burdens of the new era, the shaky international position of the dollar, and the general nervousness of the population, Burns had to concern himself with the psychological health of the financial marketplace.

In assuming such responsibility, of course, Burns, the conservative Republican, fused together another spot along the increasingly hard-to-define seam between the public and the private sectors. By establishing that the Federal Reserve was ready to go to the rescue of the financial community in a large-scale crisis of "confidence," Burns served notice that if the game was played for high enough stakes, banks and financiers could avoid the ultimate discipline of the market. Burns set the precedent. Soon federal government bailout of banks became almost routine. In 1980, the First Pennsylvania Bank nearly collapsed as a result of bond speculation losses and received $1.3 billion in aid organized by the federal government, which also provided $1.3 billion in aid to twenty-five savings and loan associations with hardly a ripple of public notice.[39]

That same year, the Federal Reserve commitment to soothing "sentiment" in financial markets was extended to helping bail out notorious high-rolling speculators such as the Hunt brothers. "Bucky" and Herbert Hunt—sons of the legendary oil billionaire H. L. Hunt—attempted to corner the silver market in the winter of 1979–80 by buying up silver contracts and then forcing up the prices. But they ran into cash-flow problems, and in March 1980 they had to refuse to take delivery on a contract for nineteen million ounces of silver. The potential loss to the brothers, who at the time held contracts for sixty million ounces, was over $1 billion.[40]

Despite the fact that they still had $8 to $9 billion in other assets to cover the silver escapade, the Hunts went to Penn Central's old friend, Paul Volcker, who was now Federal Reserve Board chairman, for a bailout loan. In late-night negotiating, Volcker, who was said to be in pajamas, agreed to support a $1.1 billion loan. It came in the midst of a national credit crunch that sent interest rates above 20 percent. Shortly before the Hunt deal, in responding to congressional criticism that high interest rates were denying funds for home mortgages and small businesses, the Federal Reserve Board piously admonished: "Banks should avoid loan activity that supports speculative activity in gold, commodity, and foreign exchange markets." Volcker denied the loan to the Hunts was for speculation; it was "to protect more securely the interests of existing Hunt silver creditors, bank and nonbank." The distinction between lending money to speculators and lending money to cover the speculators' debts seemed more metaphysical than economic. The fact was that while hundreds of thousands of small businesses were being denied access to credit on the grounds that the economy had to be made more efficient, the Federal Reserve was going out of its way to reward the most destructive and economically de-stabilizing use of the banking system funds. Both Burns and Volcker, of course, continued to denounce federal government spending on food stamps, housing, and health care as destroyers of capitalism's moral fiber.

Then came Chrysler. The company's managers overextended them-selves in foreign markets, draining the corporation of capital for badly needed modernization of their domestic plant. And they continued to concentrate on the production of fuel-guzzling big cars when all the evidence was pointing to higher prices for gasoline. Other auto com-pany managements had made colossal mistakes in the past—for exam-ple, Ford's Edsel—but in a strong and growing market for high-profit big cars, such mistakes were not fatal. The market of the new era is not so forgiving. In 1979, Chrysler lost over $1 billion. Cash-short, debt-ridden, and without access to credit for retooling, the Chrysler executives made their trek to the U.S. Treasury led by the board chairman, Lee Iacocca. For years as a Ford Motor Company vice-president, Iacocca had been a champion of unfettered laissez-faire, passionately denouncing government safety and fuel-efficiency regula-tions in the auto industry. He was described by one reporter as the "lead tenor in a decade of whining" about government regulation. Now this same Iacocca demanded of this same government $1.2 billion in loan guarantees. He was supported by a high-powered lobbying effort that included the United Auto Workers, Detroit Mayor Cole-man Young, and nearly the entire Michigan congressional delegation. Even Thomas Murphy, the chairman of General Motors, joined. "If it were necessary for the federal government to become involved," Murphy conceded, "if it were black and white, if that were the only answer, that Chrysler otherwise could not continue . . . I guess I would have to say 'sure.' "[41] That the head of one company would agree to special government subsidies to a competitor "if it were necessary" for the competitor to continue tells us a great deal about the nature of modern "free enterprise."

Chrysler got the money. The last installment on the loan was per-sonally approved by Ronald Reagan.

The steel industry is another example of the growing fusion of public and private sectors. Characterized by obsolescence, declining productivity, poor labor-management relations, high labor costs, and a notoriously arrogant management, American steel companies have ceased to be competitive in most of the world's markets, and in much of the American market as well. The reaction of steel management and labor has been to demand both subsidies and tariff protection. The industry mobilized public officials and civic leaders from more than sixty cities around the nation into a Steel Communities Coalition to lobby Washington. The campaign was effective. It resulted in several hundred million dollars in loan guarantees for steel investment; U.S. government pressure on the Japanese and others to reduce steel imports; and a new credit gimmick in Ronald Reagan's tax package, which burst through the limits of conventional broker-state tax spending and resulted in government checks being sent to unprofitable steel companies, which then bought new equipment. As the price of passage, the tax credits were made available to every industry, opening up a new, massive loophole in the already riddled tax code. A negative income tax for corporate America.

Despite the obvious contradiction with conservative principles, the Reagan administration also extended other protection to big business. For example, in direct opposition to free-trade ideology, political pressure was put on Japan to reduce exports of autos to the United States; and new legislation was introduced to permit the President to reduce imports if other nations proved intractable in negotiations. In 1983 the Reagan administration banned imports of foreign motorcycles. As we shall see, it heaped $21 billion in subsidies on the farm industry. The protection of U.S. business interests also had a higher priority than even the holy war against communism. When the Polish government, after its brutal suppression of the trade union Solidarity and imposition of martial law, could not make its payments on loans to American banks, the Reagan administration agreed to pay off the loans without forcing the Poles to default first and risk panic among the large banks. Again, free-market spokesman Arthur Burns, now ambassador to West Germany, once more advised in favor of the bailout, warning of the imminent dangers to the fragile structures of international banking. In 1983 the Reagan administration approved expanded support for the International Monetary Fund so that it, in turn, could finance defaulting foreign creditor nations that would not otherwise be able to pay even debt service on loans from Citibank and other large U.S. financial establishments.[42]

The behavior of the American banking industry executives, and their counterparts in steel, autos, railroads, and so forth, is not perverse. From their perspective it is a sensible response to the need for order and stability. The banking system *is* overextended. A large corporate failure or the failure of a major foreign loan could kick off a massive contraction and drive the financial world into crisis. Obviously there is self-interest involved, but under the present system there is also collective interest; *without government intervention the system itself could be severely damaged.*

Thus, there is a fundamental contradiction: Our national ideology —and therefore our national policies—is out of sync with this reality. The broker state is seen as an aberration. If one is liberal, it is seen as a conspiracy of big business to subjugate government. If one is conservative, it is seen as an extension of the despised welfare state mentality, which is corrupting the private competitive sector. Always government expansion is rationalized as an exception. The political task is still defined as separating our government from the marketplace and returning to a pristine state in which the private and public sectors are distinctly different.

Lee Iacocca and thousands of other less well-known businessmen trudging to the Treasury for protection from the new economic era are self-styled "conservatives." They profess belief in the virtues of industrial capitalism and in free enterprise as a fundamental law of nature. The professions grow with every turn of the vise of economic crisis. But while our political dialogue moves backward in time, the real world economy moves on.

To maintain that America's complex interrelated economy can survive by re-creating the eighteenth-century world of Adam Smith is romantic folly for those who do not know better; it is irresponsible hypocrisy for those who do.

Observing the contradiction between the steel industry's ideology of the free market and its demand for protection, conservative writer George Will notes:

> Because the distinction between public and private sectors is decreasingly meaningful, traditional "free trade" ideology is increasingly anachronistic. And the steady politicization of major economies exerts pressure toward further politicization of the U.S. economy, which cannot be impervious to the worldwide dynamic of collectivization and semi-socialization. It is, perhaps, fitting that steel, symbol of the traditional enterprise economy, today dramatizes the metamorphosis of that system.[43]

The broker state is not just a *part* of the economic system—some separate sector that recycles taxes into one "public" activity or another over which liberals and conservatives quarrel. As we move deeper into the new economic era, the broker state is becoming the core of the economic system. Yet the gap between our professed economic principles and our economic reality creates mass confusion and encourages public attitudes that are out of touch with the way the world *really* works. It leads to a dangerous infatuation with abstract theory which, like the charge of the Polish cavalry into the German Panzer divisions at the beginning of World War II, is doomed.

Chapter 3

THE ROAD
TO DUNKIRK

The presidential election of 1980 was hailed as the triumph of a new political and economic order. Ronald Reagan's neoconservatism administered the *coup de grâce* to the tottering New Deal coalition. The ideas of liberalism—centered around a socially progressive federal government—seemed condemned by the voters as no longer relevant to the problems of the new economic era. The rest of the century seemed to belong to the Right.

During the 1980 presidential debates, Reagan had turned to the audience and asked: "Are *you* better off now than you were four years ago?" It was a smart question. Polls taken on election day showed that the voters were concerned first with their cost of living and second with the threat of unemployment. Despite the daily reminders of hostages in Iran, foreign policy was a distant third. The so-called moral majority issues—abortion, gay rights, prayer in the schools—were important only to a tiny percentage of the voters. For most voters the answer to Reagan's question was "No." They elected him President.

Two years after his inauguration, when pollsters went back to the people with the obvious question, "Are you better off now than you were two years ago?" the answer was still no. The Carter recession of 1979–80 had been followed by a deeper, longer Reagan recession. The neoconservatives had their revolution, steamrollering their program of tax cuts, military spending, and dismantling of government social programs over the hapless Democrats. But the economic crisis worsened, creating the highest unemployment rate since the Great Depression. The confident prophets of Reaganomics who had predicted an immediate return to the lost paradise of the postwar boom a year later were explaining how difficult economic problems were. The economy picked up in mid-1983, but there was no fundamental change. Despite vast differences in style and some apparent differences in philosophy,

Reagan like Carter, seemed helpless to correct the course of the drifting "stop-start" economy characterized by short bursts of recovery and longer and longer lapses into stagnation.

THE COLLAPSE OF THE HOUSE OF KEYNES

Before the decade of the 1970s, American economists had basked in the glory of the triumph of their profession. *Time* magazine celebrated the success of what was then called the "New" Economics. "Economists," it reported, "have descended in force from their ivory towers and now sit confidently at the elbow of almost every important leader in government and business. . . ." The magazine summed up the ebullient mood: "If the nation has economic problems, they are the problems of high employment, high growth, and high hopes."[1] Lyndon Johnson's Council of Economic Advisors claimed that prosperity was now the "normal state" of the American economy. In 1970, a prominent economist, the late Arthur M. Okun, reassured Americans that recessions were "fundamentally preventable, like airplane crashes and unlike hurricanes."[2]

This seeming miracle had been accomplished by the adaptation to America of the ideas of British economist John Maynard Keynes. Although it would be an error to attribute the long postwar boom solely to Keynesian economics, his ideas indisputably inspired those who managed it.

The brilliant Keynes made many contributions to economics, but the most important was his solution of the perennial problem of capitalist markets—the cycles of boom and bust. Cycles are inherent in market economies; in America there were six major financial panics and two long depressions between the Civil War and World War II. With our more refined statistical methods since World War II, we count another eight smaller business cycles.

Some economic cyclicality is inevitable. Food prices vary with the season, clothes sales change with periodic fashion, and the breeding habits of cattle and human beings create fluctuations in the price of beef and the demand for toys, sports cars, and retirement homes. But so long as the overall economy is growing, and businesses and workers can shift from declining to expanding industries, cycles in individual economic sectors are not threatening to the economy as a whole. The problem for society is the general business cycle, which creates the periodic busts of large-scale unemployment and widespread bankruptcy.

The fundamental condition that creates cyclical instability is that the expectations of individuals become out of sync with collective reality. Theoretically, so long as everything stays in balance—for example, consumers do not borrow to try to buy more than producers can produce, savings always match investors' desire for capital, and inventories keep perfect pace with sales—a boom could last forever. But in the real world things do not mesh. Each actor—business,' worker, bank, consumer—tries to outguess both the market and his or her competitors. Some will guess wrong, some will guess right. Since the system is both uncoordinated *and* interrelated, it does not take many small miscalculations to clog it. It is like rush-hour traffic with no stoplights. Each driver, responsible only for getting himself or herself home quickly, will make decisions that seem rational but that are irrational for the traffic pattern as a whole. Individuals will make wrong turns, momentary stops—small, seemingly insignificant decisions—that can end up jamming every car in the city and bringing traffic to a halt.

Businesspeople, for example, will increase inventories anticipating rising sales. From the point of view of the individual who sees a growing market, the decision makes sense. But other businesses are also increasing inventories, and new people are setting up businesses. Soon inventory growth outpaces sales growth, and goods begin to stack up in showrooms. Businesspeople then order less from factories, and manufacturers start to lay off workers and cancel plans for buying new equipment. The unemployed workers stop going to the stores. The ripple of recession spreads, leading to unemployment and bankruptcies. Sometimes the cycle is led by dramatic shifts in credit, at other times wages, at other times capital investment. But left alone, the cycle will always turn downward at some point. Underlying imbalances in the division of society's resources add to the difficulties: If consumers regularly receive incomes inadequate to purchase the things corporations make, ultimately excess capacity must emerge, retarding growth and leading to deeper stagnation.

Prior to the 1930s, conventional economic wisdom held that cycles *should* be left alone. Both friends and enemies of capitalism felt a periodic "purging" of the system was necessary to punish bankers and businesspeople for their mistakes in judgment and to discipline the wage demands of workers. The theory held that at some point business would drop prices so low and workers would drop wage demands so low that consumers would increase their buying and/or investors would begin investing again and the cycle would turn upward. In classical economic theory these adjustments happened instantaneously, but in real life such depressions could last for a decade and in fact often did not appear to turn into a recovery without some outside stimulus —a war, the appearance of a new industry, the opening up of new land. In the midst of the last Great Depression, in the 1930s, Keynes and his colleagues concluded that unemployment was not just a periodic, temporary part of capitalism but had become a *permanent feature* of the system. They demonstrated that costs, especially wages, were "sticky"; even the widespread unemployment of the Depression could not lower costs enough to rebuild the confidence of investors and consumers so that the upward movement could begin. Left to itself, industrial capitalism seemed to have a natural tendency toward stagnation.

But Keynes also had a solution. It was for government to act as the "stabilizer" of the private economy. When business and consumer spending began to contract, the government, the only institution with responsibility for society as a whole, could fill the gap by spending more money than it took in (or running a deficit). This would be a net stimulus to private demand and put people back to work. When business and consumers were spending too much, causing shortages of labor and rising prices, government would counterbalance these excesses either by taxing away some consumer purchasing power or by itself spending less than it took in (running a surplus). Because of its control of the central bank, it could also expand and contract credit countercyclically. Thus the manipulation of a few simple tools (government spending, taxes, and central bank credit) could even out the boom-and-bust cycles and create the conditions for sustained prosperity. Over the span of the business cycle, government deficits and surpluses would cancel each other, thus balancing the budget over time, although not necessarily in any given year.

Keynes personally felt that any necessary government expenditures should be for housing, schooling, public health, transportation, and the like, but he acknowledged that the *type* of spending was a secondary question. *The important thing was the spending itself.* In a famous passage, he wrote:

> If the Treasury were to fill old bottles with banknotes, bury them at suitable depths in disused coal mines which are then filled up to the surface with town rubbish, and leave it to private enterprises on well-tried principles of laissez-faire to dig the notes up again . . . there need be no more unemployment and, with the help of the repercussions, the real income of the community, and its capital wealth also, would probably become a good deal greater than it actually is. It would indeed be more

sensible to build houses and the like; but if there are political and practical difficulties in the way of this, the above would be better than nothing.[3]

Keynes offered a way to save capitalism at a time when doubts about its usefulness were widespread. Still, for most conservative American businesspeople, the notion that government, the suspected carrier of the disease called socialism, held the answer to our economic problems was a hard sell—even in the Depression. Ideological resistance to Keynes prevented his ideas from being seriously implemented during the 1930s. As late as 1938, even Franklin Roosevelt tried to balance the budget while 19 percent of the labor force was out of work, an act that began a second depression within the Depression. Luckily for FDR, growing demand for military hardware from Western Europe saved the day. It was World War II—with its large public deficits—that showed businessmen that government spending could mean high profits without socialism. The war wiped out the Depression overnight. Moreover, the savings built up during the war when wages were high and consumer goods scarce fueled the economy during the years after the war ended. Aided by Cold War military spending, the economy continued to expand in the 1950s with only minor downturns along the way. But toward the end of the Eisenhower years, economic stagnation began to appear once more.

The final triumph of Keynesian economics came with the famous Kennedy tax cut (actually passed under Lyndon Johnson in 1964), which deliberately created a peacetime deficit to stimulate the economy. When it was demonstrated to business that the economy could be stimulated by tax cuts as well as by government spending, business climbed on board. By 1971, Richard Nixon could publicly proclaim: "We are all Keynesians."[4]

The conversion of Nixon to deficit-spending economics was the high-water mark of Keynes' political influence. It came just as the new economic era tide was running out on his model.

It is important to understand that Keynes' theory accepted many of the simplifying assumptions of classical economics. One such assumption was that capital and labor are perfectly mobile between industries and regions. This ignores "bottlenecks" and uneven growth, which in real life cause prices and wages to rise in industries that are operating at capacity at the same time unemployment is widespread and persistent in declining industries.

In the short run especially, capital and labor are not completely mobile, nor are their prices set in perfectly competitive markets. Short-ages of skills and materials in some industries exist side by side with surpluses in others. Yet prices and wages do not adjust automatically to these differences. On the upswing of a business cycle, average prices rise before full employment is reached. On the downswing they tend not to fall as quickly as demand declines.

Industrial economies tend to have an inverse relationship between the behavior of prices and unemployment. The relationship is often referred to as the Phillips Curve, named for the British economist who measured the "trade-off" between inflation and unemployment over a hundred years of British history.

The "trade-off" problem is aggravated by monopoly and near-monopoly power. As Robert Lekachman has noted, the system is now honeycombed with

> an army of restrictions upon entry into unions and professions, special benefits to well-organized interests, tariffs and quotas, subsidies to defense contractors, indul-gent regulation of public utilities, raids by municipal unions on city treasuries, monopoly positions in industry, insurance, and finance, and miscellaneous extor-tions from the unprotected portions of the community. It is not an exaggeration to assert that wherever an observer's eye falls, it registers a situation of market control or actual dominance by a small number of individuals, corporations, health insurers, trade unions, business associations, or professional societies.[5]

By 1979, the *Fortune* 500 firms, representing .02 percent of all individual firms, had more than 80 percent of all manufacturing sales and more than 75 percent of all profits and employees. The four top firms controlled 93 percent of automobile production, 90 percent of electric-lamp production, 70 percent of tire and inner tube production, 89 percent of breakfast-cereal production, 77 percent of the greeting-card industry, and 87 percent of copper production. The leading *Fortune* 100 firms managed about the same fraction of manufacturing assets as the top 200 firms 30 years ago. And the manufacturing assets of the 200 largest now matched those of the top 1,000 companies in 1941.[6]

On the labor side, there are great disparities in labor power, and therefore wages. Production workers in 1981 in the steel and automo-bile industries received hourly wages 1.7 times the national average, while millions of other workers with similar skills hovered about the minimum wage.[7]

As a result of concentration, large sections of the economy have fallen under the sway of "administered pricing." Large corporations can "target" future profit levels and set prices in corporate boardrooms rather than in the hurly-burly of the marketplace. In a number of industries there is a gentlemen's agreement to follow the leading company on prices. Many giant corporations also have the power to cut production rather than prices to shore up profits during a recession. One study revealed that during the 1974–75 recession, when auto sales plunged 27 percent, new-car prices jumped an average of a thousand dollars, an obvious indication that the classical law of supply and demand had been substantially amended, if not repealed.[8]

All this creates a major problem for Keynesian economics: before a new stream of spending can stimulate new production to hire the unemployed, it regularly gets converted into high prices, wages, profits, and incomes by the more monopolistic sectors of the economy. Prices and wages rise in some industries at the same time unemployment is widespread elsewhere. The economy can *stagnate* and *inflate* at the same time, giving rise to the new phenomenon of *stagflation*. Stagflation also clearly alters the distribution of rewards. Those fortunate enough to work in the more stable monopolistic sectors absorb the benefits. Those who do not are doubly penalized—by high unemployment rates and high prices.

Keynesian theory also had no answer to sudden "jolts" to the nation's price level from outside the economy—such as the huge jumps in food and energy prices in the 1970s. In theory, these shocks should have little effect on the general price level as long as everything else remains the same. If the price of energy goes up, consumers simply have to pay more for energy and less for other things. But the effect of the energy and food shocks on demand and expectations were so great that they created havoc with consumers, high prices for the economy as a whole, and massive confusion for the policymakers.

In the early 1970s a series of weather-related crop failures in several areas of the world suddenly put Russian and Indian consumers in direct competition with American housewives for the output of American farmers. Food prices rose 35 percent in 1973–74. During the same period, the OPEC nations quadrupled the world price of oil. Average consumer prices for energy in America (heating oil, gasoline, gas, and electricity) rose 17 percent in 1973 and an additional 22 percent in 1974. Similar "shocks" in the food and energy sectors occurred at the end of the decade. In the case of food, a meat shortage that was related to the earlier high feed grain prices contributed to the 23 percent food price increase of 1978–79. And the panic in world oil markets set off by the Iranian revolution led to a 37 percent increase in consumer energy prices in 1979.[9]

The jolts from the external world rippled through the domestic economy and ratcheted prices upward. Higher food and oil prices were passed forward with markups by processors and retailers. These added to the cost of other businesses. As the cost of living rose—especially for necessities such as food, gasoline, and heating oil—workers demanded higher wages to catch up, which added to costs and ultimately led to even higher prices. Because of concentrated market power, large sectors of the economy could maintain the new price levels even when the source of the inflationary disturbances had subsided.

The jolt and spiral pattern of inflation had nothing to do with an overheated economy as described by the conventional Keynesian model. In fact, throughout the decade, America had a large and growing army of the unemployed—people willing and able to work who could not find jobs. Unemployment averaged 4.8 percent for the decade of the 1960s, 6.2 percent for the 1970s, and about 8.5 percent for the first three and a half years of the 1980s, suggesting a worsening economic trend.[10] Nor was there any indication that the physical capacity of America's plant and equipment was being extraordinarily strained. During the same period, industrial production ranged between 77 and 86 percent capacity. In 1980, some 7.6 million people were officially unemployed—while the Consumer Price Index rose 13.5 percent. In the Keynesian world, it was as if both ends of a child's seesaw were rising at the same time!

The importance of the jolts as an initiating cause of our inflation was recognized by Charles Schultze and the other Keynesians who made economic policy for Jimmy Carter. In 1978, the Report of the Council of Economic Advisors speaking of the inflation concluded that

> the dominant influence was the rise in food and fuel prices. Its force was not limited to direct effects. The pass-through of cost increases into other prices broadened the inflation, and the rise in consumer prices led to efforts by wage earners to recover lost incomes.[11]

The same point was made again in the 1980 report. Inflation was not being created by an overheated economy but by "sectoral" forces, coupled with a "downward insensitivity in wages and prices" from the growing market rigidities in the economy. These new problems required new solutions. But despite his diagnosis, in the end the main cure Dr. Schultze relied on was Keynesian: cut back federal spending and throttle back the money supply. So despite the fact that millions of Americans were without work, a Democratic administration in 1979 called for a $25 billion cut in government spending, while an undisputed analysis by the Congressional Budget Office showed that such cuts would not reduce the then double-digit increase in the Consumer Price Index by more than .2 or .3 percent. In the same year, Carter chose Paul Volcker, a conservative banker, a follower of Milton Friedman, to be chairman of the Federal Reserve Board. Volcker proceeded to tighten the money supply, driving up interest rates to record levels.

Keynesianism had in fact become a grotesque parody of itself. No longer did the Phillips Curve simply represent a small marginal trade-off between jobs and prices when the economy got close to full employment. It demanded that huge numbers of human beings be tossed into the street to appease the insatiable monster of inflation. It was certainly true that if demand was cut back enough and unemployment was allowed to rise enough, prices and wages would start to come down. But at what cost? A common estimate by the Keynesians themselves was that in order to get the underlying rate of inflation down by one percentage point it would require a million people to be out of work for three years!

The monster began to devour the Democrats. Up for reelection, Carter could not risk looking soft on inflation—which the polls told him was the number one political issue in the country.

But he was trapped: Barred from full implementation of the logic of Schultze's economic theory by the certain political defeat that would have followed a Thatcher-like policy of deflation, he was also closed off from wage-price controls and other direct interventions in the economy by his and Schultze's perceptions of the ideological limits of American politics. He could neither reduce the traffic nor install traffic lights, so the economic jam got worse. Interest rates rose to 20 percent, the housing market collapsed, small-business failures rose, the corporate bond market vanished, prices kept rising, and unemployment rose —particularly in industrial blue-collar strongholds of the Democratic Party. The country was treated to the spectacle of a Democratic administration presiding over a self-inflicted recession in an election year.*

One reaction was to blame the statistics. It was said that the unemployment figures were unnaturally swollen with too many women and young people. But these were young people not in school and women,

---

*The Administration tried to "jawbone" wages down, and it proposed a slapdash "real wage insurance" package so flimsy it was hooted out of Congress. See Chapter Thirteen.

single or married, who needed work so they could eat, pay the rent, and meet their bills, just like adult males. The Consumer Price Index was also attacked. The Carter economists complained that the complex formula overemphasized the cost of home ownership. So they forced the civil servants in charge of the statistics to come up with a new index, which assumed that the entire population rented their homes.*

Not that any of it made a difference politically. People were angry with Carter not because they read about unemployment and inflation in the newspapers but because they, or people they knew, were out of work; because inflation in general was out of hand; and because families could no longer afford to buy houses—regardless of what the Consumer Price Index said.

Inevitably, panic set in. Carter and Schultze careened from pronouncement to pronouncement, basing decisions more openly on the latest polls. They introduced a tough-sounding austerity program—a pledge to balance the budget, a hiring freeze on federal employment, a ten cents per gallon tax on gasoline, consumer credit controls, and a twenty-five-billion-dollar budget cut. When Ted Kennedy entered the primaries, charging Carter with betraying the New Deal, Carter abandoned his budget-cutting and began to shovel federal monies out to cities, states, and a variety of traditional constituencies. Once Kennedy was beaten, Carter moved back to the Right, stressing balanced budgets and conservative economics.

More and more the problem was blamed on the people. A President who was elected on his promise to make the government as good as the people was now blaming the people for not following his government's exhortations. The people were infected with "malaise." People were too lazy to conserve energy. They were too apathetic. They wanted too much from the government. They would have to make do with less. Carter's speeches were sprinkled with references to pain, discipline, and sacrifice that would be required to beat inflation.

Caught between the rock of Schultze's obsolete theories and the hard place of his own cautious politics, Carter tried to slip through the election by creating an image of decisiveness. Symbolism was no

---

*There was some merit to the point about the CPI. But the criticism ignored the fact that the index was designed precisely to measure what it would cost to buy a specific set of goods and services, including housing. Moreover, in their rush to reduce the government's own index of their inflation failures, they ignored other issues. For instance, after the shocks of the 1970s, food and energy costs played a bigger role in the family budget than the index showed—but they had no wish to revise the statistics in a comprehensive manner.

longer just a way to sell economic policy; it *was* economic policy. "We know these measures won't bring down inflation in the next several months," said a Treasury Department official to *The New York Times*. "We're counting on the emotional impact of a balanced budget to give people the feeling that something is finally being done."[12]

The image collapsed before the open snickers of the media. Carter was seen as incompetent, vacillating, and insincere. He lost forty-four states, and with Carter a group of the Senate's most liberal members went down to defeat.

THE HOLLOW "CLINK"

The Republican Right had stalked the Democratic Party for years, waiting for its opportunity. It came close in 1968 after the Vietnam War split the Democrats. But Richard Nixon decided to write *himself* into the history books instead. He recognized Red China, created a détente with the Soviets, imposed wage-price controls, and finally disgraced himself and the Republican Party with Watergate.

Nixon's opportunism was not the only obstacle in the path of the Right. In order to beat the liberals decisively, Republicans had to capture a large part of the white, working middle-class constituency, the blue- and pink-collar workers of the country's factories and offices. But the Democrats seemed to have a lock on the economic issues that meant most to these people. The albatross of the Great Depression was still around Republican necks: they were the party of big business. Conservatives such as Howard Phillips, Richard Viguerie, and others argued that the Right should concentrate on social issues, stirring up discontent in the Democratic coalition over abortion, busing, homosexuality, and the class hostilities directed not by workers against capitalists, but by the mass culture against the stereotypes of effete liberal intellectuals.

But as much as they might hate busing and despise abortions, the blue- and pink-collar workers had stayed with the Democratic Party throughout the 1960s and 1970s. Economic growth and jobs were the bottom lines in a mass-consumption culture. The Republicans, for all their professed sympathies toward working-class social values, were clearly identified by this constituency as being "for" Wall Street and the *Fortune* 500, for tight money and tight budgets, and for sacrificing workingpersons' jobs to save wealthy investors' bonds.

In the early 1970s, a number of self-styled neoconservatives began to search for an alternative to traditional Republican economics. They included Irving Kristol, former Democrat and editor of *Public Interest;* Jude Wanniski, an editorial writer for *The Wall Street Journal;* and Republican Congressman Jack Kemp, who represented a district of industrial Buffalo. A handsome ex–football hero for the Buffalo Bills, Kemp was more in touch with the anxieties of the blue-collar world than most of his Republican colleagues. He saw that in order to out-flank the Democrats, the Republicans needed a new economics that could appeal to labor's concern for jobs and security.

He found his inspiration in the Democratic Party's own Keynesian past—especially in the successful Kennedy-Johnson tax cut of 1964, which had deliberately unbalanced the budget and led to an accelera-tion of growth and jobs. It also increased government revenues, which were used to feed the Great Society . . . and the Vietnam War. Kemp and the neoconservaties saw that Keynesian economics could be used as a tool for conservative purposes as well as for liberal ones. All you had to do, or so it seemed to, was *keep cutting taxes,* thereby shrinking the government while stimulating the economy.

But the problem of deficits remained. Richard Nixon had converted to Keynesianism, but Nixon had been disgraced. And despite the success of the Kennedy tax cut, the notion of deliberately inducing deficits to spur economic growth was still not popular among Republi-cans. Deficits meant increased government borrowing, which "crowded out" the private sector from the money markets. They kept employment higher than was comfortable for price stability (if any-thing, Wall Street believed in the Phillips Curve more fervidly than the liberals did). Finally, they were bad because they encouraged cheap money, and Wall Street had fought populist politicians over cheap money for more than a century, from Andrew Jackson and William Jennings Bryan to FDR and Harry Truman. Deficits meant undisci-plined government, undisciplined labor, and undisciplined debtors. Wall Street held to the classical notion that busts were necessary to sweat out the excesses of economic booms. Deficits delayed the mar-ket's harsh, inevitable reckoning.

Even in the interests of putting a Republican in the White House, deficits would not sell on Wall Street. To fulfill his dream of a Republi-can renaissance, Kemp needed deficit spending without the deficit. Kemp found his answer to the Phillips Curve in another curve—a simple idea originally sketched on a napkin in a Washington restaurant by a young conservative economist named Arthur Laffer. The sketch showed the familiar "L"-shaped chart; the bottom horizontal line represented government revenue, the vertical line represented tax rates. A curve started in the lower left-hand corner of the chart, extended upward and to the right, and then bent backward to finish on the vertical line at the upper left. It purported to show that up to a certain point, increased taxes would result in increased government revenues, as one would expect. But beyond that point it suggested that higher taxes would decrease revenue because they would become so high that people would no longer have an incentive to produce income. If raising tax rates can actually reduce government revenue, *then it would follow that cutting taxes could increase tax revenues:* the government's revenue loss from reduced *rates* would be offset by the revenue gain from those same rates applied to increased incomes.

Laffer's point was not new. Economists have always understood that at some level taxes could become so confiscatory that people would actually work less and produce less, resulting in lower revenues for the government. But the point is relevant only if tax rates are so high that people lose their incentive to work and to invest. It is like saying that there is a point at which *another* glass of milk will make you sick— undoubtedly true, but irrelevant unless you have already had as much milk as you can drink without being sick. The question was, were we at the place on the Laffer Curve at which people were already being taxed too much? Unfortunately, you could not tell from the Laffer Curve. It was a freehand drawing, not a statistical chart. Nor did Laffer offer any evidence that such was the case. It was a theory. That's all.

The Laffer Curve was dubious economics. But it was brilliant politics. It provided a way to marry Keynes to conservative ideology. The rhetoric surrounding the Laffer Curve and its subsequent embellishment emphasized *supply* rather than demand; it was not the increased injection of demand into the economy that spurred the boom after the cut of 1964, said the neoconservatives, it was the increase in *supply* as a result of the greater incentive to work harder and to invest more because of the lower tax rates. That is, jobs were not created because sales went up, but because the marginal tax rate on profits and income went down—making it more profitable for rich people to invest instead of consume, and for working people to take jobs instead of being unemployed.

By arguing that supply rather than demand was the key to the Kennedy-Johnson tax cut, the Laffer Curve rationalized a fiscal policy that favored the rich and at the same time appealed to a broader constituency. Since the rich tend to save more of their marginal income, neoconservatives could argue that tax reductions would increase investment and therefore jobs. At the same time, unlike traditional

Republicans, they could argue that the programs that made up the working middle-class safety net—Social Security, Medicare, housing subsidies, veterans' benefits, etc.—could eventually be expanded.

Despite its common parentage, "supply side" conservatism became a political alternative to "demand side" liberalism. A growing number of neoconservative academics, working out of business-supported "think tanks" such as the American Enterprise Institute, the Heritage Foundation, and the Hoover Institution, and writing in magazines such as *Public Interest, Commentary, Harper's,* and *Reader's Digest,* begin collectively to build an argument and political support for sup-ply-side economics. Freed from the iron law of the Phillips Curve and the traditional conservative demand for austerity as the answer to inflation, the neoconservatives could now offer Republicans a magic weapon to cut into the heart of the Democratic electorate. Supply-side economics was a painless way to prosperity. Cut taxes, create jobs, and eventually have even more revenue for public spending.

Kemp joined with Republican Senator William Roth to introduce the Kemp-Roth tax bill in 1977.[13] The bill called for a cut of about one third in federal income taxes, skewed toward the upper end of the income scale. Families making $15,000 would receive a reduction of $260 in taxes; families earning over $500,000 would receive a $50,000 reduction in taxes. Four years later, a bill only slightly more modest was rammed through Congress by a triumphant Ronald Reagan.

The Democrats had prepared the table for the Republican feast. The decline in real wages caused by unchecked inflation squeezed middle-class family budgets hard, making them particularly sensitive to the highly visible bite that taxes took out of their income. At the same time, the shift of growth from Frostbelt to Sunbelt strained public finances on both ends, leading to higher local taxes.

But the Democratic Party made things worse by structuring the burden of taxes away from the corporations and the rich toward the working middle class. Despite the fact that the party held both Houses of Congress and their tax-writing committees for the entire decade of the 1970s, and the White House from 1977 on, the federal tax system became more regressive. The Revenue Act of 1978, passed by a Democratic administration and Congress, lowered the maximum rate on capital gains, removed capital gains from the list of income subject to a minimum tax, and compensated corporate stock and real estate for value lost due to inflation. Over 80 percent of the benefits from the cut in capital gains went to taxpayers with a 1979 income over $50,000.[14]

Progressive federal income taxes for the average family fell slightly in real terms between 1969 and 1979, while *regressive* Social Security payroll taxes more than tripled. At the same time, the percent of total federal revenues over the decade provided by the corporate income tax fell from 17 percent to 12 percent.[15]

The Democrats also had become a party of big business. In the election of 1980, corporate Political Action Committees gave more money to Democratic congressional candidates than to Republican. But the Democrats were *seen* as the party of big government. And the rising tax bills came from government. The average family has little control over the source of its income—for the most part the decision to create jobs is made by the actions of an invisible private-investment process over which they have little influence. The workers' decision is to apply for the job or not. Neither do they have much control over the source of higher prices. They decide simply to buy or not. They neither elect nor even know the people who make the major decisions over their jobs and their living costs. But they do have some control over their government. And government was the inevitable target for anger generated by the stagnation of the average family's standard of living.

It was particularly vulnerable because government in the 1960s had been the instrument of a series of efforts to reduce discrimination against minorities, women, the handicapped, and the poor. Scenes of welfare mothers demanding larger checks; blacks demanding school busing; and women, homosexuals, and others demanding affirmative action rubbed social nerves raw enough even in the general boom time when the economic pie seemed to be growing fast enough for everyone to increase their share. But in the slowdown of the 1970s satisfying one group's demands meant taking jobs and opportunities away from another group. In economist Lester Thurow's phrase, it had become a "zero sum" society. Without the cushion of growth, and given the increasing burden of taxes, government's efforts to make the system more equitable became a sinister threat to the middle class.

Having for decades complained about unbalanced budgets and deficit spending, the Right was in perfect position to exploit the opportunity. Inspired by the success of California landlords in passing Proposition 13 (which rolled back property taxes in many categories to 1 percent of assessed values and capped the rate of increase until the property was sold), local business groups and conservative politicians organized tax limitation efforts all over the country. During 1978 alone, thirty-six states enacted tax cuts of one kind or another. By 1980, even liberal Massachusetts—the only state that voted for McGovern in

1972—passed Proposition 2½, which severely restricted localities' ability to raise property taxes; within months Boston and other major cities in the state were struggling to keep from falling into bankruptcy.[16]

The tax revolt presaged the 1980 election, and the Republicans were swept into office on the votes of disgruntled Democrats. Supply-side politics provided the rationale for choosing the neoconservative alternative. Reagan's campaign message divided the world into two groups: those who produce and those who consume. The producers were like the hardworking ant in Aesop's fable who works all summer and in the winter feeds the lazy, irresponsible grasshopper. Since most people think that they work hard, are unappreciated, and are not rewarded quite enough, this defines a political majority. In the other group are people who do not work and receive welfare (3 percent of the population).[17] The imagery of supply-side politics had an instant appeal to the vast majority of Americans.

After the election in December 1980, David Stockman and Kemp prepared an economic plan for Ronald Reagan, entitling it "Avoiding a GOP Dunkirk," to emphasize its political nature.[18] Kemp and Stockman stated that the traditional conservative economic strategy of planned deflation—which they labeled Thatcherism—was an unacceptable course for the Republicans, who were still somewhat stained with responsibility for the Great Depression: It would mean losses in the 1982 elections and would undermine Republican strategy thereafter. Moreover, austerity could not achieve a balanced budget. Rising unemployment, they said, would increase the deficit by generating more "soup line" social welfare spending and less tax revenue. Thus, like liberal Keynesians, they argued that federal deficits were not the cause of inflation, they were primarily the *result* of slow economic growth. Conversely, an immediate large tax cut would stimulate enough taxable economic activity through Lafferite relationships to balance the budget before the next presidential election.

Kemp and Stockman then argued that a promise to cut inflation by cutting government spending (not because deficits caused inflation but because people *believed* they did—shades of Jimmy Carter's symbolism!) would inspire firms and labor unions to *expect* less inflation in the future and therefore reduce their demands for higher wages and prices. Expectations were also the key to the money market. A major cause of high interest rates, said the memo, was uncertainty about future inflation. This uncertainty caused lenders to shy away from long-term investments. The result was a rush on the shorter-term money market, which had driven up interest rates to 20 percent. If business *believed* inflation was likely to fall, long-term capital would once more flow, and interest rates would come down. Since the budget cannot be balanced in the short run anyway, the key is to show firm intention that it will be balanced in the future. It will work, they said, because people will believe it will work.

Finally, the Stockman-Kemp memo pledged support for Volcker and the Federal Reserve in a tight money policy. This, of course, would continue the Carter high interest rates. It would also act, however, as a brake on the growth that Kemp and Stockman were looking for. It was a fatal contradiction—an expansive fiscal policy and a restrictive monetary policy. Neoconservative economics, though more boldly etched in its tax and budget cutting, began to look more and more like the drab, more modest, but essentially similar economic strategy of Jimmy Carter.

Not all Republicans climbed on board. Stockman and Kemp were opposed by older economists such as Arthur Burns and Herbert Stein, whose basic loyalties were to defending the existing economic system and who were skeptical of the unproven claims of the supply-siders. To them it sounded awfully close to a "free lunch." Burns and Stein, of course, shared many sentiments with the neoconservatives. They favored cutting taxes and reducing government spending. But they were appalled by the casual attitude of the Laffer Curve analysis toward the deficit. Burns and Stein reflected the Wall Street anxiety that financing the deficit would result in the federal government squeezing private borrowers out of the money market.* The tax cuts were so generous, however, particularly those offered to the banking and securities industries, that America's financial leaders abandoned responsibility for what they called sound money, and simply went along.

As the neoconservatives saw, if federal revenues were strategically reduced, it would put the Democrats continually on the defensive by creating a constant pressure for further spending reductions. The extraordinary political skills of Ronald Reagan provided as good a test of economic theory as one ever gets in the real political world. He got

---

*Stein commented: "If the tax cut is to increase the revenue by its effect on the supply of saving and labor, that will require a much greater response of both saving and labor to an increase in after-tax returns than any investigation of that response has discovered."[19] But supply-siders cavalierly dismissed the lack of statistical evidence of their propositions. Said Irving Kristol in explaining supply-side economics to the readers of *The Wall Street Journal:* "The interactions are so subtle, the feedbacks are so complex, that we do not have any econometric model capable of handling them."[20]

everything from Congress that he asked for—the tax cuts, the budget cuts, increased military spending, and tight money from the Federal Reserve. According to the plan, the economy was supposed to take off in the summer of 1981, when the tax-cut legislation passed. Businesses would then be motivated to invest, the rich to save more, and individuals to work harder. But throughout the summer, business continued sluggish and weak, and business plans for investment did not change. Well, of course, it could not happen on expectations alone, said the neoconservatives; wait until October 1, when the tax cuts go into effect. October 1 came and went. There was activity, to be sure. The savers and investors moved existing savings into new money-market paper. Large companies bought and sold tax losses and exploited other new gimmicks. And there were spectacular corporate battles as the largest companies used their new wealth to try to buy up smaller ones. But actual economic activity not only did not grow but instead steadily dropped throughout the fall and winter. Industrial production fell 7 percent between July and December 1981, and in six months another two million workers were added to the unemployment rolls.[21] An exasperated Secretary of the Treasury Donald Regan cried: "We have carried through on our commitments . . . but where is the business response? Where are the new research and development initiatives? Where are the new plants? Where are the expansion plans? It's like dropping a coin down a well—all I'm hearing is a hollow clink."[22] A year later, industrial production had fallen another six points, and twelve million Americans were out of work.

Meanwhile, as a result of the tax cuts and higher military spending, the deficit skyrocketed, roughly doubling the deficit of Carter's last year. Ronald Reagan, who had solemnly told the American people a year earlier that the federal deficit was the cause of most of our troubles, abandoned almost all pretense that he would ever balance the budget at any time throughout his term—even though in 1981 he reversed himself, asking for and getting the largest tax increase in American history. Stockman himself, as he admitted in an embarrassing interview published in the *Atlantic Monthly*, had abandoned the supply-side theory even before he submitted Reagan's first budget to Congress. Reagan's tax bill, he said, was a "Trojan Horse" for the giveaways to big business, which was all they were interested in from the start. And when the legislation got to Congress, "The hogs were really feeding," he said glumly. In the space of a few months Laffer's theory was a piece of intellectual junk.[23]

Inflation did fall, of course. The Phillips Curve "trade-off" proved right after all—throw enough people out of work, and the demand for goods and services will fall far enough to stabilize the price level. Reagan was helped by a temporary series of bumper harvests that lowered food prices and by quarreling among OPEC members, but these factors simply meant that the unemployment rate did not have to rise even farther.

It was reasonable to expect, of course, that the recession would bottom out at some point, and a turnaround of sorts did begin in mid-1983. But the economy was still on the bumpy, drifting, "stop-start" patterns of the previous decade, with unemployment reaching new depths in the trough of each recession. In 1983 Reagan also changed his position slightly on the jobs issue, accepting a token spending program that made him a less vulnerable political target. The tremendous increase in military spending, too, could be expected to stimulate the economy in conventional Keynesian fashion, but if it did so to a significant degree, interest rates and prices were likely to accelerate—so Administration policy was to try to keep growth slow and unemployment high. The massive deficits also kept long-term interest rates up, undercutting investment and deepening the trend of stagnation. Reagan and the Republicans were caught, as Carter and the Democrats had been. They could reduce prices at the cost of high unemployment and business bankruptcy. Or they could really put people to work and stimulate sales at the price of inflation. But they could not solve the fundamental problem, at least not in *their* terms of political reference.

Irving Kristol had already suggested what would be the consequences if the Reaganomics gamble ultimately failed. He had written in *The Wall Street Journal:*

A skeptic might inquire: What if this new conservative political economy doesn't work? To which one can only reply: It had better work. It is the last, best hope of democratic capitalism in America, and if it fails—well, then conservatism can concentrate on nostalgic poetry and forget all about political economy. Someone else will be in charge of that.[24]

Chapter 4

THE ECONOMICS OF DECLINE

The first Reagan priority was the deficit, yet, his initial two years in office were a vivid economics lesson, demonstrating that federal deficits were not the cause of inflation. A member of his own Council of Economic Advisors dismissed decades of Republican dogma: "We shouldn't worry about a direct relationship between deficits and inflation. It just is not in the data . . . and it is not something in which I think there is any special reason to be concerned."[1] Reagan himself sighed and said the deficit was something you had to live with "in the real world."

But the lesson did not seem to sink in. Keynesian economists agreed that near-term deficits were not a major problem in an economy that was operating with so much slack. They argued that future "out years" deficits had to be closed to reduce long-term interest rates. By and large, however, such distinctions were lost in the popular political debate as Republicans and Democrats alike rushed to avoid being labeled "big spenders." Without apparent embarrassment, most Democrats who had ladled more tax cuts from the Treasury to big business than even Reagan had asked for in 1980 now castigated him for a deficit that undermined the economy.

The ongoing metamorphosis of the U.S. economy cannot be accommodated within the ideological framework of the broker state. Hiding behind the myths of a laissez-faire past, the broker state is self-indulgent and politically undisciplined in a world that increasingly requires competent government. The broker state nourishes the wrong behavior in the country's leadership; the politician constantly campaigning against government spending whose political life is spent looting the Treasury for his own constituency is not capable of serious political leadership in the new economic era.

The broker state is the handmaiden of big business, but its deficiencies have not gone unnoticed in corporate boardrooms. As the more observant businessman looks around the world he cannot help but see the evidence of what George Will called the "worldwide dynamic of collectivization and semisocialism."

American business now competes with foreign corporations that operate as part of their nation's overall economic strategy. It was not some smart European entrepreneur who outmaneuvered American grain dealers in 1972, it was an agency of the Soviet Union. It is not private oil companies we deal with in Saudi Arabia, Kuwait, and Venezuela, it is the government. The expansion of the Japanese steel industry, which helped devastate the American steel industry, was the result of an economic strategy designed by the Japanese government. It is not some private foreign corporation American Motors had to bring in as a partner in order to survive—it was Renault, wholly owned by the French government. In almost every economically important nation in the world, governments have become inextricably involved in the planning and financing of their major industrial sectors.

The degree and efficiency of formalized planning vary from nation to nation, but in all cases there is close collaboration between government and big business, with organized labor's role depending on where the political pendulum is at the moment. In Western Europe, only Great Britain and Italy have failed to establish a workable system. In some cases, such as Sweden and France, the planning, though different in bias, is relatively formal and open under both conservative and socialist governments. In others, such as West Germany, it is a combination of informal relationships between businessmen and government officials and formal worker collaboration in the management structure of large corporations. In Japan, planning is done through a subtle but disciplined system of financial controls; companies whose plans are not consistent with the long-term industrial plans of the government find it difficult to get credit. The specific mechanisms are grounded in each nation's institutions and culture, but the core idea is political agreement—sometimes implicit, sometimes explicit, sometimes coerced, sometimes voluntary—among the various sectors of the economy over the allocation of resources and, often, even markets themselves. The purpose is to encourage productivity and to eliminate duplication and waste (particularly in export industries) and to stabilize the overall environment so that the private actors in the system—business, labor, consumers—can themselves plan for the future with more confidence.

All this, of course, is an explicit rejection of the "invisible hand" of laissez-faire capitalism. And it is the logical evolution of the corporate-dominated broker state, the elevation of the political deal to a grand scale—a deal between classes. And though, as we shall see, it is not without major problems, its superiority to the broker state is evident. In 1980 eight nations—Sweden, Switzerland, West Germany, Denmark, France, Belgium, Norway, and Luxembourg—had already surpassed the United States in per-capita income, with the Netherlands a few dollars behind. In each case government represents a much larger share of the national economy than it does in the United States.[2]

THE UNEASY PLANNERS

Growing awareness within the business community of the advantages of government-managed economic planning has led to an ideological crisis. Professor George Lodge of the Harvard Business School—who teaches students how to get to the top of the corporate ladder—observes that corporate leaders are suffering a "schizophrenia" as they seek to sustain outworn ideas in the face of new economic conditions. The old ideology emphasized individualism, property rights, competition, the limited state, and scientific specialization. An ideology that accommodates the new reality of our economic world requires an emphasis on communitarianism, rights of membership (entitlements), community need, a holistic view of science, and the recognition of the state as planner. Moreover, just as Cantril and Free (see Chapter Two) discovered in their survey of the general population, Lodge found that business leaders are torn between their *ideological* attitudes against government and their *operational needs* for more help. "The fact is," writes Lodge, "that the new planning role of the state is virtually upon us, but its ideological underpinnings are still missing. Without them it will lack legitimacy and will tend to be misunderstood, mishandled, and totally inadequate."[3]

While Messrs. Simon, Kristol, and other defenders of corporate capitalism were vigilantly guarding the boardrooms from left-wing attack, the ideological foundations were beginning to crumble from within. Wassily Leontief, a Nobel Prize winner in economics, commented in the mid-1970s that a planned economy will emerge in America "not because some wild-eyed radicals demand it, but because businessmen demand it to keep the system from sputtering to a halt."[4]

Leontief was on target. The first serious public call for economic planning since the end of World War II occurred at the halfway point of the decade of the seventies when a number of prominent business leaders began to say publicly what a few short years before the business press would have denounced as Bolshevik madness.

Here is investment banker Robert Roosa, partner in the investment firm of Brown Brothers, Harriman:

> The time has come, in my view, to develop a truly homegrown American form of national economic planning. Practically all the pieces of a planning process already exist. They are just not pulled together. The choice I see today is not between plan or not plan; but between coherent planning and chaotic planning.[5]

Thornton F. Bradshaw, then president of Atlantic Richfield, now head of RCA:

> Since so many government regulations are nothing more than stopgap efforts to compensate for failure to plan, it follows that government economic planning of a high order—including, especially, the setting of specific goals and plans for achieving them—would *reduce* the amount of government regulation with which we have to contend. I advocate such national planning as a means of saving the very market system so often considered to be inconsistent with it. . . .[6]

J. Irwin Miller, chairman of Cummins Engine Corporation:

> Government must now become the systems manager of the total potential of its society, establishing objectives, setting limits, monitoring incentives and allowing all the forces to work freely where they are appropriately effective.[7]

Felix Rohatyn, partner in the investment house of Lazard Frères: "What many will call state planning would, to the average family, be no more than prudent budgeting."[8]

Seconding the call for government planning were such other business leaders as Henry Ford II; William May, chairman of American Can; and W. Michael Blumenthal, later U.S. Secretary of the Treasury and at the time chairman of Bendix. The result was a specific design for economic planning in the United States, the Balanced Growth and Planning Act of 1975. The Act proposed that a planning agency be set up in the White House to construct a six-year economic plan that would be revised and extended every two years. The plan would have to be approved by Congress. Once approved, it would guide U.S. economic policy, setting objectives for the allocation of capital, natural resources, and labor to specific sectors of the economy and establishing long-range goals for production and consumption. It was not authoritarian. No one—neither consumers nor corporations nor workers—would be forced to do anything. But given the importance of the federal government in the economy, a plan to guide its actions would have a powerful effect on who gets what. The bill was introduced in Congress by the late Senator Hubert Humphrey and Senator Jacob Javits of New York. Appropriately enough, the sponsors represented the two wings of the Keynesian post–World War II era, big government and big business. In its politics as well as in its substance, the bill reflected an initial synthesis of the economic future envisioned by the two wings of the informal "party" that dominated most of postwar America.

The Humphrey-Javits "trial balloon" burst. Ideological hostility to planning among businessmen was still widespread, particularly in the rising conservative tide of the late 1970s. Business instead would have its last ideological fling with the Reagan variation of the broker state, which promised the best of both worlds—a government that took care of business without requiring anything in return.

But the idea of planning could not go away, not only because planning was necessary to run the economy, but also because it was necessary to run the business corporation as well. Advanced, complex technology is the undisputed centerpiece of our multinational economy. It requires large amounts of capital and long lead times. The amount of capital investment per worker required in U.S. industry rose from $5,931 in 1950 to $46,151 in 1980.[9] And the time required for the introduction of an innovation—the research, the trial and error of production systems, the market testing, the establishment of complex financing, sales, and distribution networks—has grown enormously. But the investment of large amounts of capital over time increases the risk of loss from changing economic conditions over which the investor has no control. Accordingly, the modern corporation must attempt to forecast the future with precision, and it must attempt to *influence* the future as well. As one executive for J. C. Penney put it: "We think it is important not to be taken by surprise."[10]

The main point of corporate planning is to minimize uncertainty and competition in the market. Comments John Kenneth Galbraith:

> The modern large corporation and the modern apparatus of socialist planning are variant accommodations to the same need. It is open to every free-born man to dislike this accommodation. But he must direct his attack to the cause. He must not ask that jet aircraft, nuclear power plants or even the modern automobile in its

modern volume be subject to unfixed prices and unmanaged demand. He must ask instead that they not be produced.[11]

There are a variety of planning styles and levels of competence among modern corporations. There are good plans and bad plans, short-term plans and long-term plans. And to avoid some of the psychological resistance to the word "planning," the function often goes under the euphemism of "corporate strategy." But planning it is, and every major corporation tries to do more, not less, of it.

The planning process has been greatly assisted by the explosive growth of computerized communication and data processing. This permits the use of more information—including political and social variables that affect markets and widen the "horizon" of long-term corporate decision-making. As *Business Week* tells us,

sophisticated tools and techniques permit analysis of business, forecasting of such things as market growth, pricing and the impact of government regulation, and the establishment of a plan that can sidestep threats from competitors, economic cycles, and social, political, and consumer changes in an erratic environment.[12]

But no matter how sophisticated they may be, no matter how much market they control, corporations cannot by themselves—or even in collusion with each other—do the planning for the system as a whole. And that level of planning is increasingly necessary to keep the system from stagnating. Daniel Bell, a neoconservative admirer of corporate organization, writes:

Every major corporation today necessarily operates in accordance with a one-year fiscal plan and a five-year market strategy in order to meet competition or to expand its size. Each company plans singly and each introduces its own new technologies —yet no one monitors the collective effects. The same is true of the planning of various government agencies. In considering social effects, one finds this kind of planning unsatisfactory.[13]

Like the economies of other Western countries, the U.S. economy has become so integrated and interdependent that it is one big system in which many industries, firms, unions, government, consumers, workers, and so forth, are dependent for economic survival on each other. When the consumer buys a car, for example, he or she is not simply buying a product but a whole system—the wages of the salespeople; the rent on the showroom; the cost of delivering the car from the manufacturer; the wages, rent, and profits of the companies; the building and maintenance of highways; insurance; street lights; oil companies; gas stations; garages, and so on. To a certain extent, of course, this has always been true. The purchase of a carriage was also the purchase of a system that included the hayfield, the stable, the blacksmith, etc. But the modern economy is so much larger and more complex—and has so many fewer self-reliant units—that its inter-dependence is of a higher order.

When the typical American manufacturing corporation was con-cerned only with future demand for a few products in one industry, and when its planning information consisted of the seat-of-the-pants guesses of a few older salesmen about what next season's sales might be like, management's concern with government was typically limited to support for probusiness candidates and dues to an industry associa-tion concerned with keeping tariffs high. But when the postwar boom expanded that corporation to an international conglomerate with hold-ings in a variety of countries, with a sophisticated management that understood that an increase in the federal health budget might help their sales of hospital equipment but also put some of their cosmetic products under more scrutiny, and that a change in government policy producing a rise in the value of the dollar might decrease the sale of its exports but also decrease the cost of a proposed takeover in another country, then the government became an integral factor in their busi-ness decisions.

The uncertainties generated by the new economic era have inten-sified problems by undercutting the assumption of the stable future that corporations need to plan long-term growth. It is thus not that modern corporations are any more anxious to use the government for their own ends than they used to be; the Morgans, the Rockefellers, the Vanderbilts, et al., were hardly political shrinking violets. What is different is that the size and scope of the modern corporation force its leadership to be more concerned with the system as a whole. The government is the only institution with the legitimacy and authority to address systemwide problems. In their drive for higher profits and more growth corporate managers *must* try to influence government; it is the only institution with responsibility for the overall economy and thus capable of providing a climate of stability.

Just as the need for a growth strategy forced the neoconservatives in the Republican Party to abandon old prohibitions against deficit spending, so parts of the business community have slowly begun to abandon their professed faith in the market as the supreme institution of social order. The root problem is not that government is *too big*, it is that government is too weak and incompetent. The broker state is piecemeal and haphazard, lurching from ad hoc compromise to ad hoc compromise with no strategy or goal other than to get through the next election. Even Ronald Reagan, so appealing to business, who seemed so strong and decisive, was willing to gamble the stability of the entire system on a slapdash, contradictory program created not on the basis of thoughtful economic analysis but by politicians willing to promise voters the world.

The ideological dilemma facing business leadership has thus sharpened: they recognize the centrality of growth, but their anti-government ideology prevents competent planning necessary to accommodate the large-scale investment realities of the modern national and multinational corporation. The result is a confused groping to find a path that can provide subsidization for corporate goals, restrain destabilizing inflation, and maintain social peace—*without dissolving the political protection that antigovernment attitudes provide to the business sector.* They must find a way to maintain ideological proscriptions *against* government "interference" while increasing operational government support *for* business goals.

The most outspoken of the group of businessmen who recognize the need for strong government economic leadership is investment banker Felix Rohatyn. Bright and sophisticated, Rohatyn headed the Municipal Assistance Corporation—the consortium of bankers who refinanced, and took over fiscal supervision of, New York City after its near bankruptcy in 1975.[14] Rohatyn's major proposal is for a new version of the Reconstruction Finance Corporation (RFC) begun by Herbert Hoover to help out failing corporations in the early days of the Great Depression. The RFC was expanded by Franklin Roosevelt and became an instrument of federal economic planning during World War II. Its assets, which included 50 percent of the U.S. aluminum capacity, nearly 100 percent of the synthetic rubber capacity in the United States, and large investments in chemicals and other defense-related industries, were sold off when the postwar boom seemed to eliminate the need for government help to big business. The agency was abolished in the 1950s by the Eisenhower administration, which felt that the RFC was no longer necessary.[15]

Noting that government aid to corporations such as Chrysler was being handled on an inefficient, case-by-case basis by a Congress ill equipped to function as a lending officer of a bank, Rohatyn proposed that the government establish and capitalize a new RFC to provide loans and even equity investments to large firms whose survival is deemed to be in the national economic interest. It would also help in the long-term financing of public infrastructure essential to private productivity—roads, bridges, etc. For Rohatyn, the planning implications are clear:

> There can be no denying that such an organization . . . can be perceived as a first step toward state planning of the economy. Yet the time may have come for a public debate on this subject. Our economy is today subjected to certain traumas which have nothing to do with the result of free market interaction. The oil cartel and the prices of other basic commodities that directly affect our economy such as phosphates and aluminum are the result of political rather than economic decisions, and are totally beyond our control. . . .[16]

Similar proposals have been offered by others: a group of Senate Democrats headed by Edward Kennedy, a coalition of House Democrats from industrial states, the AFL-CIO, economists Lester Thurow and Robert Reich. And the general idea was endorsed by most of the Democratic candidates running for president in 1984.

A related set of planning proposals was presented by the editors of *Business Week* in a special issue of its magazine entitled "The Reindustrialization of America." As conceptualized in *Business Week*, "reindustrialization" is a concept that avoids explicit use of the term "planning," yet endorses an industrial policy, or plan, for increasing domestic and international growth of the private sector. The contradictory formula also shares some major assumptions common to the supply-side conservative position. It assumes that the key to a revised economy is more private capital investment and that the way to increase investment is to reduce the competition for resources coming from the public sector. The general formula is the same: Cut government spending and cut income and corporate taxes.

Business Week's editors do not by any means argue that all our problems are a result of big government. To be sure, they think there is too much regulation and an unfortunate tendency to "unproductive" social programs. But government is here to stay, and to finance it they advocate higher payroll and new sales taxes, which shift the tax burden further to workers and consumers. They also recognize the failure of business management itself to reinvest and plan for the future. They criticize American management for being obsessed with short-term profits. Another problem is the creaky structure of collective bargaining, which precludes the kind of cooperation between labor and management that the Japanese and the West Germans enjoy. *Business Week* even goes so far as to say that the failure of U.S. wages to keep pace with inflation has been making labor cheaper than capital

and has therefore undercut the incentive for investment in more productive plant and equipment.

The most important aspect of "reindustrialization" is explicit recognition of the need for a government role in allocating the broad pattern
of capital investment. Say the editors of *Business Week:*

> In the ideal world of David Ricardo, who more than 150 years ago formulated the
> well-known law of comparative advantage, there was no need for an industrial
> policy. Free trade ensured that all nations concentrated on what they were best at
> producing. But in the less than ideal world of the 1980s, the unfettered market has
> become obsolete. The industrial plans of other nations, enforced by a growing web
> of subsidies, tax incentives, and other arrangements, mean that international compe-
> tition is becoming increasingly influenced by government policy. And the U.S. has
> no real option but to develop its own industrial policy to avoid falling behind. The
> U.S. response so far—protectionism with apologies—has mainly been a way to
> avoid the serious issues.[17]

Interest in a national industrial policy aimed at going toe-to-toe with
Japan has spread through the ranks of Democratic politicians looking
for an economic horse to ride to power. It is reminiscent of Stockman
and Kemp several years earlier. One faction, which includes Representatives Timothy Wirth and Richard Gephardt and Senator Paul
Tsongas, stresses that revitalization of the U.S. economy depends
mainly on our ability to hold the lead in high technology. Originally
dubbed "Atari Democrats," their basic argument is that the United
States must make long-term strategic decisions to build up "winners"
—industries with the potential to expand their share of international
markets—and that the nation accept the decline of "losers" who have
little chance for trade expansion. Workers in loser industries would be
provided with retraining and assistance in moving to areas where the
jobs in growth industries are expanding. Other Democrats, under
pressure from traditional auto workers and steel unions, and seeking
votes in the declining Midwest, call for protection of "basic" industries
and join Rohatyn in urging RFC loans to help restructure and preserve
such less-high-technology firms.

The reindustrialization ideas of the corporate industrial planners are
a halfway effort to bring the economic institutions of the United States
up to date with the "worldwide dynamic of collectivization and
semisocialism." But they are a far cry from a competent planning
system. First and foremost they do not confront the basic dilemma of
the system—*how to have high growth, full employment, and price stability.* The corporate planners as a group leave us still hung up on the

Phillips Curve with neither a clear strategy to achieve high growth, nor any way other than recession to control inflation. Rohatyn's RFC attempts to rationalize broker state subsidies, but rational or not, such subsidies can at best only affect a small segment of the economy. High-technology jobs, for instance, amount at best to 3 percent of the U.S. economy (depending upon how they are defined). Many are in low-skilled, low-paid assembly work. Moreover, as the departure of one of the Atari company's California assembly facilities for Hong Kong illustrated in 1982, it is by no means clear that substantial numbers of high-technology production jobs can be kept in the United States in the absence of much more fundamental strategies. Nor, clearly, does assistance to the faltering auto and steel industries add up to a comprehensive strategy. In order to have a major impact on the way the overall economy behaves, the RFC would have to become a gigantic financial institution well beyond the selected industrial targeting dreams and intentions of its advocates. Other than the tax proposals, which Reagan by and large implemented in 1981, the reindustrialization program—*relative to the larger problems the corporate planners acknowledge the economy faces*—is surprisingly minor, despite the public attention it has received.

THE POLITICS OF DECLINE

It was opposition from within the corporate business class that led Rohatyn and others to abandon overall planning. And, in large part, it is their unwillingness to discipline the most destructive and antisocial behavior of specific industries and corporations that hobbles the reindustrialization program. For example, businessmen and bankers in private will bitterly denounce the economic plundering by the oil companies that has made the energy substructure of the entire economy vulnerable and drained huge amounts of consumer spending out of the domestic economy. But few reindustrializers can contemplate even the lightest controls on the major oil firms. Likewise, even after several years of murderously high interest rates imposed by the banking community led by Paul Volcker, the reindustrializers—many of them financiers themselves—could not bring themselves to consider any serious effort to dilute the independent control over credit and monetary policy exercised by the Federal Reserve Bank. The crucial difficulty in the reindustrialization program is what is *left out*. Reindustrialization ignores the central problem of achieving full employment, stable prices, and rising real incomes in the new era. Proposals to accelerate the growth of high-technology firms or to revive older smokestack industries aim at a relatively narrow sector of the economy and have little to say about the trade-off between unemployment and inflation. Nor do the proposals represent a strategy for sustaining long-term growth. Even a "successful" industrial policy that aided certain manufacturing industries could exist side by side with a stagnating economy seesawing between deep recession and bursts of inflation. On the campaign trail everyone is "for" full employment and price stability. But without a specific solution to the prices–jobs trade-off problem, there is no solution to the crisis.

Reindustrialization as presently conceived will do nothing to halt the system's incapacity to resume serious improvements in real income. Irrespective of their different public images, all three major variants of orthodox economic wisdom—the burned-out Keynesianism represented by Charles Schultze and Jimmy Carter, the neoconservative contradictions of David Stockman and Ronald Reagan, and the uneasy planning compromise proposed by Felix Rohatyn and *Business Week*—all point to an overall economics of decline and a politics of divisiveness. This grim direction is well symbolized by the gruff, cigar-smoking banker's banker from New York, Paul Volcker. Volcker was appointed by Carter and reappointed by Reagan to the Federal Reserve Board chairmanship. His tight-money policies were the anti-inflationary linchpin of Reagan's program. And Volcker personally helped the bailouts of Penn Central, Chrysler, the Hunt brothers, and the savings and loan associations. Volcker uttered the essence of American economic policy since the new era began when he said in 1979: "The standard of living of the average American has to decline. I don't think you can escape that."[18]

Because a relatively small percentage of the poor vote, the antipoverty efforts of the Great Society were slashed. Unfortunately, the savings still to be made by eliminating public spending on the poor are small potatoes. Rohatyn has identified a number of places where cuts have to be made in the middle-class standard of living in order to get more capital for industrial and infrastructure subsidies. These include a major new tax on gasoline, large cuts in farm price supports, significant income reduction in Social Security, and the imposition of a military draft (which reduces the cost of paying for the volunteer army). But the savings needed to finance Rohatyn's programs are not easily obtained here; the middle class votes and resists Volcker's dictum of a lower standard of living. When Reagan cut Social Security benefits for the children of deceased or disabled workers, which primarily affected blue-collar families, there was little opposition; and a

1982 compromise permitted small additional savings and temporary postponement of cost of living adjustments, but no large-scale Social Security cuts are likely to occur. And when Reagan tried to scale back loans to college students, there was a roar of opposition from the middle class, and even hard-line congressional conservatives had to break with the President.[19]

To sell its program to the people, reindustrializers have explicitly included *organized* labor in their social contract.[20] Based on the kind of arrangements that exist in Japan and Germany, their assumption is that a deal can be made by having the leadership of the business community sit down with the leadership of organized labor. But there are obvious problems with this strategy in a situation where success requires a cut in the workers' standards of living. Rohatyn himself maps wage restraint as the price of RFC loans, and other corporate leaders, already able to force unions to "give back" previous gains in new contracts, are seeking more oppressive action.

Moreover, neither business nor labor is sufficiently organized to deliver their constituencies to an economywide bargain in an era when real wages are already dropping and corporations see opportunities for breaking union power. The United States is not like Japan or Western Europe, where bankers and businessmen all come from the same few schools and form a tight social system. The overwhelming majority of the fourteen million businesses in the United States are small and unorganized by unions. These businesses are unwilling to let a few corporate leaders—most of whom manage firms that *are* organized—represent them in a deal with big labor. Reindustrialization proposals are still too much the product of eastern financiers and midwestern durable-goods manufacturers at a time when the dynamism of American capitalism has shifted west and south, into oil and real estate and the growth of the Sunbelt money centers in Miami, Atlanta, Houston, Phoenix, and Los Angeles. In many of these newer centers of corporate power, even limited reindustrialization smacks suspiciously of a plot to bail out the old industries of the Northeast and Midwest and is resisted.

As for labor, unions represent only about 20 percent of the labor force; even if a deal is cut with this group, it is likely to be insufficient. The expansion of private-sector jobs in America over the past decade has come in the low-paying, unorganized service sector. The increase of eleven million jobs between 1973 and 1979 was concentrated in the nonmanufacturing sector of the economy, primarily services and retail trade. As economist Emma Rothschild points out, *increases* in employment in eating and drinking places over that period were greater than the *total* employment in the auto and steel industries combined in 1979. For the most part restaurants and similar services generate low-wage, often part-time jobs. A large percentage of such jobs go to women who need them to maintain family living standards or to support themselves and their children.

The new workers represent an element in the increasingly *dual* nature of the labor force. At the top is a layer of well-paid unionized or professional employees whose incomes have kept pace with, or even outpaced, inflation. On the bottom is an expanding layer of lower-paid workers, less skilled and/or less organized.[21] People at the bottom tend to eat at home; those at the top go to restaurants. People in the lower end wash their own clothes; those in the upper end take their woolens to the dry cleaner. The various investment tax subsidies originally proposed by Carter, expanded and enacted by Reagan, and supported strongly by the corporate planners will—to the extent they do affect capital investment—aggravate unemployment problems. They increase the use of automation and other more efficient (labor saving) technology at a time when the general demand for labor is sluggish, further limiting growth of employment in the capital-intensive industries. Shrinkage in industrial employment under such circumstances in effect changes high-paid steelworkers into low-paid laundry workers. Indeed, there is growing evidence that the combined effect of slow growth, automation, and the shift to services is depleting the middle class itself. Between 1960 and 1975 the number of people earning incomes in the middle range—roughly 20 percent below average to 20 percent above—shrank by 23 percent. The number of people in the top range rose by 8 percent while the number at the bottom expanded by 17 percent. The accelerated loss of manufacturing jobs since 1975 has aggravated the situation. Thus, there is a growing population of frustrated, insecure, and potentially very angry people desperately trying to hang on to middle-class status on unstable lower-class incomes.[22]

In the absence of a planning capacity capable of delivering sustained growth in real income, racial tensions within the work force also exacerbate the problem of achieving a social deal over labor's share. In theory the burden of limiting labor's income might be distributed equally among all workers. But it is more likely that such pressures will intensify conflict within the working class, dividing worker from worker both within and between income groups. A 1980 *New York Times* survey found a direct relationship between fear of unemployment among whites and negative attitudes about blacks. Whites personally worried about unemployment tended to believe that the unemployment rate for blacks was the same as or below that of whites. Whites who were *not* worried about unemployment held a more accurate picture of the black unemployment rate—which is regularly roughly double the white rate. When asked what was the cause of unemployment among blacks, 50 percent of the worried whites cited "laziness," as opposed to 38 percent of the unworried group.[23]

Under any circumstances, one would expect that affirmative action —the notion that members of a group who have been historically discriminated against deserve some special compensation in the present—would meet with resistance. But a decade of slow growth in real income and a slowdown in social and economic mobility among the white middle class brought support for affirmative action to a standstill. A Gallup Poll in 1977 found that only 11 percent of respondents agreed that "women and members of minority groups should be given preferential treatment in getting jobs and places in college."[24]

Recognizing that a corporate-oriented industrial policy will intensify the economic pain among a wide variety of groups, *Business Week* comments: "Thus the major challenge will be to establish a framework for national industrial planning that neutralizes the traditional interest groups." "Neutralizes"? "Traditional interest groups"? Who are they? Not business, of course. But, surprisingly, not labor either. Not even the educational establishment. The following is *Business Week*'s solution for achieving a social consensus:

> The leaders of the various economic and social groups that compose U.S. society should agree on a program for reindustrialization and present that program to Washington. *Neither Congress nor the Administration is capable of providing the leadership necessary to form a national consensus.* Business, labor and academic leaders should establish a forum to hammer out a new social contract for the U.S. Special groups must recognize that their own unique goals cannot be satisfied if the U.S. cannot compete in world markets. The drawing of a social contract must take precedence over the aspirations of the poor, the minorities, and the environmentalists. Without such a consensus, all are doomed to lower levels of living, fewer rights, and increasingly dirty air and water.[25]

After a hundred pages of a tough-minded if business-oriented analysis of the nation's economic problems, and innumerable suggestions for this or that public intervention in the market, the reindustrialization proposals thus fade into a vague scheme for leaving the fate of the nation in the hands of an ad hoc collection of unidentified leaders whose avowed purpose is to draw up a social contract that excludes the nation's poor and minorities (who together make up some 21 percent

of the population—forty-seven million people)[26] and environmentalists, who on many issues make up a majority of our people. Moreover,
it excludes from participation the government—the only legitimate
institution for the formulation of national policy and the institution
that is supposed to carry out the policy of reindustrialization. It would
be hard to imagine a process with less chance of achieving a lasting
social consensus for policies that demand great pain.

America seems on its way to repeating the experience of Britain as
we move toward the final years of the twentieth century. Prior to the
election of Margaret Thatcher, a succession of alternating British governments of Right and Left created a pattern of "stop-go" economic
policies in which Labor governments pushed for slightly expansive
policies mixed with industrial planning measures, and Conservative
governments slightly restrictive. Since neither had much of a mandate,
neither had much political elbowroom in which to maneuver. The
1970s were treated to the spectacle of Labor governments forced to
impose wage austerity on the unions and Conservative governments
overseeing the nationalization of companies such as Rolls-Royce. The
government of Margaret Thatcher, elected on a promise to curb labor
and lessen the power of the state, adopted a hard-line monetary policy
that sent unemployment rates to the highest levels since the Depression. High interest rates also destroyed large numbers of small and
medium-sized businesses. Antagonism between labor and capital worsened, with workers striking out in blind anger against reforms that
might make industry more efficient, and the capitalist class seeming to
relish mean-spirited policies to punish the labor force as much as to
discipline it. The economic crisis in turn periodically exacerbated
growing race conflict, something Britain had historically been able to
avoid. In the spring of 1981, Great Britain saw her first modern riots
—a confused mixture of both class and racial strife. Only the war fever
built up by Thatcher's "tough" stance in the Falkland Islands, and the
division in the opposition parties, rescued Thatcher from the oblivion
the polls had predicted as her economic policy collapsed.

Since the end of World War II our sense of community in America
has depended on material growth. Differences in race, ancestors, lan-
guage, and region were smothered by the materialism of the great
boom. Our food, our education, our jobs, our very landscape—the
highways bordered by Burger King and Kentucky Fried Chicken and
Exxon—were homogenized. However one might feel about the quality of that culture, it provided a sense of the familiar, and in a time of

great change it has, in its odd way, provided some sense of stability. Mass culture was a readily understood metaphor for progress and personal opportunity. Combined with the boom-created mobility— Americans hopping back and forth across the country, meeting each other on buses, in restaurants and airplanes, at conferences and conventions, and most of all seeing people from other regions night after night on television—postwar commercial culture offered a sense of sameness cemented together with expectations of more consumer goods, better jobs, and a decent retirement. America became a global village of its own, people connected by a trust that tomorrow would be better than today.

The trust has faded. As the tide of crises rises, the American Dream of infinite upward mobility is disappearing. In the past only the poor, the marginal people living in the lowlands of the economy, had to struggle to keep their heads above water. But now the waves are splashing into the foothills of the great middle class.

"We are not middle, we are not mobile, and we are not affluent," says a university professor. "We are up against the wall and are going nowhere—and neither are our kids."

"There was a time, before the children arrived, that I felt middle class," says a postal clerk, "but I don't anymore."

An out-of-work business executive tells what it feels like to be facing unemployment for the first time, to lose health benefits, to be months behind in bills, to face foreclosure of the mortgage: "And in the late evening when your household is quiet and you switch off the bedroom light, it's to be alone, alone like you've never been before. To lie there looking at the darkness and wonder if you're going to lose the home . . . the only equity you've been able to accumulate in 30 years of work and raising a family."[27]

Those higher up the economic elevations stare uneasily at people caught in the swirl of troubles below. The TV flashes on angry auto workers, farmers being foreclosed, the face of a mother whose baby was bitten to death by rats, or a ninety-year-old woman jailed for three days for stealing fifteen dollars' worth of food. People at the top of the economic mountain speculate in real estate, Impressionist paintings, gold, some uneasy in the knowledge that these efforts to save oneself make it worse for everyone else.

In America, inner-city neighborhoods have long been festering sores of unemployment and pain. Antidiscrimination laws have made it easier for the exceptionally gifted and aggressive minority people to escape, but the masses of the black and Hispanic poor remain trapped in a world dominated by crime and drugs and dwindling welfare checks. Old people live in terror and young people without hope. Violence is everywhere, for the most part hidden and private—muggings, robbery, and rape, daily occurrences that rarely make the newspapers, much less the headlines. "The riots of the sixties never ended," one policeman points out, "they just became spread out, decentralized, into a one-on-one thing."

The prospect of violence also undermines support for both democracy and civil liberties. The continuation of a relative quiet, observed a government Task Force on Disorders and Terrorism as early as 1977, is a "false calm and we must see in the current social situation an accumulation of trouble for the future."[28] It urged federal, state, and local governments to plan for an inevitable social explosion. Suggested procedures include giving governors the power to impose curfews, requiring citizens to carry identification papers, temporarily suspending some legal rights, spying on suspected terrorist groups, and creating more efficient "last resort" military forces to assist the police.

For a President, the person in the American system nominally in charge of maintaining social cohesion, the great temptation is, of course, to sustain national unity by finding a foreign enemy. Foreign policy is a grand stage, more removed from stalemates on the home front, for national adventure and leadership heroics. Gerald Ford's dramatic "rescue of the *Mayaguez*" was the most popular action of his Administration despite the forty American casualties. The Navy's shooting down of two antiquated Libyan fighter planes in the summer of 1981 and the invasion of the tiny island of Grenada bolstered Reagan's sagging popularity in the polls. Discussing the terrible temptation of foreign policy for contemporary presidents, Richard Barnet has observed of Lyndon Johnson:

> He could do something. He did not have to "sit in my rocking chair" (to use Johnson's words) and admit that he, the President of the United States, was as powerless to influence the dangerous outside world as he was to change America . . . If he claims to be winning the "war on inflation" it is possible to determine the accuracy of his claim at the local supermarket. But who can successfully challenge his claim to be winning the hearts and minds of Southeast Asia by improving the "kill ratio"? Only when a foreign war meets with obvious disaster does the President lose his firm (and exclusive) grip on the flag.[29]

In *preparing* for foreign dangers, however illusory, there is a clear advantage: As a job-creating quick-fix, military spending has considerable short-term attraction. Although shifting resources away from productive investment to the military sector ultimately weakens American productivity, military necessity provides the least difficult political rationale for spending—and for the stimulative policies needed to pull the economy out of stagnation. The major insight of Keynes in this regard has not been disproved. If reliable growth does not come through "supply side" tax incentives or "reindustrialization," there is another option: an even greater increase in military spending, under threat of new international crisis, imagined or real, is *the* economic ace in the hole, the ultimate card for the entire spectrum of strategies we have been examining. As it is, the shrinkage of manufacturing jobs, the general shifts to low-paying services, and the cutbacks in student loans and aid to education mean that millions of American high school graduates now face the grim choice of dead-end service jobs or joining the army. Carry a mop at McDonald's or carry a rifle.[30]

Writing in *The Wall Street Journal*, Irving Kristol proclaims nothing "relevant" to the state of the world except "an American foreign policy in which power, and the readiness to use it boldly, will play a far more central role than has ever before been the case in our human history." Kristol's rationale for a permanent state of war preparedness is a call for violence as the only solution to the fundamental problems of the new economic era.

> *Nor will the United States really have any alternative but to use such power to recreate a world order it can live with*—a world in which there is relatively free trade and relatively free access to the world's resources . . . Our economic growth will henceforth be as dependent on our foreign policy as on our economic policy. And if we fail to establish the conditions for such growth, our democracy will itself unravel, as economic pressures give rise to political polarization, at home and abroad.[31]

Recession at home and aggressiveness abroad are on the same political and economic continuum. As economic anxiety grows, it is not too much to imagine that there might come a time when we will feel the need to put our foot down, to demand a strong leader, someone who knows how to get things done, someone to unify us, make us feel good to be Americans again, show us which foreign devil is the cause of our troubles. There could come a time when we will feel that both democracy and peace are luxuries, slightly impractical—like a job for everyone, stable prices, clean air and water, and other extravagances we no longer seem able to afford.

Part II

An organic commonwealth—and only such common-wealths can join together to form a shapely and articulated race of men—will never build itself up out of individuals but only out of small and ever smaller communities: a nation is a nation to the degree that it is a community of communities.

MARTIN BUBER,
Pathways in Utopia

Chapter 5

A COMMUNITY-SUSTAINING ECONOMICS

Crammed within the limits of obsolete ideologies, conventional economics' failure to escape the worsening "trade-off" between unemployment and inflation has substantially narrowed our vision of the future. The public debate no longer concerns how to use this rich nation's natural and human wealth to create a bountiful, just, and ecologically rational society. Those who represent the variations of the economics of decline—Volcker, Schultze, Stockman, Rohatyn—are obsessed with the problem, in Schultze's words, of "how to allocate the pain." The "zero sum" society has become a self-fulfilling prophecy. The central question is: Who suffers? Economics is once more the dismal science.

Yet the objective facts of our economic potential tell a different story; they show that even if we simply operated our economy closer to its existing capacity, we could generate the resources needed to sew up the ripping seams of our social fabric. Economist Frank de Leeuw has demonstrated, for instance, that had we reduced the average unemployment rate between 1970 and 1979 by just a little over one percentage point (from 6.2 percent to 5 percent) we could have enjoyed almost $500 billion worth of additional goods and services. The American people would have had an additional $310 billion in income to spend and/or save, and the cumulative federal deficit for the period would have been $177 billion less.[1] After studying the relationship between economic growth and unemployment during the twenty-year postwar period from 1956 to 1976, Professor Steven Sheffrin of the University of California concluded that had we been able to lower the U.S. unemployment rate to levels *achieved by most European nations in the same period,* we would have enjoyed an additional $3.8 *trillion* worth of goods and services over the period, plus an additional $750 billion in federal revenue. By 1976, *annual* federal tax receipts would have been almost $100 billion above what they actually were, with no change in tax rates. With such revenues we could have completely eliminated poverty (at a cost in 1976 of $16 billion), raised the rate of public antipollution programs to a level that would have substantially cleaned up the environment by 1985 ($18 billion annual cost)—and still cut individual federal income taxes by over one third.[2]

In early 1983 roughly 11 percent of Americans who were willing and able to work were out of a job—about twelve million people.[3] Had we enjoyed full employment we would have added, conservatively, $400 billion to our Gross National Product and another $125 billion in federal tax revenues—enough to cut substantially the then estimated federal deficit. Yet the American political debate was not focused on the central issue of how truly to maximize our output, but on the question of how to cut costs and trim losses. Both the Republicans and the Democrats were mesmerized by the prospect of Ronald Reagan's presiding over a massive deficit. It was understandable that Democrats would want to hoist Reagan by his own petard, but it was essentially a sideshow, diverting attention from the enormous waste of resources accepted by conventional economic wisdom on both sides of the political aisle.

Looking at the American economy as a manager might look at a business enterprise—in terms of its assets, labor force, skills, and so forth—rather than through the ideological prisms of our politics, it is obvious that our economic problems lie not in what we are but in what we do. There is no *intrinsic* reason for anyone in America who is willing and able to work to be out of a job. There is no intrinsic reason why every American should not have access to the basic necessities of life. In the face of this nation's enormous wealth, any economic ideology that cannot produce employment and a decent minimum standard of living for all Americans willing to participate in the work of our society is a failure by the simple test of common sense.

TOWARD A NEW PARADIGM

The task ahead requires America to choose, to allocate resources, to plan in a way we have never done other than in wartime. To do so also requires a greater degree of national unity than we have ever had before. Hamstrung by obsolete ideologies, mainstream economic strategies cannot offer a program that can provide sustainable benefits to a majority, and thus there is little prospect for an operational mandate for effective and fair planning. We grasp at small, temporary economic improvements while the larger trends continue. It boils down to waiting for crisis—the *deus ex machina* that can solve the problem for us. Says Rohatyn: "Although it is impossible to predict whether it will be monetary or military, in the Middle East or in Cleveland, the potential for military, economic, or social strife is probably too great to be avoided. When a crisis of sufficient magnitude creates the possibility for fundamental change, it will carry with it enough of a popular majority for action so that a President with a real vision of the future will be able to put his program through."[4]

Yet in a volatile and unstable world, a crisis great enough to force national unity might well destroy us. Moreover, a consensus created out of crisis lasts only so long as the crisis itself lasts. And our dilemma is not a short-term one. We will be facing the problems of the new economic era for as far as we can see into the future. This requires a consensus that can endure—that will not disappear when the headlines fade, or at the first signs of discomfort and strain. This is also quite different from a narrow-interest group deal. Professor Theodore J. Lowi reminds us of how inadequate such arrangements are: "The very success of established groups is a mortgage against the future of new needs that are not yet organized or are not readily accommodated by established groups."[5] . . . "Group needs for stability seem to be so great that they have helped to convert modern governments into additional means of system maintenance for groups *rather than for the society at large.*"[6]

Nor will a solution be found in restricting democracy. The roots of freedom and sense of the right to protest and oppose are too deep in America simply to limit; they must either be cut back severely, or extended. If we are to save democracy in the new economic era, we must expand it. In a democratic society an operational mandate for effective policies and an enduring consensus can come only from an individual's sense of responsibility to a common interest, a willingness of people to support public decisions as legitimate even when they disagree on details. Such support comes voluntarily from a deeper sense of commitment to shared values.

Values are not window dressing; they cannot be added after the fact, once the technical economists have done their work. Here is where another "neoliberal" thread gets lost. The work of MIT Professor Lester Thurow, for example, represents a perspective on economics that is technically competent, and reasonably uncluttered with old ideology. Thurow finds interest-group deals repugnant and he respects informed, expert decision-making. Yet having identified as crucial the issue of consensus in his *Zero-Sum Society,* he throws up his hands in despair at our political institutions and retreats into a weak hope that we will adopt a parliamentary system that seems more likely to encourage party discipline and somehow force choices. This is Thurow's mistake: at the critical place in his analysis, he turns back. Thurow's analysis is partly correct, but his solution cannot be taken seriously. The problem is not the "failure" of something called "politics." Nor is it a failure of economics per se. The problem lies in the *limits* of an economics which, when it uncovers the critical question, declares itself to have reached the edge of its intellectual jurisdiction. It is no answer to admonish politicians to get their house in order. Since consensus is lacking, even if we were to adopt a parlimentary system, we are again left waiting for the Godot of political crisis to liberate the experts so they can apply their solutions without interference from the messy realm of an ineffectual politics. Economic planning lies in wait for political agreement.

The fundamental question is how to *establish* and *maintain* sufficient social agreement to produce an operational mandate for sustained economic progress. And this in turn requires policy alternatives based on different principles from those that undergird our failing ideologies. The steady metamorphosis of the advanced industrial systems toward de facto, if hobbled, planning is grinding up the real-world basis for traditional theories, rendering them more and more obsolete before our eyes each day. This opens the door to—and requires—a parallel metamorphosis in our politics. But it does not guarantee one; nor does it point toward an equitable or democratic solution.

The dominant realities of the final years of the twentieth century require us consciously to accept planning as a central element of a new paradigm. Not that markets are irrelevant. Quite the contrary; the market is a powerful, useful, and important mechanism in any society, capitalist or socialist. It is only when the market is urged as the "be all and end all" of economics that it blinds us to what is true about the world. An essential first principle therefore is that we relinquish the myth that our own government must stay free of the economy and that responsibility can be abdicated in favor of an "invisible hand" unguided by conscious decision, plan, or principle.

A second principle follows directly from the first: if conscious human choice—rather than the unguided, mechanistic workings of the market—is to play a strategic role in economic policy decisions, then the values that inform human choice must be *explicit.* We must cease to promote the illusion of value-free, technically objective economics as if it could operate in pure abstraction, divorced from human concern. This includes honoring the values at the heart of the liberal and conservative traditions—but *in ways appropriate to the new conditions we face.*

The corporate planners do not address this issue. In the absence of the tightly knit class systems of Western Europe and Japan, where one large room often can hold the people necessary to reach agreement on major issues, the American social contract will have to be more open and its benefits spread widely. And it must recognize at the outset our historic commitment to freedom and decentralization. This is the starting point for a reconstruction of political-economic ideology in the era of planning.

FREEDOM AND COMMUNITY

The traditional problem of freedom is how to protect the individual *both* from authoritarianism, the excessive power of the state, *and* from anarchy, the absence of state power. Freedom is a complex value. And it certainly does not manifest itself in the economic dimension alone. A sense of individual freedom is rooted in a great many factors of human life that economic policy cannot hope to influence intelligently. But in the economic dimension, there are certain fundamental requirements for the exercise of human freedom.

Traditional conservatism, for instance, emphasized the importance of the individual entrepreneur as the condition of political freedom. Yet the malfunctioning of the broker state economy has increased the bankruptcy rate of small business to a fifty-year record. Fewer than one in five small businesses now survive for more than five years.[7] The monetarist illustration has sentenced tens of thousands of small businesses to bankruptcy court. And it has largely eliminated going into business for oneself as an option for most people. An alternative strategy must minimally be more serious about the conditions needed to sustain individual entrepreneurs in the new economic era.

Still, only 8½ million individuals call themselves entrepreneurs in America today.[8] How can freedom in its economic dimensions be made real to the rest of the nation?

A central building element of the American political system historically was the notion of private property, generally understood in the eighteenth century to be arable land. Without secure economic footing anchored in land, the individual was lost. Jefferson, Madison, and the majority of the early architects of the Constitution believed that in an agricultural society, an inalienable right to property in land was necessary if the individual were to survive independent of the approval and sufferance of the state. At the same time, the right to property gave the masses a stake in social stability and order that protected the state against anarchy. During the 1787 Constitutional Convention, Noah Webster put it this way:

> In what does real power consist? The answer is short and plain—in property. A general and tolerably equal distribution of landed property is the whole basis of national freedom.[9]

The foreign and domestic policy of the United States for its first hundred years involved a series of government programs to maintain this condition by providing land-ownership opportunities for the burgeoning population. The Louisiana Purchase, the rejection of slavery, the Homestead Act, and the Farm Credit Acts were major landmarks in the evolution of economic freedom. Widespread distribution of land into small individual holdings was the conscious policy of the United States government to support economic growth *and* democracy.

The accumulation of the nation's capital in the hands of large corporate agricultural institutions that hardly existed at the time of Jefferson have made his model of citizen-farmer obsolete, and the industrialization of America has made the question of land ownership more symbolic than real. The self-sufficient farmer owning his own land has evolved into the wage-earning suburbanite owning a fraction of an acre. In more recent times, the federal government, focusing on the symbol of land rather than the underlying issue of a stake in the production system, has helped to finance housing. Encouraging widespread home ownership is still a reasonable goal for government policy, but it does not provide the protection from state power that farmland once did.

In late-twentieth-century capitalism the job is comparable to private *real* property in the late eighteenth century. For the overwhelming majority of modern Americans, economic survival—and therefore freedom and independence—now depends on access to work. Jefferson understood the two had similar functions:

> The earth is given as a common stock to man to labor and live on. If for the encouragement of industry we allow it to be appropriated, we must take care that other employment be permitted to those excluded from appropriation. If we do not, the fundamental right to labor the earth returns to the unemployed.[10]

And the modern business consultant and writer Peter Drucker observes:

> For the great majority of people in most developed countries, land was the true "means of production" until well into this century, often until World War II. It was property in land which gave access to economic effectiveness and with it to social standing and political power. It was therefore rightly called by the law "real" property.
>
> In modern developed societies, by contrast, the overwhelming majority of the people in the labor force are employees of "organizations"—in the U.S. the figure is 93%—and the "means of production" is therefore the job. The job is not "wealth." It is not "personal property" in the legal sense. But it is a "right" in the means of production, an "ius in rem," which is the real definition of real property. Today the job is the employee's means of access to social status, to personal opportunity, to achievement and to power.[11]

If independence and freedom are to have meaning for the vast majority, the right to a job is a central principle of a new paradigm. It has limits, of course—just as real-property rights do. In today's society there are constraints on an individual's right to pollute and defile the land, or to use it in a way that seriously disturbs one's neighbors. If the landowner does not pay his taxes—the price of public protection—the land can be taken away by the community. In the same manner, the right to a job cannot mean the right to get drunk on the job, to give less than an honest day's work, to be uncooperative or otherwise unproductive. The right to a job means simply that everyone must be able to count on the opportunity to earn a living if the condition of economic freedom is to be met.

If freedom is to be grounded in the real world rather than used abstractly as a rationale for broker state indulgences, we must also explore its meaning in other economic aspects of the ordinary citizen's life. The prerequisites for independent decision-making for most people boil down to some practical considerations: enough income to pay the rent, to put food on the table, to be free of worry over medical bills, to afford a child. In practice a sense of freedom means most of all a life that moves toward expanding options—one in which it is possible to exercise free individual choices between work and leisure, between going into business and working for someone else, between taking care of one's children and having a career, between short-run higher income and investing in one's skills through more schooling. These are the nitty-gritty economic freedoms of everyday life. On any moral scale, an economic strategy that aims to establish secure footings to enable everyone to exercise such freedom holds more weight than the provision of still more income and wealth to those who already enjoy an immense amount of freedom of economic choice. Social justice is a condition of community.

For this reason, and since freedom in modern society is also to a substantial extent a function of money, the distribution of income and wealth must become a legitimate subject for democratic planning. It is a topic in which there are no absolutes. Rewards and incentives are necessary to encourage individual performance in our culture. But in the name of incentive we have created an economy that has one of the most unequal distributions of income and wealth in the industrialized world—along with one of the slowest rates of economic growth. In the name of incentive we have maintained extraordinary earnings and wealth gaps between races and sexes. In the name of incentive we have perversely shifted the tax burden from unearned and inherited wealth to earned income, a socially regressive step that is gradually hardening class lines.

The Consumer Price Index also offers one practical measure of economic freedom: when costs for the basic necessities increase, day-to-day freedom for most Americans diminishes rapidly. The prospect of old age becomes not a period when the rewards of a life of hard work are reaped, but the choice of begging from one's children or living in misery. Again, trying to maintain one's living standard in the face of a deliberate effort by the central bank to force it downward is exhausting and constraining. Gradually the future appears not as a place for expanded freedom but as a prison.

Freedom does not mean that everyone must have a *right* to a high standard of living or to success in business. But if economic freedom means anything, it must be associated with the ability to bargain with the world for an increase in real income in return for an increase in real work. For the majority of Americans such a bargain is harder and harder to make.

The elements needed to undergird economic freedom in the modern era suggest one set of requirements for planning. At the same time, we must address the threat that increasing government power inevitably poses. There are, of course, constitutional ways of limiting and checking government. In the past few decades, for example, procedures for due process, public hearings, appeals to the courts, and extensions of legal assistance have been developed to protect the right of citizens and corporations against arbitrary government action. Although such mechanisms are essential, exclusive reliance on them to defend individual freedoms generates delay and constant appeals to the courts. America is already the most litigious society in the world. We have three times as many lawyers per capita as West Germany, seven times as many as France, and twenty times as many as Japan.[12] Our obsession with laws, lawsuits, and legal battling is not by any means solely a function of enlarged government; still, it is clear that the use of essentially negative legalistic mechanisms is inadequate to the challenge of constraining centralized authority.

In continent-spanning America, a nation twice as populous as Japan and four times as populous as West Germany, we need to develop an approach to planning that self-consciously holds economic strategy accountable to the principles of decentralized power. This requires an enhanced sense of the importance of locality, a concept traditional conservatism also understood very well. "Democratic process is an invention of local bodies," wrote the founder of the Chicago school of economics (and Milton Friedman's teacher), H. C. Simons. "Modern democracy rests upon free responsible local government and will never be stronger than this foundation."[13] An emphasis on localism rests upon two principles. One is that individuals can participate in public decisions most effectively at the local level. The second is that in modern society strong local governments are needed to prevent a large central government from destroying individual freedom in the name of democracy.

Conservative sociologist Robert Nisbet adds the warning that "the longing for community which now exists as perhaps the most menacing fact of the Western World will not be exorcised by incantations drawn from the writings of Bentham, Mills and Spencer."[14] Nisbet's concern is that the communityless, alienated individual in unstable mass society can be manipulated into an experience of artificial community by those with access to central power, the mass media, and the other instruments of totalitarianism.

Nisbet also rejects the idea that freedom for the individual can be achieved simply by removing government from the environment. "Economic freedom cannot rest upon moral atomism or upon large-scale impersonalities," he concludes, "it never has." "Economic freedom has prospered, and continued to prosper, only in areas and spheres where it has been joined to a flourishing associational life. Economic freedom cannot be separated from nonindividualistic aspects of association and community of moral purpose."[15]

Conservative and neoconservative ideologies have distorted the legitimate fear of centralized government as a way to attack programs they oppose. But fears of "big government" could not be manipulated to stalemate progress if there were not a real issue at its core. The key to balancing the interests of the state with the interests of the individual in the new economic era lies in strong intermediate-scale units of society, both local and regional. Republican administrations from Richard Nixon's and Gerald Ford's to Ronald Reagan's have emphasized the importance of returning decision-making to state and local governments. Yet it is conservative economic policies that undermine the economic foundations of locality and thus destroy the capacity of local institutions to protect people from the arbitrary power of the state. The conservative insistence on the absolute mobility of capital contradicts the conservative insistence on stable local institutions.

It is one thing to return decision-making to localities; it is quite another to let them hold the bag for a failing economy and a national cut-the-budget political strategy. Ultimately, communities in decay will turn to Washington for assistance, and with this turning inevitably come the bureaucratic strings and centralized tendencies of the broker state. Local economic health is a precondition of local political independence. Therefore, planning that takes decentralized decision-making and *local* democracy seriously must necessarily assure that the economic underpinnings of local communities' independence are secure. For most entrepreneurs—grocers, retail clothiers, service station owners—the central economic issue also is whether their local environment is secure. Furthermore, intermediate-scale institutions—churches, neighborhood organizations, labor unions, local governments—do not exist in the abstract; they flourish only in a healthy local economic climate. "Conservatives who aimlessly oppose planning, whether national or local, are their own worst enemies," Nisbet observes: "What is needed, however, is planning that contents itself with the setting of human life, not human life itself."[16]

Theologian Martin Buber put the essential principle in these words: "The primary aspiration of all history is a genuine community of human beings—genuine because it is a *community all through*. . . . A community that failed to base itself on the actual and communal life of big and little groups living and working together, and on their mutual relationships, would be fictitious and counterfeit. . . ."[17]

Any effective strategy for dealing with the economic crisis that does not threaten democracy must provide for a compensating counterweight to the inevitable centralizing tendencies of planning by strengthening the economic basis of local communities. The principle of community cannot be an afterthought of economic policy—tacked on at the end of a program to keep the mayor happy. It must be an organic part of the way we plan.

A SUSTAINABLE SOCIETY

The twenty-first century will be characterized by the exhaustion of some of the natural resources that now sustain us. Hence the 1980s and 1990s are transitional. At the same time as we must provide jobs and full production to avoid economic and social chaos, we must simultaneously shift the *way* we produce. At the same time as we are developing new technologies and resources to substitute for old ones, we must practice resource conservation. It is not simply that we lack the oil to fuel our auto fleet and heat our homes, it is rather that the entire ecological system that sustains society is threatened. "We're coming now to a situation where the water, the farmland, the energy, the resources, the pollution dissipation capacity clearly cannot continue to be used at the increasing rate that we have been seeing," warns MIT professor J. W. Forrester.[18]

Both renewable and nonrenewable resources are under severe pressure as rising demands begin to push biological systems to the limits of their productivity and beyond. The results are apparent in deteriorating soils, declining fish catches, and deforested hillsides. Numerous expert studies—from the United Nations, the World Bank, the International Union for the Conservation of Nature and Natural Resources, the Worldwatch Institute, and many other organizations—have pointed to an impending ecological crisis.

Economic stagnation is no answer to the problem. In modern society, unemployment and widespread economic insecurity are even greater political threats to an ethic of ecological sanity. It is in economically stagnant towns and cities that we find people willing to foul the air and contaminate the water for the sake of a few jobs. It is in hard times that people are willing to trade their children's birthright of the continent's natural beauty for a few pennies off the electric bill. Conversely, concern with clean air and water blossomed into an environmental movement during the 1960s—our longest period of sustained prosperity. It was not because the problems were more acute. The major cities of the nation were dirtier and more full of choking pollutants earlier in the century than they were in the 1960s. And the rivers of the country had been open sewers for decades before Rachel Carson wrote *Silent Spring*. What was different was the willingness of Americans to pay the costs of cleaning up their environment and protecting it.

Full employment and high growth rates must not mean a return to wasteful, ecologically destructive policies of the broker state. Indeed, destruction of the environment is not an efficient way to produce goods and services. Carefully planning our jobs for more solar converters and fewer gas guzzlers, for more recycling facilities and fewer throwaway plastic containers requires decisions as to the kinds of things we want our economy to make, and as to the means we need to make them.

Moreover, there is simply not enough land at the beach for everyone who wants to have a vacation home there. There is not enough water in Arizona for everyone who is rushing to live there. There is not enough gasoline for everyone who wants to drive a big car and live thirty miles away from his or her job. If we destroy the water and land we need to produce food, all of us shall be threatened. If the air is so polluted that cancer becomes endemic, none of us shall be spared. If we continue to dump poisonous toxic wastes into the land, water, and air, no individual alone can escape. If we waste the limited hydrocarbons we still have left, the energy available to fuel our existing industry and transportation will be gone. Without a sense of community and a conserving ethic, without giving up some part of our right to consume resources to a larger community, we have a formula for unending conflict.

The market is "no respecter of carrying capacity," Lester Brown observes. It has "no alarm that sounds when the carrying capacity of a biological system is transgressed." Only after the system collapses do prices soar. The market also has no ability to take into account the external costs associated with economic activities, such as industrial air pollution. Dumping poisons into the air is often the least costly and therefore most "economic" strategy from the point of view of a steel industry executive—but it may destroy freshwater fisheries, agricultural crops, and the exterior home surfaces downwind for others. Soil conservation practices can be expensive to the farmer facing a tightfisted banker—yet, if ignored, they will add extraordinarily to the costs borne by the overall society within two decades.[19]

Planning is essential, but just as serious respect for the problem of managing the overall economy in ways that *support freedom and decentralization* leads to a dual emphasis, so too planning for a sustainable society must also respect locality and individual responsibility. Community requires participation. We know that participation is enhanced in small human-scale units, as is an ethic of cooperation and conservation. It is also necessary that there be scope for individual autonomy, initiative, and choice—scope for, but not total, autonomy. Both work best not in such abstractions as a continental "nation" of 235 million people, but down to earth in local places. As Bruce Stokes writes:

> People can create local solutions to global problems by taking charge of the process of problem solving and by changing their values and behavior in response to today's economic and social conditions. By so doing, they can mold more democratic, self reliant societies.[20]

Yet communities cannot even plan long-range land use, solar, waste recycling, and other ecologically balanced strategies if the local economy is continually disrupted and the social fabric weakened. Again, we need a particular kind of planning that manages national decisions in ways necessitated by ecological limits—yet preserves local and decentralized decision-making.

A natural tension between the two principles must also be recognized. "What I wish to emphasize is the duality of the human requirement," Friedrich Schumacher wrote. "When it comes to the question of size there is no single answer. For his different purposes man needs different structures, both small ones and large ones, some exclusive and some comprehensive." Schumacher did not share the anarchist antigovernment ideology of some of his "small is beautiful" followers. "The whole crux of economic life—and indeed of life in general—is that it constantly requires a living reconciliation of opposites which, in strict logic, are irreconcilable," he wrote. "In macroeconomics (the management of whole societies) it is necessary always to have both planning *and* freedom—not by way of a weak and lifeless compromise, but by a free recognition of the legitimacy of and need for both."[21]

"HOLLOWING OUT" THE STATE

Managing the economic system with sufficient efficiency and fairness to prevent the disintegration of society into warring camps is a condition both of democracy and of a transition to sustainable, longer-term modes of production. It is also the minimal condition of community.

As de Tocqueville noted, the great potential of the American ideal of community was that it was practical. It was founded on the "principle of self-interest, rightly understood"—namely, that one's own welfare was inextricably bound to the welfare of the community. De Tocqueville wrote:

> In the United States, hardly anybody talks of the beauty of virtue, but they maintain that virtue is useful and provide it every day. The American moralists do not profess

that men ought to sacrifice themselves for their fellow creatures *because* it is noble
to make such sacrifices, but they boldly aver that such sacrifices are as necessary to
him who imposes them upon himself as to him for whose sake they are made.

The principle of self-interest rightly understood produces no great acts of self-
sacrifice, but it suggests daily small acts of self-denial. By itself it cannot suffice to
make a man virtuous; but it disciplines a number of persons in habits of regularity,
temperance, moderation, foresight, self-command; and if it does not lead men
straight to virtue by the will, it gradually draws them in that direction by their
habits.[22]

The fundamental goal of a community-sustaining economics involves the creation of an economic environment that encourages "daily
small acts of self-denial" for the good of the neighborhood, the city,
the country. Given the atomized, individually oriented culture we live
in—where the emphasis is on "me" and "my" rights to personal gratifi-
cation—how do we, as a conscious act, help nurture the sense of
community we need to survive the shifts and changes ahead? Our goal
is not the complex question of the ultimate meaning of community; it
consists of some quite simple things: whites and blacks not throwing
rocks at each other's children, doctors not performing unnecessary
operations on people, businesspeople not profiting by endangering the
health of their workers, workers taking responsibility for the efficiency
of their enterprises, public officials operating honest, intelligent government.

Another American term, "teamwork," is a good word for what is
necessary—an environment in which we are responsible not only for
ourselves, but also for the creation of a prosperous, democratic, and
free society. It is not a strange or unnatural principle. In our private
lives we willingly make sacrifices for family or community if we
believe that the burden of sacrifice is fairly shared. We crave a stable
economic environment—a job we can depend on, a mortgage we
know we can pay off. We get comfort and sustenance from small,
human-scale units. We want the protection of society and the freedom
to grow, to change, to take that "second chance."

Though in our personal lives we know such values are important,
we have allowed our public ideology to render them irrelevant. We
have permitted the debate on economic policy to degenerate into a
statistical pillow fight among experts who, like the cynic in Oscar
Wilde's epigram, know the price of everything and the value of nothing. The debate is reported with a straight face by TV anchormen and
reporters cowed by their own clumsy arithmetic. Success or failure,
good or bad, is a number that goes up or down. The question of the
purpose of it all is irrelevant.

The result is a self-fulfilling prophecy. Our economic system is a purposeless enterprise. It is a perfect reflection of the governmental and corporate bureaucracies that dominate the broker state and whose only purpose is their growth. The experts raise their eyebrows. A purpose? "But the world doesn't work that way," they say. "That noise you hear is just the natural humming of the marketplace." Nonsense. The need for planning is more and more obvious every day as the economic wreckage of laissez-faire ideology piles up higher and higher around the decaying footings of the broker state. A planned economy is largely here, and its extension is inevitable. If we insist on blind resistance it will be irrational, unfair, and ultimately dangerous. If we accept it and understand how to make it work, we have a chance of controlling it.

Planning *means* human choice. If democracy is to prevail, explicit goals are crucial. Without them, we have no way to hold the system accountable. We need sharp, clear principles that are widely understood and supported—but that also make sense in the new economic era. Can our values give direction to the economic system? Can we build an economy in which the goals we strive for in our individual lives are made the explicit goals for our society?

The modern "science" of economics has never been truly divorced from questions of human values and political power. In practice it has taken on the coloration of whoever pays its bills. In the service of corporations and bureaucracy, economics is concerned only with the comings and goings of the millions of atomistic individuals, like ants in a colony. When asked whether the system is serving the ants, or the ants serving the system, the reply is a disdainful, "That's not my department." Schumacher saw through the ideological smoke screen and was not intimidated:

> What is the meaning of democracy, freedom, human dignity, standard of living, self-realization, fulfillment? Is it a matter of goods, or of people? Of course it is a matter of people. If economic thinking cannot grasp this it is useless. If it cannot get beyond its vast abstractions, the national income, the rate of growth, capital/output ratio, input-output analysis, labor mobility, capital accumulation; if it cannot get beyond all this and make contact with the human realities of poverty, frustration, alienation, despair, breakdown, crime, escapism, congestion, ugliness, stress, and spiritual death, then let us scrap economics and start afresh.[23]

Successfully solving the problem of the grim trade-off between inflation and unemployment requires us to broaden the scope of the economic policy beyond its current narrow confines. So too does the transition to ecologically sustainable production. We must break with obsolete ideological constraints and consider the direct public management of strategic economic decisions by the only legitimate institution available to us, the government—which in any case is already held responsible for the economic system. But we must do so in a careful way. Michael Walzer, professor of philosophy at Princeton, has offered a useful image. "The State," he says, "must be held tightly to its own limits, drained of whatever superfluous moral content and unnecessary political power it has usurped, reduced so far as possible to a transparent administrative shell (overarching, protective, enabling) within which smaller groups can grow and prosper. The State is not going to wither away; *it must be hollowed out.*"[24]

We cannot live in a modern society without a strong and effective state any more than we can live in a house without a roof and strong bearing walls to maintain it. But at the same time, we need not clutter and contain our lives in a maze of bureaucratic compartments and narrow hallways of unnecessary rules and regulations. The answer is to hollow it out, widen the rooms and corridors, throw out unneeded walls, raise the ceiling, expand the windows, put in plenty of wide doors and porches. We want to get rid of the freedom-limiting contraptions of the broker state but simultaneously toughen the weight-bearing walls without which the roof will collapse.

Chapter 6

PRODUCTIVITY AND STABILITY

Whatever their political persuasion, and whatever their differences on other matters, economists are agreed that increasing productivity—the efficiency with which we produce goods and services—is the essential foundation for a rising national standard of living. In the coming decades, the production of goods and services must grow faster than the population in order to avoid the social chaos of the zero-sum society.* Rising productivity is also a necessary (though not sufficient) condition for reducing inflation without resorting to recession—and thus of resolving the employment-inflation trade-off dilemma. As we shall see, a strengthening of community will be required to sustain high levels of productivity.

Our best statistical measure of productivity growth—changes in output per worker—shows that it declined substantially over the last decade and a half. Since the end of World War II, there have been three distinct stages to productivity trends in the U.S. economy. The first period, from 1948 to 1966, saw the highest productivity growth this nation has ever reached in its peacetime history, an average 3.2 percent per year increase in output per worker. Then, between 1966 and 1973, the rate lowered somewhat, to an average of 2.4 percent annually. After 1973, it dropped precipitously, averaging 0.7 percent per year. In 1974, 1979, and 1980, productivity growth turned negative —that is, the level of efficiency decreased.[1]

By most measures, the United States still enjoys the highest overall

---

*To the extent we alter our consumption patterns, substituting a different quality of individual and community living for ever-expanding national consumption, this logic can be modified over time.

level of general productivity in the world. The material foundation upon which a healthy community depends is still very solid. Our prospects for the future, however, depend upon whether we regain a steady upward growth path.[2]

The numbers on output per worker are not a complete guide to the overall efficiency of the economy. They tell us nothing, for instance, about the efficiency of producing wasteful or ecologically destructive products. Unfortunately, none of our productivity statistics measure efficiency in the service industries or in government very well. And they do not measure efficiencies in some sectors at all; for instance, the increased efficiency in running a household because of appliances is not reflected in national productivity. Moreover, the statistics reflect simply the ratio of production to the number of people working. Thus, if a major depression reduces the number of people working by 25 percent and the amount of production drops by only 20 percent, productivity statistics would register a rise per worker despite the huge drop in productivity for the society as a whole.

Despite these limitations, the numbers are a reasonably accurate guide to the direction in which productivity in the goods-producing sectors has generally been moving. It has been flagging at best, downward at worst.

Why?

On this question there is much less agreement. A number of explanations have been offered. Most of them make *some* sense; that is, they probably have made some contribution to the falloff in productivity. But there is no convincing case that any one technical factor is the dominant cause of the problem, or gives us a clear-cut answer on how to solve it.

A great deal of recent economic policy, as we have seen, has been devoted to arranging special tax deals for wealthy savers and business on the theory that such deals will spur investment, which in turn will increase productivity. Given the high interest rates, stagnating economy, and other problems since they were enacted, these have had very little effect on investment. Yet even before the tax cuts, the percentage of investment in the economy had not gone down; quite the contrary. During the period of highest productivity growth, from 1948 to 1966, private capital investment as a percentage of our Gross National Product averaged 9.4 percent. Between 1966 and 1973, while productivity growth *fell*, private investment actually rose, to an average of 10.5 percent of the GNP. It maintained itself at this historically high level, moreover, even as productivity dropped farther after 1973. In the disastrous collapse of productivity to the negative rates in 1979 and 1980, private investment rose even more—to 10.8 percent.[3] Although investment and productivity are related, there is little evidence that recent drop-offs in productivity are solely a result of declining investment.

A major factor that has contributed to the longer-run slowdown has been a change in the industrial "mix" of high-productivity and low-productivity industries. The U.S. Department of Agriculture's successful effort to raise farm labor efficiency, for example, encouraged a massive shift of workers to the cities. From 1950 to 1972, a substantial drop in the number of people working in agriculture even as output rose resulted in extraordinary gains in productivity. But by the early 1970s, the shift from agriculture was virtually complete. Most farms were already mechanized and utilizing chemically intensive technologies. Since 1972 the number of people working in agriculture has declined only slightly,[4] and the agricultural sector has contributed only modest gains to national productivity.[5]

Over the same period, the number of people in manufacturing grew somewhat. But it was the low-productivity services that saw the most rapid growth in employment over the decade. As we saw in Chapter Four, the *growth* in employment in restaurants and bars alone was greater than *total* employment in the automobile and steel industries combined. Two other service industries—health services and business services (which include building maintenance, mailing and typing services, and computer services—gained more than a million workers during the period. There are now more jobs in these three service industries than the total number of people working in the construction, machinery, electronic equipment, motor vehicle, aircraft, shipbuilding, chemicals, and scientific instruments industries.[6]

Not only are many services characterized by low wages and low productivity,[7] but they also do not contribute to broad economic growth in the way that manufacturing industries do. MIT's Emma Rothschild's calculations show that business services and medical services buy relatively little outside the services sector. Eating and drinking places spend about a third of every dollar they earn in the food industry and the rest on services, trade, and transportation. In contrast, manufacturing industries buy a large proportion of their purchases from other manufacturing industries, stimulating sales and therefore productivity improvements in a wider swath of the economy.[8]

Some people welcome this development as a higher stage of economic growth, a "postindustrial" age in which workers have been freed by technology to earn a living in more humane work than the factory. But the slowdown in manufacturing employment has not come about simply because our industrial sector has become too efficient. It has also come about because it is inefficient and is therefore losing markets. America is behind other nations not only in overall productivity growth but in manufacturing productivity growth as well. With the exception of Great Britain, the rate of growth in U.S. manufacturing productivity has lagged substantially behind that of every major non-Communist industrial nation in the world.[9] In comparison with Japan, especially, the record has been dramatic: from 1970 to 1975 U.S. manufacturing output per worker increased at an annual rate of 3.4 percent, while Japan moved ahead at nearly double time, at 6.7 percent. Between 1975 and 1980, as American productivity increased a mere 1.6 percent, Japan averaged 7.9 percent, almost five times as great an improvement *each year.*[10] Of the major industrial countries, the United States has the smallest proportion of its labor force in the industrial sector.[11] This has not been associated with a new ascendancy to a postindustrial prosperity, but with a decline in income growth relative to those in other countries. As we have seen, the United States now ranks ninth among industrial nations in per-capita income.

As the slowdown in productivity *within* manufacturing indicates, the shift to services is only a partial explanation of the productivity decline. What then is the cause of the poor performance in manufacturing?

One common political reaction has been to blame the "government." It has been held, for example, that increases in government regulation are a major cause of U.S. productivity losses. Edward F. Denison, the dean of productivity experts, has estimated the effects of the two most commonly cited federal regulatory programs on productivity. His studies indicate that the incremental costs of OSHA health and safety regulations and the antipollution regulations of the Environmental Protection Agency contributed about one ninth of the deceleration in productivity after 1973. A study by the private accounting firm of Arthur Andersen of the effect of regulation on business in 1979 found that the costs imposed by the next four most important regulatory systems (the Equal Employment Opportunity Commission, the Department of Energy, the Federal Trade Commission, and the Employee Retirement Income Security Act) amounted to less than one fifth of OSHA and EPA costs, which suggests that the overall contributions of these major government regulators to the productivity decline, while real, probably could not have caused more than one sixth of the total decline in private-sector productivity. One of the most highly regulated industries—communications—has one of the highest rates of growth of productivity.[12]

A look at a major competitor is also instructive. The Japanese government's air and water emission standards for industrial pollution are even more stringent than the U.S. government's, and government environmental planning is more elaborate in Japan than in the United States. According to an OECD study in the mid-1970s, Japan—which was invading Western markets with cheaper, higher-quality goods—was also spending 3 percent of its GNP for antipollution activities, several times that of any other member country.[13]

Excessive government paperwork is another complaint. Here again, however, there is little evidence that it is a major factor. A survey made by the federal Office of Management and Budget in January 1977 showed that federal reporting requirements took only 0.2 percent of total hours worked in the private sector. Eighty percent of the burden was accounted for by tax forms. Even if we added another 50 percent —or 100 percent—to that estimate to account for state and local government requirements, the level of paperwork is too modest to account for much of the decline. Moreover, the removal of wage-price controls after 1974 for nonenergy products, and the reduction in federal red tape—which was one of the major, if unpublicized, administrative accomplishments of the Carter years[14]—suggests that federal paperwork probably declined during the past decade.

Then there is the very general assertion that big government has decreased the economic efficiency of the private sector. Ronald Reagan, George Bush, and other Republicans have pounded away at this theme, yet the evidence from around the world is not very supportive. In fact, comparing the United States with Western Europe in the twenty-year period 1960–1980, we can even make the opposite argument: that big government is associated with higher productivity growth. During this time, productivity grew faster in most Western European countries—which absorbed larger shares of their economies devoted to government—than in the United States.[15] While Japan does have a smaller share of government spending in the economy, it has far greater intervention in private decision-making in most industries.

Another explanation of the productivity decline is the large amount of American research and development resources that are funneled into the military. Our principal commercial rivals, of course, spend much less of their most valuable scientific and engineering resources on military work. As a percentage of its national output, the United States spends about twice as much on military R&D as do Great Britain and France, five times what West Germany spends, and twenty times what Japan spends.[16]

Channeling the best, most creative technical minds to esoteric military and space problems since World War II undoubtedly has had a depressing effect on the longer-term *level* and overall quality of commercial and industrial technology in the United States. The burden of being the military laboratory for the West comes out of the American standard of living. But as an explanation for recent drop-offs in the rate of productivity growth, it falls short. The percentage of R&D spending devoted to the military steadily declined after the mid-1960s. In 1965, military R&D stood at 54 percent of total R&D spending in the United States, and by 1980 it had fallen to 32 percent. In absolute terms, military spending adjusted for inflation dropped more than 30 percent.[17] Military spending for R&D, burdensome as it is, is clearly not a major source of our recent decline. Similarly, while the long-term effects of spending hundreds of billions of dollars each year on the military in general (while our industrial rivals invest in industry) is deleterious, the fact is that the percentage of military spending in the economy went down, not up, during the sharp productivity falloff in the mid-1970s. In a similar vein, while increased investments in education contribute to long-run productivity improvements, there is no evidence that sudden shifts in educational programs are related to the big recent productivity changes.

One factor that clearly did contribute to the productivity slump was the increase in energy prices. This increased the cost of capital (which uses energy) relative to labor. The result was less incentive to buy labor-saving equipment. Dale Jorgenson of Harvard University concluded that energy prices played an important role in the decline in productivity. Although Jorgenson's general point is undoubtedly correct, over the precise impact of energy prices there is dispute.[18] As we shall explore in Part III, the problem was not so much the rise in oil prices as the way in which our government and private economic institutions reacted. Other industrial countries, such as West Germany, France, and Japan, had a greater reliance on imported oil, yet maintained higher rates of productivity growth after 1973. An influx of new workers into the labor market, the delayed effect of the baby boom, also altered the ratio between capital and labor. Some economists believe that the resultant reduction in labor costs relative to new machinery is responsible for much of the falloff in productivity. Again, this factor undoubtedly accounts for some part of the problem, but it cannot explain the major and sudden breaks in trend.

A clue to perhaps the most significant causes of recent setbacks—and more important, to potential areas for significant gains in the future—is the fact that the falloff in the 1970s was largely an across-the-board phenomenon. The slowdown was typical of the main industrial branches of the economy rather than being focused in one or two areas for which one might seek special explanations. Something that affected the economy as a whole was clearly at work—something that was the result neither of changes in the mix of low- and high-productivity sectors nor of selected sectors hit by high prices. Denison notes: "It is possible, perhaps even probable, that everything went wrong at once. . . ."[19]

Why?

As we have seen, one of the effects of the oil price shocks was that they generally retarded economic growth and, specifically, helped set off the recessions of 1974–75 and 1979–80. Business efficiency is greatly affected by whether there is enough demand for products to keep business operating at or near full capacity. Lower sales volume translates into reduced production, but when production workers are laid off, the fixed costs of doing business do not decline as much. These include costs for a substantial portion of the work force, such as executives, secretaries, maintenance workers, bookkeepers, salespeople, and security guards, as well as for such items as rent, interest payments, and equipment maintenance. We end up with proportionally larger numbers of workers supporting a reduced level of production.

Productivity, in fact, generally follows the business cycle. Even during the postwar years of generally higher productivity growth, there were peaks and valleys corresponding to the ebb and flow of the business cycle. The level of productivity growth actually dropped in six of the eight recessions since World War II. There are additional, longer-term results of cyclicality. Small business, the source of much innovation, is often badly hurt. And since business in general is faced with idle capacity, there is no incentive to purchase more up-to-date and efficient equipment, further retarding the long-term trend of improvement from new technology.

After an exhaustive examination of the data on productivity decline, economist Michael Mohr of the U.S. Department of Commerce concluded:

The evidence overwhelmingly indicates that the labor productivity slowdown in manufacturing after the mid-sixties was the result of cyclical rather than secular forces. Further, had output demand after the mid-sixties been less erratic and had firms been able to plan and adjust their input mixes for more stable output growth, the levels as well as the growth rates in costs and prices for manufactured goods would have been noticeably lower than their actual levels during the interval from the mid-sixties to 1972.[20]

Other research, by Mohr and Paul Christy, suggests that at least half of the 1970s slowdown was caused by energy and other shocks, which generated higher uncertainty.[21]

Mohr's conclusion about the link between business planning and stable growth is critical. Whatever the precise mix of factors that contributed to our past difficulties, at the heart of the recent and ongoing productivity problem is the increased uncertainty with which business management faces the future. It prevents them from undertaking the long-term investments, long-term contracts with suppliers, training of employees, experimentation with cost-saving techniques, and so forth, which are the nitty-gritty of efficiency.

Uncertainty facing the business executive in the new economic era extends in all directions—prices, raw materials, skilled labor, interest rates, and, most of all, the incomes of customers. As one businessman said to us: "I really don't care what the tax rate is—if I'm paying taxes it's because I am making money. I don't even care what the interest rate is—if the business is there, I will pass on the costs in higher prices. What I want to know is: Are there customers out there with enough money in their pockets to buy what I make?"

Expectations—or confidence in the future—have long been recognized as a key ingredient for sustaining expansion in a private enterprise or a mixed economy. As we have seen, both Jimmy Carter and Ronald Reagan attempted to revive the flagging confidence of business through various demonstrations that they shared the conservative ideology of business. Tax cuts, budget cuts for social programs, Carter's speeches on "discipline," and Reagan's union busting have all been justified as necessary to restore business confidence in the future.

But such efforts miss the point: They confuse ideological uncertainties and anxieties of business *with specific economic uncertainties.* They treat businessmen as social philosophers rather than as investors. It is not surprising, therefore, that businesspeople during 1981 and 1982 continued their personal support for Ronald Reagan, but *as business executives,* they were if anything more afraid of the future. For instance, a *Business Week* poll in the midst of the recession, nine months after Ronald Reagan's program passed Congress, found that 60 percent of top corporate executives felt that the President's economic program was working. Yet with plants operating at roughly three quarters of capacity, when asked whether as a result they were "planning for a bigger increase in capital expansion than they normally would," only 23 percent said "Yes." And when asked whether they intended to build inventories, only 7 percent said "Yes."[22]

A Congressional Budget Office report states the planning issue clearly: *"If efficiency is best served by permitting the realization of business plans,* then one major policy implication is that productivity growth would be enhanced by reducing those elements of uncertainty over which the government has some control."[23]

UNCERTAINTY AND MANAGEMENT PERFORMANCE

The pervasive effect of instability and uncertainty can also be found in other problem areas. General management failures, for instance, are often treated as if they occur in a vacuum rather than in an enveloping economic climate. In the summer of 1980, two Harvard Business School professors, Robert H. Hayes and William J. Abernathy, just back from a series of seminars with foreign business executives in Europe, wrote a widely publicized *Harvard Business Review* article that laid a significant part of the blame for America's productivity decline (as well as its lagging performance in generating new products) squarely at the feet of American business management. Hayes and Abernathy began with the simple observation that although the return on investment in American business corporations had remained roughly the same since the mid-1960s, private investment in research and development declined. "The conclusion," they write, "is painful but must be faced. Responsibility for this competitive listlessness belongs not just to a set of external conditions but also to the preoccupations and practices of American managers. By their preference for servicing existing markets rather than creating new ones and by their devotion to short-term returns and 'management by the numbers' many of them have abdicated their strategic responsibilities."[24]

The two professors struck a resonant chord in the American business community, and the quality of American management since 1980 has come under critical scrutiny in the press, in business schools, and in corporations as never before.

To begin with, it has been observed that there has been a major shift in the type of person managing America's largest corporations. The last thirty years have seen a 50 percent increase in the proportion of top corporate executives who have financial and legal backgrounds and a roughly 15 percent drop in the proportion of those who have production experience. Salaries for business school graduates who go into production are consistently lower than for those who go into finance. The corporate manager is thus increasingly detached from the process of production, with inevitable consequences for American innovation and productivity.

Moreover, America's top executives have become transients. By their nature, financial skills are mobile. A profit-and-loss statement is an abstraction that does not require familiarity with the industry and market and institutions it represents. Out of this mobility was born the idea of the professional manager who could walk into any company in any industry and run it. Professor David Vogel reports that the typical chief executive officer of a corporation now stays in his job for an average of five years, compared with ten years a generation ago.[25]

The "cult" of the mobile professional manager brings with it further pressures to reduce complex business decisions to abstract financial simplifications. Hayes and Abernathy comment:

> True believers keep the faith on a day-to-day basis by insisting that as issues rise up the managerial hierarchy for decisions they be progressively distilled into easily quantifiable terms. One European manager, in recounting to us his experiences in a joint venture with an American company, recalled with exasperation that U.S. managers want everything to be simple. But sometimes business situations are not simple, and they cannot be divided up or looked at in such a way that they become simple. They are messy, and one must try to understand all the facets. This appears to be alien to the American mentality.[26]

Business executives are also encouraged to reduce investment in people and product lines and processes that have long-term potential but that show up on the *current* quarterly financial statement only as costs. Bonuses and salaries, hirings and firings are increasingly based on short-run performance. The obsession with the short-run "bottom line" has reduced time horizons throughout the corporation, cutting back those inventions or ideas that need longer nurturing. The system provides incentives to sell off assets that are not producing immediate high returns, and in particular to avoid research and development activities where the payoff may be five or ten years away.

Another result of short-term management by the numbers is that product development becomes "market-driven" to the exclusion of efforts to improve the quality of the product itself. When new products are created solely on the basis of market research—on what customers *say* they want—a huge amount of imitation occurs, a proliferation of similar products with slightly different packaging or styling. In part this is because consumers are limited to their experience of what is— *not what might be.* But the short-run, bottom-line ideology of the modern conglomerate also discourages innovation. Coming out with a slight variation on an existing product is easier because the market is already established, distribution issues are understood, etc. As other business researchers have observed: "Inventors, scientists, engineers, and academics, in the normal pursuit of scientific knowledge, gave the world in recent times the laser, xerography, the instant photograph, and the transistor. In contrast, worshippers of the marketing concept have bestowed upon mankind such products as new-fangled potato chips, feminine hygiene deodorant, and the pet rock. . . ."[27]

The use of "hard-nosed" quarter-by-quarter numbers to make or break managers has resulted in American managers now being notorious for their "risk avoidance." The pressures and insecurities—and costs of failure—are too great, the gains of possible success too dubious. In terms of technological progress, the American automobile industry has been stagnant for twenty years. The transverse engine, front-wheel drive, overdrive, lock-up clutches on automatic transmission, and V-8 engines that can cruise on four cylinders are all techniques that were known and used in the 1950s.[28] Currently the fifty thousand deaths from automobile accidents a year provide an immense opportunity for safety innovations and fairly cry out for new technologies that can provide them. But instead of aggressively designing such innovations and using the obvious willingness of the government to encourage safety, U.S. automobile manufacturers are mesmerized both by ideological opposition to government, and by marketing surveys that not surprisingly reveal consumer indifference to untried innovations. So, as they did with the issue of fuel efficiency, American automobile manufacturers are letting Western Europe and Japan take the lead.

The deterioration in the overall performance of American management, however, cannot be explained simply by some mass personal psychological change in managers as people. If anything, today's individuals are smarter, better trained, and have wider personal horizons than their counterparts in the prosperous 1950s and 1960s. Nor can its origins be found primarily in the relative emphasis on finance versus production taught at the business schools. If American corporations began to demand and pay for more people with production skills, business schools would shift their own priorities quickly.

One major source of the problem is the growth of conglomerates as a result of the merger boom that began in the late 1960s. Agglomeration has resulted in upper management having less and less experience in the actual production of the goods and services of subsidiary companies. The many different subsidiaries of the typical conglomerate are treated not as human institutions producing goods for sale in specific markets, but as abstract "profit centers," to be judged primarily and even solely on short-run returns. The operating companies are run by the parent firms as if they were simply another investment in the corporate portfolio, little different from stocks and bonds.

This practice has in turn reinforced the merger mania by stressing investments that may or may not fall within the actual line of dominant technical expertise of the parent; U.S. Steel buys Marathon Oil because it hopes the value of oil assets will rise, irrespective of whether its own staff of managers knows anything about the nitty-gritty problems of the oil industry. In 1981 American corporations bought other companies at the rate of $82.6 billion a year—about four times what they were spending on industrial R&D.[29]

As corporations become larger and larger collections of separate, unrelated companies, bought and sold like so many trinkets in a bazaar, the identification of many managers with the long-term interests of the company is also weakened. No longer is the manager a leader in the sense of being entrusted with the responsibility for the people who make up the enterprise. "I know—we all know—of people all over this town," observes an official of an executive recruiting firm in New York, "who are running their companies into the ground, taking huge, quick profits and leaving them a shell. And when you look at their contracts, it's easy to see why. What does it matter to them ten years from now? They're building giant personal fortunes, and *appear* to be running their companies terrifically, and in ten years, when there's nothing left, they'll be long gone."[30]

Most suggestions for management reform have concentrated on how to prune the trees while ignoring the forest in which they live or die. Thus it is often proposed that corporate boards of directors should reward managers more on the basis of long-term growth than short-term profits.[31] But from the point of view of the corporation itself, the short-term, get-it-quick-and-fast approach is in fact a *rational* response to the current economic environment. In an uncertain world why should a corporation encourage its managers to make long-term investments? And uncertainty is the dominant characteristic of the new economic era.

Instability and its offspring, uncertainty, also create bottlenecks that appear in economic upturns, blocking further growth and adding to inflation. The gyrating housing industry, for instance, is characterized by excess capacity in the downturn, by sudden shortages of material and skilled labor, and by canceled deliveries in the upturn—all adding to costs and inefficiencies. Construction firms are reluctant to invest in the most modern building systems because they cannot afford the risk of expensive machinery standing idle. Cyclicality results in workers' skills getting "rusty" during long periods of idleness, leading to lower productivity, and to high accident rates when they do go back to work. The industry's instability also causes workers to demand high hourly wages to compensate for long periods of unemployment.

A constantly fluctuating economy throws firms out of sync with each other and creates a lack of confidence *within* the economy's industrial structure. Canceled contracts, sudden demands for speedup, and changed specifications poison the atmosphere of industrial cooperation. Industrial engineers have pointed out that a major advantage of the Japanese auto industry is its use of "on-time production" planning. A supplier plans his delivery time down not only to the date, but even to the hour of the day. Manufacturers can plan production months in advance without stockpiling massive inventories of material and supplies.[32]

Uncertainty also retards the rapid diffusion of available technology. For example, inherent in computer technology is the power to make small-lot manufacturing as efficient as mass production. Small-lot manufacturing accounts for more than 75 percent of current U.S. industrial output. But our system is plagued by long lead times, high in-process inventories, low machine utilization, and insufficient automation. Nathan Cook of MIT judges that use of computers and robots could reduce overall costs in this area alone by 80 to 90 percent.[33] But the investments necessary to reorganize small-lot production techniques are made haltingly in conditions of long-term uncertainty.

PRODUCTIVITY AND PARTICIPATION

Productivity improvements are by their very nature labor-saving. The degree to which workers accept—and can become sources of—changes in technology, design, and work practices is a major factor in the efficiency with which a firm and an economy operate. Lack of cooperation on the shop floor between labor and management—the difficulty of generating a spirit of teamwork in our major industries—

is a major impediment to the longer-term revival of productivity. This is another area in which Japanese and many Western European businesses have a decided advantage over American businesses, but it is an advantage that rests on far more than coaxing to change the spirit of worker-management relations.

Over the past several decades practices of industrial management have undergone a radical transformation in much of continental Western Europe and Japan. Organized workers in these countries participate in, and often have legally sanctioned veto power over, decisions that in the United States are solely the prerogative of management. In West Germany, Austria, the Netherlands, and Scandinavia, worker representatives by law are allocated up to as many as half the seats on large, private-corporation boards of directors. Worker representatives must be given information other directors get, and worker representatives have full privileges to debate and vote on corporate policies. These nations, again by law, have established some form of work council at the level of the individual factory. The oldest and most elaborate are in West Germany and are composed entirely of worker representatives elected by the workers in the plant who participate full-time at company expense. Management must obtain their approval for such major decisions as pay, work rules, health and safety, vacation and holiday schedules, overtime, hiring, firing, shutdowns, and the introduction of new equipment. Volkswagen, for example, had to get the permission of its employees before building a plant in Pennsylvania to serve the American market. The employees agreed only after lengthy discussion and a detailed examination of the company's books and cost structure, which convinced them that the choice was to build in America or lose the market altogether. In Sweden, employees of the Virsbo Iron Works—one of the country's major steel mills—rejected a management proposal to open a factory in Spain.[34]

Nor have work councils hestitated to "interfere" with basic plant operations. They have been prime movers in the development of efforts to reduce the stress, arduousness, and monotony of factory work. Under pressure from the work councils, companies such as Volvo have broken up the assembly lines for automobile engines: They are now produced in smaller work groups in which workers, rather than being slaves to the rhythms and speed of "the line," have some control over the pace of the work. Most other continental Western European workers live in a world of generous, government-subsidized pensions, health services, housing, mass transportation, education, training, and other accoutrements of the advanced welfare state.[35] It is a system diametrically opposed to conventional American notions of what makes for the efficient operation of a business and an economy —namely, unchallenged management authority and workers in constant fear of losing their jobs if they do not perform. Yet West German productivity growth has been greater than that of the United States for the past two decades, and their per-capita income now surpasses ours.

The Japanese system is somewhat different. Not so much a product of law, it is a result of the stronger sense of community that is characteristic of the large Japanese business corporation. In Japan the corporation is more than a job, it is a way of life. In fact, "lifetime employment" is a recognized right for permanent workers of large Japanese companies, perhaps one third of the labor force. When sales drop, production continues, and both government and firm look for ways to keep employees working. If they cannot maintain production, they regularly keep the worker on anyway. Says Tadahiro Yoshida, senior managing director and member of the board of YKK, the world's number one maker of zippers, "If we face difficulty, we first proportionately reduce the wages of all employees from general manager down to the lowest-paid employee." He continues: "The very basis of our company's philosophy is profit sharing with our employees. In America, in a period of recession, many companies focus only on the bottom line and, looking narrowly at the profitability over the next year, may move to cut off a production line and the people on it. This can only have a negative impact on all the workers."[36] The vice-president of Toyo Kogyo, maker of the Mazda car, observes: "In Japan, we say we prefer to sip a thin soup together in hard times. Only as a last resort are workers fired here, in contrast, I understand, to your country, where the work force is regarded as one of the most flexible elements in production."[37]

The loyalty goes both ways. A militant left-wing union leader at the same plant says: "I feel a basic love for this company. I have faith in the Mazda rotary engine, and I know whatever happens to Toyo Kogyo will happen to me because all of us in the company are in the same boat together."[38]

Life for a production worker in Japan is no paradise. Like factory work everywhere, it is hard, monotonous, and inherently alienating. And the system of lifetime tenure does not extend to the entire labor force. Still, there is little question that a sense of loyalty, mutual obligation, and fairness exists in the typical Japanese firm to a much larger extent than it does in United States business. The lesson of Japan in this respect is not that its system should be America's model, but that the Japanese have proven that job security can be a contribution rather than an obstacle to productivity.

The Japanese also give great weight to the arrival of a consensus before decisions are made. It is simply a goal within top management. To a much larger extent than in the United States, proposals for production changes come from lower levels in the hierarchy, largely through a system of "quality circles" in which workers and managers in a particular part of the plant's operation meet regularly to discuss ways to improve productivity and new-product development. Again, a key part of the process is sharing information. One American observer reports that in Japan, "workers consider it an insult for management to surprise them with decisions, small or major." A measure of the success of the system is the incidence of strikes. In 1979, strikes and work stoppages cost the Japanese economy twenty-four days per thousand workers; they cost the U.S. economy forty-two days.[39]

Turnover among blue-, pink-, and white-collar labor from one company to the other is also rare. High turnover is a negative influence on productivity; if American industry could cut turnover in half, some experts estimate productivity would rise by 30 percent in five years.[40] In part, high turnover is discouraged in Japan by the absence of transfer privileges for pensions and seniority benefits (although for most industrial workers in the United States, pensions and seniority are equally nontransferable, government-sponsored Social Security is more important in the United States than in Japan). But the major element is the sense of the corporation as a community. There is simply little reason for a worker to leave the company.

Some of the results are striking. James E. Harbour, an American automobile management consultant studying comparative practices, found that American manufacturers required 120 hours of direct labor time to build the average subcompact car; the comparable vehicle required only 60 hours in Japan. Japan's system of "defect prevention" rests fundamentally on respect for the individual worker, who serves as his own inspector for quality control. American cars on average have 3 to 5 defects on delivery compared with the Japanese rate of .7 to 1.5.[41]

European and Japanese cooperative efforts have succeeded not because their workers are naturally more pliable than ours. Traditional social class divisions are deeper in both Europe and Japan than they are in the United States, and class antagonisms are built into their social and political institutions. Much larger proportions of Japanese and European work forces are unionized, and unlike America, unions generally have a strong socialist, often communist ideology. Compared with other industrial democracies, the labor movement in the United States is weak both in numbers and in organizational discipline. Labor racketeering is more widespread. Unions are fragmented, rarely support each other in strikes, and often spend more time raiding each other's membership than organizing the vast majority of the nonunionized labor force. American labor has concentrated almost exclusively on bread-and-butter issues of pay and fringe benefits, leaving the operation of the workplace to management.

Yet, it is in America and Britain where the greatest shop floor resistance to automation has occurred—and in other Western European countries and Japan where there has been the greatest shop floor accommodation and support for it.

When evidence on the value of greater participation in Europe and Japan began to trickle into the United States in the 1970s, it was originally dismissed as appropriate only to closely knit societies with a collective consciousness based upon ethnic and national solidarity. But the stereotypical, obedient, nose-to-the-grindstone, hardworking German, Swedish, or Japanese worker was increasingly likely to be an immigrated Turk, Yugoslav, or Korean. Moreover, the history of widespread labor-management cooperation in Japan is relatively recent. Industrial relations in Japan until the early 1950s were characterized by strikes, violence, and bitter class antagonisms. The Japanese management style is not a natural evolution from ancient feudal traditions, but part of a social system created after World War II out of recognition that cooperation was essential for survival. Finally, some Japanese companies, such as Sony, have demonstrated that enormous efficiency gains are possible in the United States when the same approach is used with American workers.

In fact, many of the principles underlying the Japanese approach were imported from the United States.[42] The idea of quality circles, for example, was inspired by visits to Japan by American management specialist W. Edwards Deming in the early 1950s. Today, the award of the Union of Japanese Scientists and Engineers presented to the Japanese companies with the most outstanding achievements in quality control is the Deming Prize.

The work of Americans such as Elton Mayo, Abraham Maslow, and Frederick Herzberg, all of whom found connections between productivity and worker participation in the industrial process, have been central to the development of modern theories of participative management. There have also always been individual American companies that have incorporated some of the basic tenets in their operations. The

Lincoln Electric Company in Cleveland—the world's largest manufacturer of arc welding equipment—has for years operated with a system of employee participation and generous cash bonuses for creative ideas. Employees are encouraged to think up ways to eliminate their job, and when they do they are rewarded and placed somewhere else in the company. Lincoln Electric's productivity rate is 100 percent above the general U.S. industrial average.[43] There is even a longer tradition of worker-owned companies; a study of worker-owned plywood firms in the Pacific Northwest found that for several decades they have been more profitable and have experienced higher rates of productivity than similar-sized plywood firms owned and managed on the conventional hierarchical model.[44]

PARTICIPATION AND SECURITY

Since the 1960s, there has been substantial expansion in the number of company experiments along participation lines. They involve some of the largest corporations in the country, and the results have generally been positive. A Texas Instruments plant, for instance, organized six hundred electronic instrument assemblers into groups responsible for setting production goals and provided them with greater information feedback. As a result, assembly-line time per unit decreased from 132 hours to 32 hours, while absenteeism, turnover, leaving time, complaints, and trips to the health center also decreased. A Monsanto Company agricultural division plant in Muscatine, Iowa, increased productivity 75 percent when 150 machine operators and maintenance workers were involved in goal-setting sessions and given more autonomy in their jobs.[45] Dr. Raymond Katzell and associates at New York University analyzed 103 worker-productivity experiments in the United States between 1971 and 1975 involving increased worker participation and found that over 80 percent of the experiments resulted in favorable effects on one or more aspects of productivity.[46]

Nonetheless, despite convincing evidence that such methods increase productivity substantially, and despite an outpouring of articles, books, and speeches urging greater participation, the idea is still "experimental" in America. It is largely limited to instances where particularly inspired individuals force the change.

What accounts for this?

The answer forces us back to elements of fairness and community and again to fundamental economic conditions. To begin with, there is worker resistance to new strategies *when the benefits of increased productivity are not widely shared.* A woman worker at a glass company, who went from assembling one part to assembling the entire eighteen-hundred-piece chemical metering device, said: "When we went for the total-job concept, I thought we should get more money. You have more responsibility, you are really doing the whole job."

A salesman for a corrugated-box company tells of a special rush order that workers filled perfectly, ahead of schedule. In appreciation, the customer, a glass manufacturer, gave the salesman crates of fancy glasses to be distributed to the employees who worked on the order. The glasses were intercepted by the plant manager and kept for the executives. "Those guys get paid by the hour," he said. "This isn't in their contract."[47]

There is also resistance among managers. Permitting workers to make even *some* decisions about their workplace lets the genie out of the bottle. Workers tend to push for more and more responsibility, and sooner or later this threatens their bosses.

"It was too successful," says Polaroid's training director about their program. "What were we going to do with the supervisors—the managers? We didn't need them anymore. Management decided that it just didn't want operators that qualified. . . . The employees' newly revealed ability to carry more responsibility was too great a threat to the established ways of doing things and to established power patterns."[48]

An experiment at General Foods' Topeka plant ran into similar trouble. In terms of economic performance, the worker self-management effort was an outstanding success. Unit labor costs dropped 5 percent, saving the company a million dollars a year; turnover was reduced, and the plant went three years and eight months before its first lost-time accident. But the change directly threatened middle management. *Business Week* reported:

> The problem has been not so much that the workers could not manage their own affairs as that some management and staff personnel saw their own positions threatened because the workers performed almost too well. One former employee says the system—built around a team concept—came squarely up against the company's bureaucracy. Lawyers, fearing reaction from the National Labor Relations Board, opposed the idea of allowing team members to vote on pay raises. Personnel managers objected because team members made hiring decisions. Engineers resented workers doing engineering work.[49]

"Economically it was a success," says another ex-employee, "but it became a power struggle. It was too threatening to too many people."

Ted Mills, former director of the U.S. Productivity Commission's Quality of Work Program, observes that these programs "open up a Pandora's box from which there is no return. Pretty soon you'll have workers managing the managers. It's a first step toward encroaching on management's prerogative of controlling and directing the means of production."[50] Related difficulties have made some union officials equally unenthusiastic: They fear both elimination of jobs and threats to their own positions in the union hierarchy.

Management ambivalence also gives workers contradictory signals. Top management encourages changes, middle management discourages them. Workers are given new responsibility and then denied authority. Experiments are begun and stopped. The initially successful work humanization program at Harman Industries' auto mirror plant in Bolivar, Tennessee—which doubled productivity on some assembly lines—was neglected when the plant was sold to Beatrice Foods. Sid Harman had begun the program not as a surrogate for a speedup but because "it was right." Beatrice Foods did not share his commitment.

The short-term and narrow horizons of American managers also play a role. Work humanization programs require a "front end" investment of time and money that managers concerned with the next quarter's bottom line are reluctant to make. The redesign of the shop floor and modification of the assembly line, for instance, initially lowered the productivity at both Volkswagen and Volvo. The resultant increase in job satisfaction and loyalty can generate benefits over a longer period of time. But by the time they do, the manager is likely to be long gone; why should he spend time feathering his successor's nest?

Some American firms in growth industries, such as IBM, Black & Decker, and Hewlett-Packard, have made major efforts not only to encourage participation but also to assure long-term employment security. But such efforts can be costly when growth is slow or negative in a recession. The benefits of stability then accrue not to the company as much as to the nation as a whole. They show up on the public balance sheet, but not on private balance sheets, as lower unemployment costs. It is not surprising that in the unstable U.S. economic context, there is only very isolated interest in lifetime employment among American managers beyond the very high-growth sectors.

The effort to create participatory management will undoubtedly continue because it is a better way to manage a modern corporation whose educated workers can no longer be treated as wage-slaves. To the extent it does expand, the productivity of U.S. industry will benefit. But there are major limitations to the notion that sophisticated techniques of management alone will make a major difference in the efficiency of the U.S. economy. These limitations are not defined by the techniques themselves, which we know can be transferred among advanced industrial democracies, whether in Japan, North America, or Western Europe. *They are defined rather by the social and economic context in which the techniques are implemented.* The most important reason why such efforts have had such a difficult time in the United States is that they work best in an environment of economic security —for both workers and lower-level management—that is missing in America.

The problem is that in the absence of some form of job guarantee —which in turn requires more stable overall economic performance— increases in productivity *must* reduce the demand for labor. As one union official put it: "Substituting the sociologists' questionnaire for the stop watch is likely to be no gain for the workers. While workers have a stake in productivity, it is not always identical with that of management. Job enrichment programs have cut jobs just as effectively as automation and stop watches."[51]

The Japanese worker who is guaranteed a lifetime job so long as the company survives has a clear and direct stake in improved productivity. He shares in the profits, and the elimination of routine and onerous jobs makes his life easier. Although the jobs of Swedish and German workers are not guaranteed by their particular company, they have historically experienced a substantial government commitment to full employment. Until the mid-1970s most of the postwar period European governments managed economies with unemployment in the 2–3 percent range. They maintained labor markets so tight that they had to import workers from southern Europe. Until the worldwide recession of 1981–82, workers in Germany and Scandinavia were rarely laid off in large numbers, and when they were, their governments saw to it that they got generous severance pay and unemployment benefits designed to maintain their living standards. They also received assistance in getting not just another job, but a job that maintained their occupational and earning status.

The typical American worker—no matter how productive—has no such protection. If he is replaced by a machine, he is out in the street. If he is lucky enough to belong to one of the handful of unions with supplemental unemployment benefits (a tiny proportion of the labor force), then his income may be maintained for a while. By and large, however, the worker faces unemployment; when he does find a job, it is usually at a considerably lower wage level. Studies have shown that even prime-age white males in industries such as steel and autos lost on average roughly 45 percent of their earnings two years after being laid off.[52]

The cooperation and release of creativity on the shop floor and at the clerical desk that is the great promise of participatory management require that the payoff benefit the worker—or at the very least, not cause harm. But in the United States, the payoff is likely to be a pink slip, if not for the worker with the "bright idea," then for the person who works next to him or her—and the lesson that Mr. or Ms. Bright Idea may be next.

The basic insecurities of American economic life are not confined to blue- and pink-collar workers. American middle managers tend to be as jittery about their future as do workers. The absence of stable employment means that their jobs are vulnerable as well. The tremendous acceleration of the buying and selling of corporations has also increased the displacement among middle-level managers. It is a constant threat not only to a manager's specific job, but also to his attachment to the managerial class. Many American managers are themselves only a generation out of the blue-collar world, having been sucked upward by the postwar expansion. Fear of dropping back is always present. Sharing information and decision-making with employees is a threat to the manager's status, not just in the plant, but in his life as well.

The jungle of insecurity that American managers face is also at the root of what Hayes and Abernathy have called the "pseudoprofessionalism" of management. The image of the professional manager, the finance-oriented professional who can read a bottom line in any industry is, like any effort to professionalize an occupation, a device to build a protective wall around a class of people *who otherwise have no institutional protection.* There is less need for the career of professional manager in Europe and Japan because, by and large, management remains with the firm. The manager can invest time in learning about the specific production and marketing issues involved with the company's product because the manager expects to stay with the firm. Studies of comparative production costs in the United States and Japan have shown that the ratio of supervision to production workers is enormously higher in the United States, often as much as one to ten, as opposed to one to two hundred in Japan.[53]

The Japanese company has so far been able to offer the security that its workers and managers need because it in turn has had a commitment from the national government to maintain economic demand at high enough levels to maintain substantial full employment. For more than thirty years in Japan the unemployment rate has stayed below 2½ percent, and often below 1 percent.[54] There is obviously no way a Japanese firm could offer lifetime guarantees for very long unless it had some guarantees itself.

Nor could a Swedish or a German company submit decisions to workers unless it understood that government policies would take into account the short-run costs involved. The conditions of the new economic era are making these practices harder, to be sure. Governments in Western Europe, especially, have found it hard to stimulate investment and production in the face of world recession and the high interest rates of the Reagan (and Thatcher) governments, which draw monies out of their economies. Ultimately the Japanese miracle as well depends on expanding exports, which are rapidly reaching their limits in a stagnant world economy. But this defines the common new problem of the new economic era: Job security and stable employment are essential ingredients for social and economic stability. Whatever happens abroad (and others may well falter!), in the United States, *substantial productivity improvements are not likely to flow from the introduction of Japanese or Western European management techniques unless they are accompanied by greater economic security.*

TWO CONDITIONS OF COMMUNITY

Some American firms have taken advantage of the fear and insecurity accompanying massive recession to squeeze more work out of their employees through "speed-ups" and forced changes in work rules. These actions can achieve temporary productivity gains, but we cannot expect American industry to steadily expand its investment in new productivity-enhancing equipment for the future unless the reality of massive uncertainty it faces is altered; to wish away repeated deepening recessions, high interest rates, inflation, and contradictory government policies is to ignore the fundamental context in which basic decisions are shaped. In the absence of planning to achieve greater stability, no package of tax, loan, technology diffusion, or other "programs" can be expected to improve productivity in qualitatively important ways. Conversely, if public action establishes a believable long-term context of stability, a variety of special-tax, loan-training, and other programs can be usefully brought to bear.

A similar conclusion is obvious in connection with the second major

area of potential new productivity gains for the future: worker participation. If the new economic era is to continue to be characterized by
chronic high unemployment, prospects for cooperation and creativity
will be diminished (both here and abroad) as other nations find the
basis of training systems weakened. Conversely, if job stability is a
major focus of overall planning, the prospect of significant improvements in industrial relations offers hope of additional productivity
gains. And in such a context greater training, education, and other
efforts will also bear fruit.

Long-term productivity improvement is related not only to the
reduction of uncertainty and an increase in job security, but it is also
related to the two *taken together:* The Japanese government, for instance, has been able to make automation and robotization of assembly
lines a national goal. The result is both large-cost savings and the
elimination of much dirty, onerous, and dangerous work. Japan already has some 70 percent of all robots operating in the world, about
five times more than the United States (the Soviet Union ranks second
to Japan). Japan has been able to diffuse new technologies more rapidly
both because business has confidence to invest *and* because workers do
not fear for their jobs.

The Japanese government has so far been able to provide both the
firm and the worker with the essential degree of certainty about future
economic trends because it has a consensus and mandate to plan for
it. Fiscal and monetary policy, zoning and transportation, public infrastructure and educational investments, and government allocation of
capital are all in the service of a full production–full employment
policy. To say as much is to define elements of a basic understanding
in which labor receives full employment and job security in return for
its commitment to productivity and labor peace—and management
agrees to lifetime employment in return for labor cooperation and a
commitment that government will provide adequate financing and
plan high levels of demand. And both labor and management agree to
the government assuming the role of overall economic manager and
long-term planner.

The specific Japanese and West European models cannot be transferred full blown to the American economy. But the experience of
other nations and our own analysis of the decline in American productivity instruct us in the importance of very specific elements of community. The revitalization of national productivity, upon which our
hopes for sustained and balanced economic growth depend, requires
a degree of cooperation among capital, labor, and government that is

unprecedented in our history and that does not come naturally to our institutions. As Chapters Four and Five suggest, that cooperation cannot be based on a narrow "deal" between a few representatives of those sectors who come together in some Washington back room. It can be developed only on the basis of a social contract whose benefits and obligations are widely understood, which includes all Americans—and which is based on a careful respect for our own traditions of freedom and decentralization. Two preliminary requirements of that contract are clear: for management, a national commitment to reduce the overall level of economic uncertainty so that business can plan effectively for the future; for the individual worker, an increase in economic security so that collaboration in raising productivity will not be at his or her expense. Both require *sustained* economic stability.

Chapter 7

A FULL-PRODUCTION ECONOMY

Work in America is what binds most adult individuals to the rest of society. It is the foundation of community beyond the family. In many ways it has become a substitute for the family and neighborhood now broken up by the economic and social pressures of modern life. Sociologists tell us that a major attraction of the modern corporation is that it offers connectedness to rootless, atomized individuals.

Having a job does not by itself create community. Jobs that are dirty and exhausting, jobs that are psychologically oppressive alienate people farther from the rest of society. And much work is dull and routinized. Chained to a desk or an assembly line, we dream of being free of the routine. But when you lose your job, freedom becomes empty. Being without work makes us feel useless and left out. The unemployed speak of being out of touch. Even people who do not have to work to earn a living seek it out to provide a sense of meaning; work defines their relationship to the world.

We cannot create a sense of community if millions of Americans willing and able to work cannot find permanent, steady jobs. In the structure of a sustainable national consensus, full employment is a major weight-bearing wall.

DO PEOPLE WANT TO WORK?

In any society there are always a small percentage of otherwise able-bodied people who won't pull their share. And they seem to be quite randomly scattered throughout the population so that almost everyone is personally acquainted with someone who seems hopelessly out of sync with the work ethic—a loafer, a parasite. But the idea promoted by right-wing propaganda that most unemployment in America is the result of laziness and a defective "work ethic" is clearly a product of ideology rather than fact. To be consistent with observable reality it would have to mean that the work ethic rises and falls regularly, parallel with *but unconnected to* general economic conditions. It would mean, for example, that the 2½-million jump in the number of unemployed people in the United States between 1973 and 1975 represented a massive attack of indolence and that the 1-million drop in unemployment over the next two years meant the disease had abated, only to break out again in 1980!

Clearly, the availability of jobs is the major determinant of the level of unemployment. *But the average working American does not see the lack of jobs in the economy as a whole.* What he or she sees is that *he or she* is working and that there are people who can work and who don't. This makes the middle class easily aroused by simpleminded attacks on the unemployed as lazy. And many politicians cannot resist the temptation. During a press conference in the spring of 1981, for instance, Ronald Reagan said that "in the Sunday edition of the *New York Times*, there were 45 and a half pages of help wanted ads, and in the *Washington Post . . .* there were 33 and a half pages." If there were not enough jobs, Reagan wondered sarcastically, why are all these jobs listed in the help wanted ads?[1]

Why indeed? A look at the help wanted ads in the *Times* that day shows that the overwhelming bulk of jobs available were for highly skilled professional, managerial, and sales people. In the *Post* there were only three ads for dishwashers; ads seeking houseworkers were outnumbered by ads by houseworkers seeking jobs. Yet the majority of the unemployed are unskilled and semiskilled people with little education. In the year Reagan was elected president, unemployment for people in professional, technical, and managerial occupations made up just 10 percent of the total unemployed; *their* unemployment rate was just over 2 percent—in other words, just about the frictional level.[2]

Investigating the thesis that unemployed people do not *want* work, *Fortune* magazine reporters studied responses to help wanted ads in Middletown, New York, in the fall of 1978. Of 228 ads in the newspaper, 50 were for part-time work only, and 25 were for real-estate salesmen or other commission-type sales jobs requiring experience or a license. Only 42 jobs represented real full-time employment for unskilled workers, and the employers offering this work were "swamped by a tidal wave of applicants."

Within 24 hours after the local newspaper published an ad by the Diplomat Motel for a $3.00-an-hour night clerk, for example, 70 people responded. The *Fortune* article concluded that behind Middletown's seeming prosperity lay a world of scared, anxious, unemployed people searching in vain for jobs of some kind. "These are not people who are out of work because they are overly fussy about how they earn a living; they are people who are eager, even desperate, for jobs that pay $3.00 an hour."[3]

At about the same time Reagan made his remark about newspaper want ads, 5,000 people applied for 90 job openings at a car battery manufacturer in Toledo, some of them waiting in line for 18 hours.[4] And the president of Zayre Corporation told *Fortune* magazine:

> I was in Chicago a few weeks ago, and I want you to know that it was simply heartrending to walk into an empty store and see 500 to 1,000 mostly black people lining up for maybe 100 jobs. I have seen lines that stretch nearly one-quarter of a mile, with people waiting for hours in the hope of landing a job that pays near minimum wage.[5]

Inevitably, many able-bodied people who are out of work find their way to unemployment compensation, food stamps, and the like, producing resentment toward the unemployed for "living off the rest of us." The idea that able-bodied people are unemployed because they want to be and that their unemployment is encouraged by social transfer payments has visceral appeal. To someone who feels exploited and unfairly treated, the sight of someone ahead in the supermarket line paying with food stamps aggravates his sense of unfairness. "Why should I," he asks, "have to get out of bed in the morning, fight the traffic, take abuse from customers and arrogant bosses, use up the best hours of my day and the best days of my life when someone else can collect a check from the government for doing nothing? If he *really* wanted to work, he'd find a way. . . ."

As the new economic era squeezes the real income of the average family, moral outrage against "welfare chiselers" has also become a major factor in the neoconservative assault on the human services side of the broker state. The *Wall Street Journal, Reader's Digest,* popular newsmagazines, TV specials, and radio talk shows have exploited it fully by repetitious stories about a gravy train for the unemployed. "To the average American," writes George Gilder in his conservative best seller *Wealth and Poverty,* "unemployment [has come] to mean not joblessness, but a nice weekly paycheck . . . and the average family receiving it now has an annual income well above the national median."[6]

The statement is simply not true. In 1979, the year Gilder refers to, average weekly unemployment benefits amounted to $89.67, or $4,663.00 per year. This represented 36 percent of the average recipient's wages when he or she was working. Since no one was permitted to collect unemployment compensation for more than 39 weeks, the most one could amass in that way during that year was $3,497.00. But if someone could have stayed on the dole all year, their income still would have been up to $1,369.00 less than someone working full time at the minimum wage that year. It would also have been about $40.00 per week below the federal poverty line for a family of four.

Fewer than half of those who are unemployed, moreover, actually collect benefits. In a special survey done on this issue by the Bureau of Labor Statistics in 1976, it was found that only 36 percent of the unemployed had received income from unemployment compensation the previous month, that only 13 percent had received food stamps, and only 12 percent some other form of public assistance. The median family income for all unemployed workers that year was $450 per month from *all sources* (including borrowing, help from friends, etc.), or $5,400. Overall median family income in 1976 was $14,958.[7]

In 1980, the National Advisory Council on Economic Opportunity commissioned a survey of the human costs of unemployment. The survey found that far from being the long-term paid vacation pictured by Gilder, unemployment resulted in a loss of self-esteem and a major increase in depression, personal stress, and mental and physical illness. Strong associations were found between unemployment and homicide, robbery, child abuse, narcotics abuse, alcoholism, and breakdown in family life.[8]

The attack on "lazy welfare cheaters" is even farther off the mark. With the exception of unemployment compensation, the overwhelming bulk of social programs have gone to people who *cannot* work—either because they are too old, too young, too disabled, or are female heads of households who cannot find day-care facilities for their young children. In 1980, even before the Reagan cuts, these programs included:

- Social Security, $118 billion. Ninety-nine percent of the benefits went to persons who were over sixty-two, or under eighteen, or were still in school, or were children of deceased parents, or were disabled.

- Medicare, $35 billion. All of the recipients were over sixty-five.
- Workers' compensation, including payments to black-lung victims, $15 billion. Only the certified disabled received benefits.
- Railroad retirement, $5 billion. All beneficiaries are over sixty, with at least thirty years' service.
- Aid to Families with Dependent Children, $12 billion. Sixty-nine percent went to children and another 28 percent to female heads of households.
- Food stamps, $9 billion. Ninety-two percent went to poor households with children. Maximum monthly income, $306 per month for a single person; $596 per month for a family of four. Maximum amount of assets other than a home people were allowed to have was $1,500, or $3,000 if they were over sixty.
- Medicaid, $14 billion. Fifty-one percent went to children or the aged, 29 percent went to the blind or otherwise disabled, and the remainder went to parents receiving AFDC.
- Supplemental Social Security, $7 billion. All recipients were over sixty-five, blind, or disabled.
- Veterans' benefits, $12 billion. At least 82 percent went to those who were disabled or their dependents.[9]

Thus, of the $227 billion in the public-transfer payments to individuals in existence when Reagan took office as President, only 6.6 billion, 3 percent, seem to fall into a category of able-bodied people.[10] This does not mean that none of the other 97 percent would be unable to work if the demand for labor were strong. After all, there is nothing magical about the age of sixty-two or sixty-five that prohibits people from doing productive work. Adequate day-care facilities would also enable many AFDC mothers to take jobs. And, of course, there are degrees of disability. Highly handicapped people often find certain jobs they can do—again, *if* the demand for labor is strong enough.

Taking all of this into account, Sheldon Danziger, Robert Haveman, and Robert Plotnick of the University of Wisconsin surveyed the large numbers of recent studies bearing on this issue. They calculated the effect of all the above social programs on the labor supply—in other words, on the amount of work that people might have done had there been no transfer programs and had there been jobs available. They estimate that the total declined by 5.4 percent due to the existence of the programs surveyed. In the most politically controversial areas—AFDC, food stamps, and housing assistance—the amount of labor held back by recipients was reduced by 1 percent and .5 percent, respectively.[11] Obviously such programs fall far short of being an important reason why people do not work.

That people generally want to work if jobs are available is also documented by evidence from other Western industrialized nations that have much more generous social services programs—government-supported pensions, unemployment compensation, national health insurance, public housing, liberal programs for the elderly, and so forth, yet normally have unemployment rates substantially lower than in the United States. While official unemployment between 1973 and 1980 averaged almost 7 percent of the labor force in the United States, the comparable number for France was 5 percent, for West Germany 3.3 percent, and for Sweden—the prototypical welfare state—an incredible 1.5 percent.[12] Great Britain, despite its economic troubles, averaged 5.4 percent unemployment. With the exception of Britain, all of the countries also outperformed the United States in productivity growth during the period.[13]

It is sometimes argued that if wages were lowered, making labor cheaper relative to capital, more workers could be hired. But such a substitution of workers for machines would by definition lower productivity. And it would mean decreasing wages still farther in that sector of the economy that does not now pay enough to maintain a decent standard of living. The point of economic policy is to raise incomes, not to lower them. The increase in jobs would in all likelihood be small and the cost in community large: Young teenagers would replace some middle-aged, family-supporting adults, for instance, if a subminimum wage were allowed in many industries.

There is one other related rationale for unemployment; it is that the unemployed are inherently unproductive. If they had more skills, had a better attitude, were smarter, would work harder, etc.—they would be "worth" hiring. Pointing to the unremarkable fact that those who are out of work tend to be less skilled and less experienced, some economists have held that the *source* of the problem of unemployment lies in the characteristics of the unemployed. The answer, therefore, is to change the character of the unemployed by giving them more education, job training, and attitude counseling. From 1962 to 1981, $63.3 billion in federal dollars were poured into local schools, antipoverty agencies, and training subsidies to business to upgrade the skills of the unemployed and "disadvantaged" young people to make them worth hiring.[14] The programs had the support of a progressive segment of the big-business community and were a mainstay of domestic economic policy through the administrations of Kennedy, Johnson,

Nixon, Ford, and Carter. In modified form, they have recently become the Reagan administration's token substitute for jobs programs.

The unemployed also tend to have other characteristics that employers use to screen job applicants, either because of direct prejudice or because, in the employers' experience, it is assumed that these characteristics are associated with inferior skills and performance: They are the wrong race or the wrong sex, have a physical handicap, etc. Since these are characteristics that cannot be trained or counseled out of the unemployed, the conventional liberal answer has been to attempt to root out such bias with lawsuits, regulatory agencies such as the Equal Employment Opportunity Commission, and "affirmative action" programs that demand some form of preferential treatment as compensation for historic bias against a population group.

There is little doubt that training programs and affirmative action efforts have helped some people get jobs and promotions they would not otherwise have received. Moreover, the attack on racial and other forms of discrimination has opened up new opportunities for people who have the skills and ability to compete successfully but who have been prevented from doing so because of their sex or race or age. On the grounds of simple justice, as well as the general economic health of the nation, these efforts have been worthwhile. But as a solution to the problem of unemployment, their contribution has been—and must be—marginal.

So long as the number of people looking for work exceeds the number of jobs available, some people *have* to remain out of work. The labor market is similar to a line outside a movie theater. If there are three hundred seats in the theater and four hundred people waiting in line, a hundred people will not get in. If there are ninety million jobs and a hundred million people looking for work, ten million will be unemployed. Structural programs mainly have the effect of shifting people around on the line. Poverty and unemployment are concentrated among minorities and households headed by women because they are the least attractive to the employers—they are at the end of the line. To the extent that training and affirmative action programs succeed in making these people more competitive, they exchange their place with someone else.

Where there are genuine skill shortages, of course, increased training and education can create new jobs. But by and large, disadvantaged people are trained for entry-level jobs for which there have usually been plenty of applicants. An estimate by economist George Johnson of the University of Michigan is that the reduction of the unemployment rate as a result of training given to one million people for one year would be less than one hundredth of a percentage point.[15]

Without jobs for graduates, training programs become warehouses for the unemployed. Gradually, the programs become little more than ways of getting income to young, inexperienced, unemployed people. Young people are recycled into and out of them. Demoralized teachers and demoralized students become mutually cynical about each other and the system. Moreover, to the extent that affirmative action efforts have been successful in moving blacks, Hispanics, and women up the line in the employment market, they have meant an increase in job insecurity for blue-collar white males. The essence of affirmative action is that people get placed in certain jobs *because* they are black or female. Without an increase in the total number of jobs available, this "reverse discrimination" inevitably means that other people do *not* get the job because they are white or male.

"My father worked here. My sister works here. My brother-in-law works here," a blue-collar worker at a Westinghouse plant in Pittsburgh complains. "I'm just an average guy. All I can give my son is the fact that I have been a good worker for thirty years in this plant. That was always good enough recommendation for anybody's kid. Now it's not worth anything."

Economic rivalry between blacks and whites, men and women, is a problem at any time. But in times of slow growth and slipping real incomes it erupts into a source of social conflict undermining community. It has also had enormous political repercussions within the Democratic Party. Old alliances between labor and civil rights groups were strained during the 1970s as their constituencies fought over the small number of high-paying jobs, particularly in the manufacturing and construction sectors.

Some people saw the problem early. In 1964 Sargent Shriver and other members of Lyndon Johnson's staff proposed that he begin a large-scale direct job-creation program financed by a tax on cigarettes. Johnson refused. He had vowed to eliminate poverty in America but was not willing to alienate the tobacco industry to do it.[16] Later, when it had become clear that job training and affirmative action do not create jobs, a modest effort was made to create public-service employment as part of the Emergency Employment Act of 1971 and its successor, CETA (Comprehensive Employment and Training Act). These were jobs, primarily in state and local governments, paid for directly by the U.S. Department of Labor. The program was a qualified success. Over a period of six years, 5.4 million jobs were created in police stations, hospitals, parks, housing, and so forth.[17] But acquiescence to conservative ideology and business fear that the jobs would raise wage levels in the private sector forced a series of restrictions. Full-time public-sector employees were also threatened; in a situation of general unemployment they feared less-expensive federally supported workers might take their permanent jobs. The restrictions—the most important of which was to limit any job to one year's duration —underscored that the jobs were "make-work," that they were created to put people to work, not for their value to society (despite the fact that they did have value).

The worth of the worker is obviously only partially a function of his or her innate productivity. It is also a function of the demand for the job itself. And for the most part the demand for a particular job is outside the influence of the worker and, indeed, outside the influence of the employer, too, in times of recession. Over the past decade the demand for engineers, keypunch operators, architects, librarians, and those in a host of other occupations fluctuated wildly. In the early 1970s, demand for engineers fell. In the late 1970s, it rose.[18] Neither had anything to do with the inherent productivity of engineers. Yet at one time they are worth hiring; at another time, they are not.

Once we acknowledge the factor of the demand for labor in the equation, the idea of intrinsic economic worth becomes quite slippery. In 1974, five million people were not "worth" hiring. In 1975, almost eight million people were not worth hiring. In 1979, six million were not worth hiring. In 1982, eleven million were not worth hiring. If the government, through tight fiscal or monetary policies, forces the demand for labor to fall far enough, then more people will not be worth hiring. If, on the other hand, the government promotes expansion, the same people will be worth hiring.

This does not mean that some people are not more productive than others and work harder and produce more value for their employer. Those are the people generally at the front of the labor market line. But the distinction we are concerned with here is between those who are working and those who are not. And *that* distinction is clearly a function of the overall demand for labor.

A STEADY ECONOMIC LOCOMOTIVE

Jobs are created when the economy is on the go. But people, and particularly corporate and private investors, can have confidence in the future only to the extent that they have assurance the rug will not suddenly and repeatedly be pulled out from under them. A storekeeper will make improvements in his store if he has a long-term lease rather than a short-term one. A petrochemical company will be more willing to expand if it has an assured supply of petroleum than if it does not. A homebuilder will take a risk and build houses "on spec" if the largest employer in town is known to be expanding. In the same way, the nation's corporations and businesses—*as a collectivity*—can make necessary long-term investments only if they have assurances that the economy as a whole will experience steady, upward expansion.

The private sector cannot provide that assurance to itself. By its very nature, the marketplace is volatile, changing, and uncertain. The more competitive it is, the more volatile, changing, and uncertain it is. In the new era of increasing uncertainty, neither frightened businessmen nor debt-burdened consumers can lead the economy forward *in a sustained fashion.* We have learned this the hard way from the failures of the Carter administration and the waste of Reaganomics. Slowly, painfully, economic downturns usually right themselves over time. But the only institution capable of taking a sustained lead is the government. The public sector must therefore become a reliable economic locomotive if it is to pull the private sector steadily into full production.

It must begin with its own long-run capital-investment program. How and where capital gets allocated determines the pattern of economic growth and therefore the character of the society. It is *the* society-shaping decision. The investment choices we make today will determine whether tomorrow we will have healthy, competitive industries with up-to-date technology. They will determine whether we can enter the 1990s free of dependence on foreign oil, or whether we will continue to be hostage to foreign governments. They will determine whether we will have jobs for unemployed, restless teenagers, or whether five years from now they will still be hanging around street corners, five years older, five years more alienated, and five years more dangerous. Investing in real-estate speculation rather than public housing, automobile restyling rather than public transportation, or cosmetics rather than preventive medicine not only alters the distribution of income and wealth in favor of some and against others, but also determines the way in which all of us work, live, and play. The house we live in, the shape of the rooms, the distance to work, our jobs—even what we know and how we think—have been to a large degree shaped by highway, housing, educational, and business investment decisions made long ago. Our future and the future of those who come after will be shaped by our investment decisions. Choosing capital investments means choosing the future.

There is no permanent answer to the question of what is the best way to create an ongoing environment of certainty and sustained production. Striking the balance between consumer spending and government spending, private investment and public investment, is *the subject* of planning; and the answers will depend on a mixture of economic and political conditions. The issue is not just one of mounting a temporary jobs program. It is how to maintain a *permanent, sustained lift to the economy*—the kind of lift that can be counted on.

American University professor Nancy Barrett estimated in early 1983 that a carefully scheduled five-year program of public investments of an average of $50 billion per year would have brought the economy to 4 percent unemployment.[19] Combined with appropriate tax reforms it could also have returned enough revenues to radically reduce the federal deficit. The result is achieved in part because high employment yields high tax returns—as we have seen, roughly $25 billion to $28 billion more goes to the Treasury with each percentage point that unemployment is reduced. In part the gains come about because the enormous tax losses of the Reagan program are reduced; in part they occur because direct investment expenditures have a much higher economic "multiplier," producing more jobs per dollar—and thus greater tax returns—than indirect tax cuts (especially for high-income groups that spend relatively small percentages of their benefits). A sustained public investment effort could be augmented by additional revenue gains from greater tax reform and military expenditure cutbacks; the primary choices are political, not economic. In the tax area, for instance, Brookings economist Joseph Pechman and others have identified tax loopholes easily worth over $100 billion that could be closed—if there were a will to do so.[20] (This is a conservative estimate of potential areas for saving from among the $388.4 billion of "tax expenditures" in the 1984 budget.)

A *strategic* plan for sustained growth transcends the dreary liberal-conservative debate over whether to cut the deficit by increased taxes or reduced spending. *Both* in fact reduce economic stimulus and, when unemployment is in the 8 to 10 percent range, sacrifice full employment to conservative politics. The fear that long-term interest rates due to deficits can abort a recovery is real—but if stimulus is reduced, an economic slowdown can reduce tax flows and *increase* the deficit. A coherent plan that gives strategic emphasis to full production is the only way to guarantee the tax flows that are the underlying condition of reducing the deficit and long-term interest rates.*

Professor David Linowes of the University of Illinois has also demonstrated how such an effort can be cost-effective in areas that

*See Chapter Thirteen for a discussion of monetary policy and interest-rate issues in such a plan.

involve high investment leverage, such as housing. If, for example, mortgage interest rates are 14 percent, a $65,000 home requiring a 5 percent down payment payable over a 30-year period is within reach of 4.5 million families. But if interest rates are directly subsidized by 6 percent through a federal investment program, another 12.5 million families become eligible. If 1 out of 10 of these additional potential homeowners enters the market, the result is 800,000 new housing units, representing $52 billion in housing sales and an overall economic stimulation of $102 billion and 1.2 million new jobs.

The cost to the public initially is $3 billion, but new tax revenue from the increase in business comes to $2.5 billion. Moreover, the 1.2 million new jobs include jobs for a number of people presently getting unemployment compensation, food stamps, and other forms of social welfare. The increase in employment therefore saves the government more money—which Linowes estimates at $800 million. Under these conditions, the investment of $3 billion generates revenues of $3.3 billion—a $300 million profit to the public Treasury.[21] Finally, there is no reason that the Treasury cannot also recover the original cost of the direct subsidy expenditure when and if the house is sold by the original buyer.

Conservative ideologues often criticize the increase in public expenditure programs during the 1960s and 1970s. Yet it was precisely during these years—when state and local expenditures increased from 7 percent of the GNP in 1956 to 10.2 percent in 1971, and federal expenditures increased from 17.1 percent of the GNP to 20.4 percent —that the economy boomed and unemployment averaged 4.8 percent. In Part III we shall examine in some detail the fallacious argument that public expenditures—rather than such sectoral factors as food and oil shocks—initiated most of the inflation of the 1970s. Suffice it to note here that the average inflation rate during the boom period 1960–69 was a mere 2.8 percent.[22]

The present general problem is quite clear; as we look down the remainder of the 1980s, we know that the American economy must to some degree be reshaped and changed in order to prosper. Since the critical decisions are investment decisions, we require a plan for capital spending targeted at those investments that can also shape the production side of the economy to meet the demands of the new economic era. This is different from reindustrialization planning, which is concerned primarily with shifting income to investors, not guaranteeing *investment* itself. It is also different from traditional Keynesian attempts to stimulate sales in order to put people back to work. Our problem is to put people back to work *permanently to make our economy more efficient, ecologically balanced, and community-sustaining.*

The prolonged attack on the public sector from the Right has led to a drastically declining share of our Gross National Product being devoted to domestic public investments—and it has defined this as an area of obvious immediate significance. In 1980, for instance, when private investment in plant and equipment as a percentage of our GNP was at a postwar high, public domestic investment in physical facilities dropped to 2.2 percent—almost half of what it had been in 1966, and the lowest point since just after World War II.[23]

Simply totaling up the obvious investment needed to rebuild our national infrastructure provides us with one list of priorities which not only are themselves essential for high growth in the private sector but also represent enough new jobs to bring us close to full employment rapidly.[24] For example:

- Fixing the 40 percent of the bridges in the United States that are in need of repair (many of which are unsafe right now) would produce 100,000 new jobs.[25]
- Maintaining the present level of highway and road conditions through 1995 would put about 550,000 people to work, and a modest expansion of the highway system, according to the National Transportation Policy Study Commission, would create another 575,000 jobs.[26]
- Repair, modernization, and expansion of railroad track to keep up with increased traffic between now and the year 1990 would produce 241,000 jobs per year.[27]
- Dredging just six Atlantic and Gulf Coast harbors to handle cargo ships of up to 150,000 tons would put 44,000 people to work a year.[28]
- Moving the mass-transit share of trips in urban areas to 7 percent through expansion of rail systems and maintenance of bus lines would create 170,000 jobs.[29]
- Construction and repair of waste-water treatment facilities, sewers, and storm-water runoff systems necessary to serve the population through the year 2000 would generate an additional 250,000 jobs per year.[30]
- Meeting the repair needs of water supply systems in the nation's urban areas would create at least 50,000 jobs, even before the major issue of meeting regional water shortages is addressed.[31]
- Meeting water pollution standards over the next five years would create 84,000 jobs.[32]

Some idea of the crisis at the municipal level can be gleaned from the following report on New York City's public-works needs:

> Over $40 billion must be invested in New York City alone over the next nine years to repair, service, and rebuild basic public works facilities that include: 1,000 bridges, two large aqueducts, one large water tunnel, several reservoirs, 6,200 miles of paved streets, 6,000 miles of sewer, 6,000 miles of water lines, 6,700 subway cars, 4,500 buses, 25,000 acres of parks, 17 hospitals, 19 city university campuses, 950 schools, 200 libraries, and hundreds of fire houses and police stations. Because of its fiscal condition, New York City will be able to invest only $1.4 billion per year to repair, service, and rebuild these facilities.[33]

In addition to investment in much-needed public facilities, there are major expenditures necessary in certain "basic necessity" goods that, as we shall see in Part III, form a major part of a strategy to control inflation as well as to support a sense of community and stability for individuals and the neighborhoods in which they live. Production of solar energy hardware and a full-scale weatherization and conservation program sufficient to reduce substantially U.S. energy consumption in 1990, for instance, would create an additional 2.9 million jobs per year.[34] Many of the latter—plus reforestation, watershed maintenance, and other conservation efforts—are also "fast-start-up" jobs that can be quickly initiated in time of recession. They are also areas in which large numbers of unskilled and semiskilled workers can be employed.

Leaving aside investments in road and highway expansion and the large investment needed to solve the regional water problem, the basic public-housing, conservation, and investment needs of the country could alone generate the equivalent of 5,620,000 in net new full-time jobs in the United States per year for the next decade.[35] When combined with the multiplier effects of secondary jobs produced by such efforts, this would more than eliminate unemployment in America. The mix of investments in a comprehensive plan to achieve sustained full production obviously also includes private investments facilitated by housing and industrial loans and loan guarantees, and by other procurement, tax, and regulatory measures. A carefully scheduled investment plan should phase in fast-hitting, fast-start-up jobs at the outset and then reduce these in a coordinated fashion as longer lead-time projects come onstream.*

---

*See Chapter Fifteen.

PUBLIC AND PRIVATE BALANCE SHEETS

Market mechanisms are and will continue to be a primary arrangement for distributing and producing most goods and services in America. We are a people dedicated to the opportunities of business entrepreneurship. Most markets are more efficient when competitive. But obsession with the ideal of the marketplace has prevented us from understanding the essential and mutually reinforcing interrelationship between the public and the private sectors in all but military areas of the economy. The ideology that sees the generation of income and wealth as a purely private phenomenon, operating in a self-contained world into which public spending can intrude only as a drain on productive activity, gives an extraordinarily narrow focus to policy. Efficiency is seen only in terms of private profit-and-loss statements— and public policy only in terms of its effect on the private balance sheet.

As a result, our official economic statistics have no categories for accurate measurement of the comprehensive impact of public spending on the economy. As we have seen, productivity, for instance, is measured mainly by output per worker *in the private sector of the economy.* The value of public goods and services is defined tautologically, as their cost; improvements in actual productivity always wash out, since input and output never differ in the statistics. Measuring productivity solely as a private phenomenon means, moreover, that government, by definition, *cannot* be productive!

This, of course, is nonsense. Government spending on education, health, and research and development is a direct and major determinant of technological progress. In the long run, productivity expert Edward Denison judges that education is the single most important contributor to productivity. And, of course, public physical investments in roads, transportation, ports, bridges, and the like are critical to the functioning of an efficient economy. One bridge in Duquesne, Pennsylvania, that is now too fragile for heavy trucks costs U.S. Steel Company $1.2 million per year. In Manhattan, private companies lose $166 million per year for each additional five-minute delay on the subways and buses.[36] The notion that a tax break to stimulate private real-estate speculation is productive, and that a comparable public expenditure on a bridge or subway is not, is patently absurd.

The fiction that the public sector is unproductive is reinforced by a government accounting system that does not distinguish between capital and current spending. No one could effectively analyze a business if dollars spent for current operating expenses, such as wages and consumable supplies, were indistinguishable from dollars spent on long-term capital improvements, such as a new factory or a major piece of machinery that will generate income through the years. The average family also understands the obvious difference between borrowing for a capital investment in a home and current spending for clothes, food, or a vacation. If it tried to pay for a home in one lump sum, it would be absurd; it *must* be "in deficit" for such a long-term capital investment. The federal budget, however, makes no such distinction. Spending is added up into one unwieldy total in which a new bridge with a thirty-year life is treated the same as a welfare payment to an AFDC mother or a cotton farmer, or the salary of an FBI agent.

Because capital expenditures are carried as current ones, the federal deficit is thus always misleading. The federal budget does give a rough measure of the direct demand on resources coming from the federal government, and therefore some general picture of how much the federal government is competing for resources with the other sectors. But here again, the federal budget is politically the focal point of interest only to the extent that it impacts on the balance sheets of the private sector. No one is concerned with the *public* or overall taxpayers' balance sheet.

The absence of a truly public accounting system ensures the illusion of an inefficient public sector at the same time as it militates against effective, direct action. It is one of the main results of an obsolete ideology. Public spending is seen as a *residual,* a surplus generated by the tax revenue of the "producing" private sector. This is then distributed by the public sector on the basis of special-interest lobbying of politicians. The model makes it easy to jump to the false conclusion that it is the private sector that alone produces and the public sector that alone consumes.

When, however, we look at the allocation of capital from the perspective of the *country's profit-and-loss statement,* we see that our problem is not one of insufficient incentive. There are plenty of rewards for the risk-taking investor in America. Nor is it a problem of misallocating resources to public social welfare spending. By the standard of almost every other industrial nation (most of which have outperformed us in productivity growth), the United States remains parsimonious with its social welfare spending. From the perspective of a total public accounting system, the most obvious problem is extreme economic *waste.*

Repeated recession, stop-start growth, unemployed people, factories operating with unutilized capacity, reduced tax flows—all are the price we pay for indulging our fantasies about the superior value of anything private over anything public. The capital we need for new public and private investment is frittered away both by absurd tax waste and by allowing the economy to stagnate. It is the cost of treating the public sector both as an object of moral scorn and at the same time as a fool to be cheated and exploited for anyone and everyone's private benefit. The political and economic realities of our time demand that government take clear responsibility for prosperity. But our ideological phobias have created a class of technocrats and politicians obsessed with the narrowest definitions of efficiency and progress—yet almost blind to the real cost of the resulting haphazard, irrational, and bizarre responses to the pressures of the new economic era.

We are, in fact, recklessly dissipating the precious capital needed to create a stable and prosperous future. The country needs to put its unemployed to work, but the broker state answer is to lavish reduced taxes on the private sector—which ends up with few jobs after subsidizing the assets of private corporations by increasing the liabilities of the public sector.

The country desperately needs new sources of energy. The broker state answer has been to stimulate a massive transfer of funds from consumers to oil companies in the hope that the latter will reinvest the money in domestic oil production. Yet only a part of the billions in new revenues the oil industry received was used to drill for more oil, while oil company after oil company speculates in the purchases of circuses, retail chains, and real estate.

The country faces a shortage of housing for low- and middle-income people. The broker state answer is to flood the housing sector with generalized tax subsidies, which the market then uses to fuel the fires of real-estate speculation. The result is that a huge amount of the nation's capital is poured into the housing sector, but fewer and fewer houses are built.

The product of this wastefulness is confusion, uncertainty, and economic instability—the characteristics of the new economic era.

A FULL-PRODUCTION ECONOMY

As we have seen from Professor Sheffrin's calculations (see Chapter Five), a full-production economy in the past would not only have put the unemployed to work, it also would have generated a huge increase in goods, services, and public revenues that could have raised the standard of living of all Americans substantially. Professor Sheffrin's projections for the future suggest potential gains that are even more startling. The difference, for example, between sustaining a 5.5 percent unemployment rate over the final twenty-five years of the century and the 2 percent "full employment" level that was common in many European countries and Japan for much of the postwar boom would be $6 trillion in GNP and $1.3 trillion in additional federal revenues. The difference between such a full-employment rate and a 9.9 percent unemployment rate (which results from a simple extension of the average U.S. growth rate for the previous two decades) is $15 trillion in accumulated GNP and $3.2 trillion in federal revenue.[37]

How close the United States can come to eliminating all but frictional unemployment is unclear. Otto Eckstein has recently proposed the older 4 percent goal as a feasible target.[38] High levels of employment are, of course, possible only if accompanied by comprehensive programs to fight inflation, the subject of Part III. But one key to achieving sustained gains under any employment target is increased certainty. Entrepreneurs are cautious risk-takers; they are not gamblers. They are encouraged not by extraordinarily high odds but by a feeling of certainty, of stability. Business confidence cannot be bought by giving away the Treasury in tax spending. Neither can it be conjured up with media hype. Gerald Ford tried it with "WIN" buttons. Jimmy Carter tried it with inspirational messages about discipline and sacrifice. Ronald Reagan tried it with ideological fervor. The investment response to them *all* was a hollow "clink" and the slow, agonizingly painful restarting of economic activity after reaching lower and lower levels each decade.

FULL PRODUCTION AND TRADE

A determined, competent federal government is the only institution that can provide sufficient confidence in the ongoing economic future to open the way for the known human, financial, and technical resources now bottled up in America. A fundamental requirement of a community-sustaining economics is a national decision to do what it takes to achieve that result. A commitment to establishing a concrete plan for sustained full production is also the key to a new approach to trade and to America's overall role in the world economy.

Since the mid-1970s the United States has been importing more than it has been exporting. The balance of merchandise trade, which was a favorable $9 billion in 1975, was a negative $28 billion in 1981; it is expected to range between $70 billion and $100 billion by 1984. So long as American manufacturing dominated world trade, almost everyone believed in the free and unfettered international marketplace. But the decline of America's relative share of world trade and the takeover of many domestic markets by foreign goods has cracked this unanimity. Both unions and management in autos, steel, textiles, shoes, rubber, electronics, and other industries now demand trade barriers to protect their jobs and investments.

The United States' position on trade is tinged with hypocrisy. We have established elaborate efforts to achieve the results of protectionism under the guise of voluntary import reductions. Prompted by the drive of the United Auto Workers to pass "domestic content" legislation that would require a certain percentage of every auto sold in the United States to be made here, for instance, the Reagan administration forced Japan to agree to reduce "voluntarily" the number of auto imports to America. Restrictions by a "free trade" administration have also added motorcycles, sugar, steel, and other items to the list of foreign-made products that find it increasingly difficult to enter the U.S. market. In 1982 the Reagan administration tried to force European firms to stop work on the Soviet natural gas pipeline as punishment for Soviet transgressions in Afghanistan and Poland—while at the same time it insisted on selling the Soviet Union surplus American grain in the name of free trade.

On the other hand, most other industrialized countries are more protectionist than we are. Sheila Page of the British National Institute for Economic and Social Research estimates that more than 46 percent of all trade is currently controlled by governments through tariffs, quotas, and other barriers.[39] Japan, for example, imposes complex and costly inspection procedures and arcane standards for consumer goods that only Japanese firms can meet. The onset of worldwide stagnation has increased pressures in *all* countries for higher trade barriers—barriers that feed on each other as internal demands for protection in one country force other governments to follow suit.

Given a prolonged period of stagnation, it is doubtful that the theoretical principle of free trade can withstand the operational reality of protectionism. In this there are parallels with the theory of the free market and the increasingly obvious realities of broker state planning. And the stark choices posed over the appropriate posture for the United States in acrimonious debate between protectionists and free traders increasingly confuse the discussion of real world options—in much the same way that our internal economic dialogue between conservatives and liberals confuses the issues posed by the emerging planning metamorphosis at the heart of the domestic system.

Our own history, for instance, refutes the overly simple idea that free trade is synonymous with growth and prosperity. America's industrial base was developed behind tariffs that protected our industries from competition with European rivals. A major economic cause of the Civil War was the South's resentment against having to buy high-cost textiles and other goods from the North while being forced to sell its cotton in the free market. Especially in the conditions of the new economic era, successful economic development often requires a country to nurture new industries for a while against stronger foreign competitors. Another limitation on free trade is national security: Would the United States really want to depend on Japan and South Korea to produce the steel, aluminum, and motor vehicles necessary to fight a war even if all were cheaper to make overseas? Even in peacetime, as the experience with OPEC has shown, it is not sensible for a nation to rely completely on foreign suppliers for essential goods. Furthermore, to the extent inadequate foreign production can create bottlenecks in scrap steel or even imported cement, economic upswings can be throttled and planning for sustained full production made impossible.

The pitfalls to a nation that excessively emphasizes production for export are also well recognized. Export subsidies and special encouragement of industries that cater to world markets tend to distort economic growth and nurture specialized high-price, high-wage sectors at the expense of the rest of the economy. These sectors are extremely vulnerable to sudden shifts in world conditions. When a nation's balance of trade depends on them, they eventually hold the economy hostage for more and more subsidization. Jane Jacobs' brilliant essay *The Question of Separation* illustrates how success in international trade among developed nations depends, rather, on creating a rich entrepreneurial mixture of small and medium-sized companies. She compares Norway's economic development with Canada's. Despite disadvantages, the latter has in many ways been more successful because it has been based more on a diversified domestic economy and to a lesser degree on large companies whose main purpose is export production.[40]

Totally free trade also hampers a nation's ability to conduct its own monetary and fiscal policy. If one country decides to increase its rate of growth while its neighbors do not, for example, increased incomes will lead to imports increasing faster than exports. Unless restrictions are placed on imports, faster growth is doomed. In the absence of international coordination of economic policies, this tends to keep everyone's economy at the level of the slowest-growing major trading partners. Fear of balance of payments problems stemming from inflation led the Federal Reserve Board to establish high interest rates in 1979—which initiated the ongoing economic slide of the early 1980s. Economists at Britain's University of Cambridge have shown that a carefully managed policy of reducing the *percentage* of imports in a nation's economy can moderate balance of payment problems and is therefore an alternative to induced recession. The resulting possibility of a higher-growth, full-production strategy can in turn lead to a higher overall *volume* of imports and of world trade than the alternative of stop-start growth or stagnation that accompanies classical free trade in the modern era.[41]

Other complications challenge the traditional paradigm—such as the fact that currency fluctuations, which have a profound effect on trade balances, often have nothing to do with the relative production efficiencies of the countries involved. Tight money policies have also caused a substantial portion of the worsening of the U.S. balance of trade in the past several years: Between 1978 and 1982, U.S. high interest rates led to a global demand for dollars, helping raise the dollar's value against other major currencies 20 to 25 percent (and more against the Japanese yen). A Toyota produced in Japan at a cost of $10,000 in equivalent labor and capital could be sold in the United States for considerably less because the yen was so cheap. A number of studies suggest that (with a one- to two-year lag) the U.S. trade balance tends to deteriorate by about $3 billion for every percentage point the U.S. dollar is overvalued. A 20 percent overvaluation will lead to a $60 billion trade deficit, which in turn means a loss of 1 to 1.5 percentage points of the GNP and one to two million jobs. C. Fred Bergsten, director of the Institute for International Economics, calculates that three quarters of the U.S. economic decline between the beginning of 1981 and late 1982 was due to this factor.[42]

Stop-start economic growth, as we saw in Chapter Six, also undercuts the long-term investment needed to improve overall productivity, and therefore U.S. competitiveness. And to the extent economic policy is geared to slow domestic growth rates by monetary-policy and exchange-rate factors, still other burdens are placed on U.S. manufacturing. When the economy is functioning at stagnation levels (and high interest rates undercut auto sales to boot), Detroit produces five million autos a year rather than ten million. There is no way to maintain high-efficiency, low-cost production in such circumstances. Half the factories are empty—yet the price of each product must cover the cost both of idle and of operating facilities. If during the late 1970s and early 1980s the U.S. auto industry has had to bear, say, a 10 percent inefficiency burden in its cost structure compared with Japan's (which continued to sustain a full employment, full production economy), the price of each car sold had to reflect some of this "stagnation overhead" factor. When combined with the effect of an overvalued dollar, the Japanese advantage—independent of labor costs and manufacturing methods—is very substantial indeed, both in the U.S. market and in competition for third-country markets.

Free traders argue that competition by foreign firms helps keep U.S. productivity growing and that global economic efficiency is improved by an international division of labor that shifts production to countries with comparative advantages in specific areas. Although there is some truth to both arguments, they can easily be overdone. In a country such as the United States, with a very large domestic market, there is a great deal more internal competition than in other nations. Furthermore, nothing stops foreign companies from investing here and introducing new technologies and management techniques to challenge U.S. firms. That part of their competitive advantage that foreign companies derive from cheap labor poses a different issue. Advocates of free trade maintain the United States should keep moving up the technological ladder so that workers displaced by technology or low wages are given new jobs. But if U.S. technology cannot improve fast enough in relation to other nations to do this (and, given the quick transfer of technologies abroad by our own multinational corporations, other nations now catch up very fast), what is to happen to American workers? In practice, free trade then means that workers in poor countries with depressed standards of living must increasingly displace American workers, whose wage standards reflect the historic level of the American standard of living. The classical mechanism of adjustment —changes in currency relationships—are supposed in theory to reorient trade among nations. But the reality is that classical mechanisms of adjustment no longer flow easily.

Perhaps the most basic difficulty with our public debate on America's role in the world economy is simply the excessive emphasis given to trade-related issues. Some economists and many politicians argue that expanding U.S. trade is so important that it must dominate all other considerations. Exports grew from 3.9 to 8 percent of GNP between 1960 and 1982.[43] But the total is still a relatively small share of the giant U.S. economy. The exports of West Germany, France, and Great Britain, for instance, amount to 27, 18, and 21 percent of their GNPs, respectively. Moreover, roughly 19 percent of our current exports do not involve manufactured goods; they are agricultural (nearly 29 percent of imports are energy-related products).[44] Contrary to a commonly held view, Japan is *not* massively dependent on exports. Only 13.5 percent of her GNP is so oriented. Japan's modern export strength, moreover, was built significantly on the productivity gains of a sustained postwar resurgence of growth *within* her internal market—a resurgence that was bolstered by import-limiting restrictive trade policies. To the extent that the Japanese economic miracle is taken as a model for U.S. policy, such facts give pause to the argument that export-led revitalization of the U.S. economy, and free trade, are *the* answers to all our problems.[45]

It is not so much that the specific points made by each side in the debate over America's role in the world economy are wrong. It is that their perspective is wrong. It is self-evident that slow growth, stagflation, and inappropriate fiscal and monetary policies have reduced overall U.S. productivity and the ability of U.S. industries to compete. But because we have no comprehensive planning framework, this fundamental issue has been downplayed and the debate has become focused on secondary questions. In a country the size of the United States— with its enormous capacity to determine its own fate—trade policy should be the natural outgrowth of full employment and price stability policies. Full production planning is the first requirement of U.S. trade policy.* Industrial policies that increase investment and technological innovation can also have a positive effect on our balance of trade. But such policies must be governed by a comprehensive plan. It is not possible, for instance, for the computer and robotic industries of all the nations of the world to become "No. 1." An unplanned scramble to do so can lead only to a massive waste of resources, a number of losers, and ultimately to more protectionism for industries that did not quite make it and whose abandonment would be impossible after the funds had been spent building them up.

Within the context of a comprehensive production plan, it clearly will serve both America and the world for us to relinquish our share of less technologically sophisticated industries to Third and Fourth

---

*Furthermore, as we shall explore more fully in Part III, to the extent that balance-of-payments problems can hamper growth, the most important—and economically appropriate—components of a full-production investment strategy may be those that reduce imports (for example, oil). Also see Part III for a discussion of the role stabilizing price rises in energy and other key sectors can play in reducing the overall cost structure of U.S. exports relative to those of other nations.

World producers over the longer haul. Depending on an analysis of the public balance sheet, temporary subsidies and import restrictions are natural elements of transitional policies. In almost any scenario a full-production economy will require a substantial heavy-industry sector for some time.* The question of national security is a separate one. If the maintenance of a larger steel industry is essential for national security, then necessary subsidies should come out of the military budget. If the fear of unemployment can be reduced, declining industries can be more easily shrunk and made competitive in smaller, high-technology specialty parts of the industry. But everything we know about human behavior tells us that only in an atmosphere of stability and security—where the people involved know that the cost of socially necessary economic change will not be borne by them alone —can the hard decisions about which industries should expand and which should decline be made with a minimum of disruption and wasteful resistance.

Given the interconnectedness of national economies, it is obvious that the United States cannot go it alone. No one can go it alone— especially (as the unsuccessful French effort to reflate its economy in 1981 demonstrated) in a global environment of stagnation and high interest rates. Sustained global growth requires a coordinated effort among Western industrial nations.

Although the United States cannot dictate terms to the rest of the world, we have a unique impact on the international economy. It was largely our domestic decisions that in recent years turned what might have been a difficult but short-lived recession into a world crisis. High U.S. interest rates both slowed world growth directly and led to a contraction of lending within other countries as they were forced to raise their rates to keep capital from flowing to America. Third and Fourth World countries that depend on high growth in the industrialized world to market their goods were decimated by the worldwide recession. Their inability to service long-term debt to private and international governmental lending institutions, in turn, has had ramifications on financial management within the industrial world. Conversely, any diplomatically competent American government committed to a full-production strategy could play a central role in leading a coordinated global recovery.

---

*Moreover, it is to a large extent the existence of large-scale heavy industry that creates the economic demand for high tech. For example, 30 percent of industrial robots are sold to the automotive industry in the United States. And in Japan it was the need to reduce cost in the expanding manufacturing field that provided the major impetus for the development of robotics.

The future of the weakest members of the global economy cannot be separated from the role of U.S. multinational corporations and American military support of regimes that resist reform.* How to achieve real reform and sustained development are not easy questions, but there is no way to solve them in the desperate and hostile context of worldwide stagnation. Nonetheless, as the Brandt Commission and others have urged, a program of aid, loans, and technical assistance is of vital importance. Other necessary reforms include increasing substitution of special drawing rights for the dollar as a de facto international reserve currency, expanding the resources of the World Bank and the IMF, and cooperative efforts to stabilize international exchange rates. Targeting assistance to improve Third World energy production and conservation, to remove bottlenecks in strategic materials production, and the negotiation of stable and fair commodity agreements all would also facilitate global expansion and help rebuild a positive sense of global economic community.†

---

*See Chapter Eleven, page 202.

†The details of such policies are beyond the scope of a book aimed primarily at issues of domestic economic policy. They have, however, been well described elsewhere. See, for instance, William Brandt and Anthony Sampson, eds., *North-South: A Program for Survival* (the report of the Independent Commission on International Development Issues) (Cambridge, Mass.: MIT Press, 1980); Ronald E. Muller, *Revitalizing America* (New York: Simon & Schuster, 1980); Roger H. Hanson, ed., *U.S. Foreign Policy and the Third World Agenda, 1982* (New York: Praeger, 1982, for the Overseas Development Council); Richard Barnet, *The Lean Years* (New York: Simon & Schuster, 1980); Michael Moffitt, *The World's Economy* (New York: Simon & Schuster, 1983).

Chapter 8

COMMUNITY FULL EMPLOYMENT

The necessity for a strong public-sector locomotive to pull the economy to high levels of sustained productivity, production, and job security brings us to a fundamental issue. If, as we have argued, healthy local government and decentralized intermediate-scale institutions are major protectors of democracy and freedom, how can we defend them against the abuses of a centralized power? How do we prevent undemocratic instincts from dominating national economic planning? And, further, how do we prevent competent centralized planning from being undermined because of legitimate fears of big government in alliance with big business? The questions return us to the *conditions* of community.

MOBILITY AND COMMUNITY

The people of Youngstown, Ohio, later referred to it as "Black Monday." It was the day in September 1977 when more than four thousand steelworkers were permanently laid off at the giant Campbell Works of Youngstown Sheet and Tube Company—a subsidiary of Lykes Corporation, a New Orleans conglomerate. Youngstown is a medium-sized industrial city anchoring the southern end of the Mahoning Valley, where they have been making steel for more than a century. Many of those laid off on Black Monday were third-generation steelmakers whose immigrant grandfathers from Ireland, Italy, and Poland found work in the giant blast furnaces and raised families in the neat single-family-house neighborhoods. And there the families remained. "When I look out the door of my house," said the wife of one laid-off steelworker tearfully, "I see my mother's house across the street, my sister-in-law's down the block, and the neighborhood full of people I have known all my life. Everywhere I look there is love. And now we have to move. God knows what will become of us."

Youngstown was not alone. In that same year, Bethlehem Steel laid off 3,500 workers in Lackawanna, New York, and another 3,500 in Johnstown, Pennsylvania. Newark, New Jersey, suffered major plant closings by Westinghouse, Stauffer Chemical, and the Wiss Company. During just the first half of 1982, over 200,000 auto workers were on indefinite layoff, with General Motors soon to lay off 60,000 more workers. Massive layoffs were announced by General Electric, Honeywell, and Caterpillar Tractor. Even high-technology companies were not exempt from trouble: Texas Instruments laid off 3 percent of its work force, 2,700 employees, and Control Data, the Minnesota computer company, announced 9,500 layoffs. Month after month, the story was the same. Over 40,000 manufacturing employees lost their jobs every month from July 1981 through December 1982.[1]

Industrial layoffs are only the most dramatic reflection of community instability. In the 1950s America saw the largest internal migration in our history as millions of southern rural, primarily black workers and their families were forced off the land by the mechanization of the cotton and tobacco fields. Largely uneducated, inexperienced in urban living, and suddenly torn away from their extended families, they poured into the ghettos of New York, Philadelphia, Cleveland, Detroit, Chicago, Los Angeles, and other cities at just about the time when jobs for the unskilled were rapidly shrinking. The not surprising result was an explosion of crime and welfare dependency.[2]

America has always been a country on the move. That is one of its great attractions. Our culture celebrates the pioneers who moved West; the farm boy who makes it in the big city; the couples who go back to the land, dropping out of the urban rat race; the loser who starts a new life in another town. America will always be the land of the second chance. But if we are serious about the issue of community, we must recognize that most people would like to stay in their communities if decent jobs were available. The various studies made on why Americans move all conclude that for those under fifty-five by far the dominant cause is employment. Concludes researcher Gary S. Fields, "Workers move to where the jobs are."[3]

Labor and capital mobility are important in a market system. Market prices are signals to tell resources where they are most needed. When the demand for boots rises relative to the demand for shoes, boot prices increase. Manufacturers, seeing the potential to make more profits in boots, shift their production. Likewise, when the demand for oil rises relative to the demand for boots and shoes, the oil industry will pay higher wages to lure workers to offshore drilling rigs. Mobility is necessary for progress and change. If capital could not pull out of shoes and boots and move into electronics, if labor could not move from the dying mill towns of New England to the high-technology firms lining Route 128 in Boston, the changing nature of the new economic era could not be accommodated.

It is one thing to recognize that change is inevitable, another to make it a fetish. This is what conventional economics does when it ignores both the costs of mobility and the extent to which public decisions affect the choices people have about where to live and work. One widely publicized example is the report produced in 1980 by the Commission for a National Agenda for the Eighties—a prestigious bipartisan presidential commission of businesspeople, academicians, and labor leaders. The report of the commission's Subpanel on Urban America assumes that recent migration to the South and the Southwest is the result of a natural law of expansion and decline—we have arrived at a "post-industrial society in which Boston, Cleveland and Detroit stand as 'bricks and mortar' snapshots of a bygone era." It therefore recommends that large cities in the Northeast and Midwest be shrunk drastically if not totally abandoned by actively encouraging people to leave. Public policy, intones the report, should follow the "natural forces" of the marketplace. "Recognition should be made of the near immutability of the technological, economic, social and demographic trends . . . that are responsible for the transformation of our nation's settlements and life within them."[4]

Yet the forces of migration to the Sunbelt are not simply the results of natural play of immutable free-market forces; they were substantially influenced by fifty years of investment by the federal government in the economies of the West and the South. These investments include:

- Military and space spending, which beginning in World War II created jobs and has since subsidized electronics and other high-tech industries.
- The national interstate highway system, which permitted the decentralization of industry from its origins in the Northeast and Midwest.
- Subsidization of rural electrification, the Tennessee Valley Authority, and federal and hydropower projects.
- Billion-dollar water projects.

- Subsidization of oil, tobacco, cotton, sugar, and other Sunbelt industries.
- Subsidies for ports and waterways on the Gulf Coast and along the Mississippi River.
- Tax laws that favored the construction of new buildings over the rehabilitation of the old.

Moreover, the report is oblivious to the fact that throughout U.S. history economic policies have been deliberately used to foster and channel internal migration. Federal investment in canals and turnpikes, vast subsidies to railroads to "open the West," the location of military facilities, and so forth, were deliberate efforts to get people to move from one part of the country to another. And even when the intent was not so deliberate, haphazard broker state policies have been major forces behind the huge internal migrations of the recent past. The migration of rural black people to the cities of the North and Midwest after World War II was not simply the work of some natural invisible hand in the marketplace; it was produced by the very visible hand of the U.S. Department of Agriculture, which subsidized the development of the new labor-saving technologies and then helped finance both the introduction of the machinery and the buying up of suddenly inefficient small farms by larger ones.

The report is blind not only to such sources of Sunbelt prosperity but also to the real cost of the massive shift in population encouraged by its policy recommendations—what Los Angeles Mayor Tom Bradley calls the strategy of "throwaway cities." The direct unemployment caused by layoffs represents only the initial cost for cities being thrown away. Laid-off workers spend less locally, generating more layoffs. Firms that sell supplies, materials, and services to major employers also begin to lay off people. Bank deposits decline and more consumer loans and mortgages become delinquent. Tax revenues are off and local governments are faced with curtailing services or raising tax rates. School budgets, fire and police protection, and public services are cut. Perhaps more important, young people and prime-age workers with families begin to move out. They cannot wait for something to show up. Gradually the community loses its more productive people—its steady, middle-class leadership. Children begin to disappear; neighborhoods grow old. The sense of cohesion provided by different generations living side by side is lost. Crime increases. Values of residential real estate drop. Those who are left—the least skilled, the elderly, the handicapped—have a feeling of bitterness and despair. The community can no longer support itself; it literally becomes a burden on the rest of the country. It was estimated at the time that the layoffs in Youngstown referred to at the beginning of this chapter cost the government a minimum of $70 million in the first three years in unemployment compensation, welfare payments, lost taxes, and other costs. In January 1981, the unemployment rate in Youngstown was over 15 percent, the highest level since the Depression.[5]

At the same time that houses, factories, stores, schools, sewers, hospitals, streets, bridges, water lines, etc., in Youngstown and Detroit begin to experience disrepair and underutilization, corresponding facilities must be rebuilt at enormous capital cost (and at 1980s prices) in Phoenix, Houston, and Los Angeles. And in the long run the latter cities—winners in the competition for growth—may turn out to be losers, too: other major areas of the booming Sunbelt are falling behind in efforts to maintain public services and decent housing. In California's Santa Clara County, home of Silicon Valley, the cost of a middle-class house jumped to $150,000, with large numbers of new homes waiting in line for basic service hookups. In Houston, which is expected by the year 2000 to have grown to six times its 1950 level, a thousand new people a week are adding to congestion, pollution, water shortages, overcrowded schools and hospitals, and a huge run-up in real-estate values. At the same time, 25 percent of the city's streets are unlighted, four hundred miles of road are unpaved, and some four hundred thousand people are crowded into a seventy-three-square-mile slum. Because of excessively rapid growth, a city industrial and real-estate commission—usually a bastion of progrowth boosterism—took the almost unheard-of step of recommending that large industrial corporations be encouraged to locate outside the county; the new tax revenue from industrial employers was just not enough to offset the costs of growth.[6]

The haphazard growth of population and industry in the Sunbelt is also rapidly creating another problem that on its present course could produce a massive drain on the U.S. Treasury. The problem is the scarcity of water. There is simply not enough to accommodate population and agricultural growth there. Some parts of the South and Southwest, for example, are depleting their aquifers at rates that would leave them largely without water by the year 2000. Although conventional market "theory" says the price of water will rise in areas of scarcity, reality says the broker state must respond. The solution? Pressure is already building for the federal government to invest billions simply to allow new migrants to turn on the water tap the way they did back home.[7]

The unrestrained geographic mobility of capital also can destroy vital economic linkages among businesspeople—the cultural and social foundations of economic activity. Contrary to neoconservative imagery, the average businessman is not the Lone Ranger. He does not ride into an industry, make a quick deal, and then ride out again while people ask, "Who was that masked man?" If they didn't know who he was, they wouldn't make a deal with him. Business is as much a matter of social relations as it is of purely economic ones. The typical businessman is part of an extensive network of people who are also in "business." Whether it is selling cloth or manufacturing computers or paving highways, business success hinges upon others. Dealmaking is the essential activity of business. Precisely because the objective is to get the better of the deal, it requires certain rules of honesty without which the game could not go on. This in turn requires trust. And trust can come only from having experienced the honesty and reliability of another. Most industries and subindustries in America are composed of vast, complex networks of manufacturers, jobbers, brokers, suppliers, salespeople, factories, bankers, technical consultants, skilled workers, and so forth. Typically, relationships among these people are built up over long periods of time. As they get built up they get faster and more efficient. When a jobber has worked with a manufacturer for twenty years, he can make a deal in five minutes over the phone. If he has had no experience it may take five weeks while he inspects the plant, looks at samples, checks his references, clears him with the bank, and so forth. Over the long run, reputations become critical. Company A does good work, but you can't rush them. If you need something in a hurry it's best to call Company B, but expect a high percentage of rejects. These relationships are both institutional and personal; salesmen are clothed in the reputation of the company they join and often take their clients with them when they leave a company.

Such linkages and connections allow industry to operate with skill and flexibility. They permit people to enter an industry or spin off a new product without having physically to perform all the tasks themselves. A physicist around Boston's Route 128 with a new design can start a business with a minimum of capital by jobbing out the manufacturing to a firm that knows the materials and machinery involved and by using a broker rather than his own salesman. Linkages also make up the living culture of fast-changing information, ideas, and discussion without which real innovation and change do not occur. It is not an accident that computer specialists in Southern California build their new companies near others. They need other people and workers who know the game if they are to keep abreast of new ideas.

Conventional wisdom fails to recognize such facts because, reflecting conventional economics, it places no value on community. In recommending that aid be given to the growing areas of the South and West and that some implicit form of "triage" be administered to declining urban areas, the President's commission report repeats again and again that it favors policy that assists "people" rather than "places." Since the people are going to the Sunbelt, it argues, this means giving individuals aid to leave the Midwest and the Northeast. Nowhere is there acknowledgment of the fact that society is not simply a random, unconnected collection of atoms each with its own private path in the universe, but a set of relationships among people that primarily take place in very small human spaces—neighborhoods, offices, shop floors, store counters. To the degree that these relationships are strong and stable, they obviate the need for action at larger, bureaucratic, inhuman, and abstract levels. The nation doesn't need to build more mental-health centers if we can go next door and talk out our problems with a neighbor. The nation doesn't need to pour money into more police and prisons if our neighborhoods are watched over by people who know each other.

The process of community uprooting has been greatly accelerated by the transformation of many single-industry companies into conglomerates and holding companies whose capital is disembodied and abstracted from the industries that feed them. Just as U.S. Steel is no longer just a steel company but an investment conglomerate, so it is no longer just a Pittsburgh company with roots and long-term interest in the economic health of Pittsburgh. When capital moves, typically a local firm does not simply move from one area to another in a way that relocates the entire business with its key people and equipment. The process is more subtle. A business will buy or start another plant in another state and gradually shift its production to the new area while allowing the old plant to deteriorate and gradually letting its labor force go.

Given our lack of concrete interest in community, it is not surprising that there is no comprehensive economic information on how much of American business is owned by people and corporations neither personally connected with nor located in the area in which the business is located. We do know from the few isolated peeks we have had at economic ownership in individual states that it is substantial. A study of absentee ownership of manufacturing firms in Maine, for example, found that 60 percent of the medium-sized companies and 76 percent of the large firms were owned by companies with headquarters out of state. Earlier studies showed even more concentration of absentee ownership in neighboring Vermont and New Hampshire.[8] MIT researcher David Birch judges that half of all the employment growth in the South between 1976 and 1979 was in corporate branch plants or conglomerate subsidiaries, the large majority of which were located in the North. From a Federal Trade Commission study of some eighteen thousand mergers between 1955 and 1968, when the location of the headquarters was known, another researcher concluded that four of five states experienced an outward shift of corporate control.[9]

Whether business is owned locally or by an absentee has important implications. Studies have shown that the bulk of new jobs in the economy are created by small- and medium-sized entrepreneurs operating out of one location. Independent entrepreneurs are much more likely to *re*invest in their original business location than in a conglomerate. Partly, this is obviously because they lack the reinvestment options open to the multinational corporations. But they are also likely to have a personal identification with a particular business in a particular community. The business is their "baby," their achievement, their life. It is what provides honor and status in the community.

Locally owned firms are also much more inclined to stick it out through an economic downturn or slump in a particular industry than are conglomerates, which have plenty of other places to put their capital at any given time. A study by Professor David Barkely of the University of Redlands in California illustrates the connection between entrepreneur and community. Barkely surveyed manufacturing industries in rural Iowa that employed more than twenty people between 1965 and 1975. As might be expected, he found that small- and medium-sized businesses had a higher failure rate than absentee corporations, primarily because of limited access to capital. But plants that were subsidiaries of larger, more successful absentee companies closed at a higher rate than did those owned by smaller companies.[10]

Local ownership of capital has other ancillary benefits for the community: Local firms tend to bank locally, to hire local lawyers, local accountants, and local architects. Management is more likely to come up through the ranks, creating more opportunities for promotion for younger people. As a result, income generated by the business itself—above and beyond profits—is also more likely to stay at home. A study of mergers in Wisconsin found that 70 percent of the companies that were bought out by conglomerates changed banks and accountants, and 75 percent changed lawyers. A study in Nebraska revealed similar shifts, including the fact that 45 percent of the firms changed to centralized purchasing of supplies and materials. Management can now sit in New York, London, or Tokyo and make major investment decisions that used to be made at the level of the plant. Local economic concerns that used to be a factor in investment decisions are now in the hands of strangers who may never have seen the plant—or even the community in which it is located.[11]

Professor Willard Mueller at the University of Wisconsin observes:

> The removal of a business' headquarters from a community has secondary and tertiary effects as it dries up demand for functions previously performed by local attorneys, accountants, banks, advertising firms and the like. . . . Local management and labor, accustomed to bargaining on the profits of the company and the productivity of the labor force, suddenly find the bargaining dominated by a conglomerate balance sheet which considers products, plants and losses the local people will never see or know anything about.[12]

The results can be bizarre. The employee of a paper mill in northern New England whose conglomerate headquarters is in the New York area reported that there had been a bomb scare at the plant. "The supervisors called New York to get permission to evacuate the mill," she said. "And it took them a half hour to get it. There was a bomb, but it wasn't wired properly. If it was, we'd have been blown to pieces before we got permission to leave."[13]

THE LOCAL PUBLIC BALANCE SHEET

Spreading plant closures over the past decade have stimulated a number of efforts to save a local economy by invoking an implicit public or community balance sheet. From the strictly private financial point of view, it may make no difference to an investor whether he invests in a local enterprise or a faraway one, as long as his returns are the same. But clearly it makes a great deal of difference to the community. In Youngstown shortly after the closing of the Campbell Works, a coalition of steelworkers, local businesspeople, and other community organizations led by a group of local clergy proposed that the plant be reopened under the ownership of a new, locally based corporation. They argued that the fact the plant had been closed by an absentee conglomerate, Lykes, did not prove that it was not profitable. Lykes, after all, was controlled by a large holding company that was interested in more than just a profit; they wanted the *highest possible* profit. The people of Youngstown, on the other hand, might be willing to settle for a smaller profit as long as it was positive, if their investment resulted in a stable local economy. They raised some $7 million in local "Save Our Valley" pledges and with the help of a planning grant from the Department of Housing and Urban Development hired consultants to design a modernization plan for the mill. A number of leading steel industry experts concluded that the plan was feasible, but opposed by steel industry giants such as U.S. Steel and Republic, the community was turned down in its request for federal loan guarantees.

The overwhelming concern of the federal bureaucrats, from low-level proposal readers to Cabinet secretaries and members of the White House staff, was: How much profit would the new plant make for private investors? How can the government justify the investment when the private sector does not think it is sufficiently profitable? The answer is that the government should have been concerned with returns to the total public—the taxpayers—not just the private investors. In this case, it should have started with the $70 million in government spending that occurred automatically because of the layoffs. These liabilities are not reflected on the balance sheets of Lykes or any other private firm. They are the cost of doing business (which includes the cost of ceasing to do business), which the political economy now automatically transfers from the private to the public sector. Any reduction in these costs represents real dollar income for the public. So, for example, had an investment been made that simply broke even but that maintained employment in the steel mill for three years, it would have represented a $70 million return for the public.

Just as our national accounting framework (as we saw in Chapter Seven) is extraordinarily deficient in this area, so too are the standards we apply to local economic issues. In 1977, it cost the government 6.7 percent to borrow for three years in the money market. The break-even point for the government—a 6.7 percent return to the taxpayer on the investment—would have justified an investment of roughly $350 million. On the private books, however, to break even at the level of the firm represents a loss, in this case at least 7.25 percent—the interest rate that could otherwise have been earned investing the same money in high-grade corporate bonds in 1977. The proposed Youngstown investment was designed to do a great deal better than to break even, but the point illustrates the difference between a private firm's set of books and the public balance sheet in the case of any investment.[14] This accounting does not include the costs to the nation, its taxpayers, and its capital markets of wasted in-place capital (housing, roads, schools, etc.) that will have to be replaced elsewhere and that will increase overall financial pressures and thus, ultimately, interest rates.[15]

If instability has costs, stability has gains. The experience of the community of Herkimer, New York—a small city not far from Syracuse—also illustrates the broader return to the local public balance. The nation's largest manufacturer of library furniture, a Sperry Rand subsidiary named the Library Bureau, was located in Herkimer. In 1975 the parent company decided to shut down the plant because it was not producing the 22 percent return on investment that Sperry Rand required of all its subsidiaries. Closing the 250-worker plant would have devastated the little community, so after several futile efforts to change Sperry Rand's mind, the workers and small businessmen in the town decided to buy the firm and run it themselves.

The spark plug behind the effort was John Ladd, a stocky, outgoing, ruddy faced local businessman with a flair for politics. Ladd and his group formed a corporation and sold $1.5 million in $1 and $2 shares to the workers and local residents of Herkimer. They borrowed $2 million from local banks, another $2 million from the U.S. Department of Commerce, and bought the plant. When the dust settled, the employees owned some 30 to 40 percent of the shares, and their neighbors in Herkimer owned the rest. A shareholder was limited to a total of $500,000 in shares.

During the first full year of operation, the new worker/community-owned company earned 17 percent on its investment. Seventeen percent was not good enough for the multinational Sperry Rand looking for faraway places in which to invest the profits. But it was plenty good enough for the people and workers of Herkimer, who saved their jobs and their town.[16]

How we calculate profit and loss, as the Youngstown and Herkimer experiences show, is a function not only of the nature of the enterprise but also of the nature of the investor. When the public sector—either a government or a collection of people connected by their geographic community—is seen as an investor in its own right, perception of profits can change dramatically. The Library Bureau's plant is the same enterprise for both Sperry Rand and John Ladd's group of local investors, but the value they place on all of the benefits generated by the plant is radically different.

Upon close examination, it is clear that the automatic assumption of conventional economics that mobility equals efficiency must at the very least be modified. We must separate the clear case for *industrial* mobility from the not-so-clear case for *geographic* mobility; the need for capital to flow from declining to growing industries is not the same as the need for capital to move from one city or region or country to another. Stable communities are not *ipso facto* inefficient, and efforts to channel capital so that they remain stable may often be a more efficient use of capital than the thoughtless encouragement of community destruction under the banner of general mobility.

PLANNED CONVERSION

Yet there is clearly a trap here. Once we admit public-sector benefits into the calculation, it becomes easier to argue that almost any business should be subsidized. And once the precedent of the government saving a business in order to save jobs has been established, there is no end to the political pressure that can be generated. One argument that was used in Youngstown and Herkimer to justify federal intervention on their behalf was that the government did it for Lockheed and Penn Central and the Franklin National Bank: Why can't it do it for us? The result can be bailouts and barriers to the mobility of capital among industries and among technologies which will slow overall economic growth. And when subsidy is not enough, the next step could well be the European direction, in which declining industries have been nationalized or otherwise propped up in a process aptly described as "lemon socialism."

The dilemma was dramatized in the debate over the subsidy to Chrysler.

The "conservative" position in the debate held that Chrysler should pay the price for its failure to compete successfully in the market. It was unfortunate, perhaps, that thousands of workers and their families would suffer unemployment and loss of income, that communities would lose their tax base, or that suppliers and ancillary industries would collapse along with Chrysler. But capitalism doesn't work without risks. This view was held by many people who were not stereotypical "conservatives." Ultimately, both Ralph Nader and the *Wall Street Journal* argued that we should simply let Chrysler go down the drain.

The "liberal" position held that the company's destruction was too high a price to pay for an abstract theory of the market. First of all, the workers, communities, suppliers, and so forth, were not the people who had made the mistakes. Yet a tremendous burden of punishment fell on their shoulders. Second, the government itself had at least partially contributed to Chrysler's demise by maintaining low gasoline prices and thereby artificially stimulating demand for larger, gas-inefficient cars. Third, when the costs to the nation of unemployment, reduced taxes, welfare payments, and housing market collapse were added up, in the long run a bailout was cheaper for the taxpayer.

The liberal position also had its odd political bedfellows. In the forefront, of course, were the Chrysler management, the United Auto Workers, the company's suppliers and dealers, and politicians from impacted communities. The loan guarantee proposal also had wide support elsewhere among organized labor in the major industrial states. As we have seen in Chapter Three, it even had the support of the chairman of the board of General Motors.

The liberal position won; it convinced Jimmy Carter, and as we have seen, Ronald Reagan ultimately supported the loan as well. The workers and communities in whose name the company was propped up, however, will not escape damage even with the loan guarantee. Chrysler eliminated more than 43,000 jobs.[17] And the company's troubles are not over despite the fact that it recovered and paid back its loan. Given the long-run prospects for the auto industry, there is a substantial prospect that Chrysler will not last another decade. By the end of the 1990s it is likely that the world auto market will be divided among a handful of multinational giants, only one of which, General Motors, is sure to be American.

Neither the liberal reindustrialization nor the traditional conservative solution fills the bill. The liberal solution has already solved the wrong problem. *At best* it will have saved the company, its management, and its shareholders, while reducing the labor force and the economic viability of communities dependent on the industry. At worst it is a temporary holding action that will discredit itself in very short order.

The conservative solution is no solution at all. The logic of accepting the "judgment of the market" condemns workers, communities, and the related small businesses to the folly of nineteenth-century economic illusions. That is why in the real world—the one in which people always value the flesh-and-blood lives of themselves and their families and their neighbors above abstract economic theory—the conservative options are so often rejected in the end. They also, of course, violate any commonsense idea of economic prudence. The so-called efficiency of the market simply ignores the empty houses, deteriorating roads, and empty schools and hospitals that will have to be rebuilt at substantial private and taxpayer expense.

On the basis of a comprehensive accounting the correct question is not "Do we save the Chrysler Corporation?" but rather "What can this collection of people and machines produce that the country needs and can afford?" It is the same question that a small manufacturer will ask when his market goes soft: "What can I do with my labor force and my machinery that will make a profit?" For the nation, the fact that we no longer need the machinery, tools, buildings, and a hundred thousand Chrysler workers and managers to serve our automobile needs is an *opportunity* to allocate those resources to producing something else. The sensible planning answer clearly is to shift the money and physical capital involved in making cars to making something else —*in Detroit.* By raising community stability to an equal rank with capital mobility as primary goals of economic planning, we could free the resources represented by Chrysler and increase capital mobility among industries and technologies. Moreover, the huge amount of both labor and capital used in building up and throwing away stores, businesses, schools, etc., in the process of capital mobility could be saved by the nation and invested in more industrial efficiency and in making life better for people where they are.

Researchers Dan Luria and Jack Russell took essentially this perspective in a 1981 report on the redevelopment of Detroit called *Rational Reindustrialization.* They found that a whole new emerging growth sector of American industry seemed ideally suited for Detroit's skills and facilities. Products included pumps, engines, compressors, tubes, and other equipment for deep-well oil and natural-gas rigs; cogenerators for capturing the heat loss in homes and factories; and gasifiers, which convert coal to natural gas at the mine site. All of these industries have healthy growth rates and bright prospects. And their location in Detroit could contribute considerably to the conservation of urban capital. Luria and Russell estimate that these industries could produce some one hundred thousand jobs for Detroit workers.[18]

Not all industries can be located anywhere, of course. But there is little doubt that for many firms seeking to start up, expand, or relocate, a variety of places fit the technical requirements. If this were not true, the bargaining that regularly goes on between companies and communities would not take place. Moreover, since World War II locational options have been getting wider. The building of the federal highway system gave a great many communities access to industrialization, weaned industries away from the railroad, and opened up vast areas for development. The revolution in communications and transmission of documents has further increased such flexibility. Just as it was no longer necessary to be on the rail spur, so it is no longer necessary to locate all of a company's management under the same roof. In improving the geographic options open to corporations, such improvements have given them bargaining chips in negotiating with communities. But this increase in flexibility also could give public planners an increased ability to encourage the location of expanding industries where the jobs are needed.

The analysis of Detroit's potential for conversion made by Luria and Russell was conservative in the sense that it did not make assumptions about additional investment in areas of national priorities. But, as we have seen in Chapter Seven, overall national growth requires a sustained locomotive of public investment if we are to achieve increased stability and higher productivity in the uncertainties of the new economic era. By linking the public investment necessary to achieve national goals to the local goal of stability, the way is opened for an explicit strategy of planned industrial conversion that gives equal emphasis to community economic health. In such planning the target of sustained *national* full employment—which can mean averaging 15 percent in Detroit with 2 percent in Houston—must be augmented by a more sharply focused criterion. *Community* full employment, defined as a minimum floor level of unemployment for communities above a certain size, puts the appropriate new edge to policy.[19]

Consider that the nation needs expanded rail, mass transit, and other nonautomobile transportation facilities for the coming decades. But we currently have capacity to manufacture less than five thousand buses a year (while the West European community, with roughly the same population, produces a hundred thousand). We import subway cars and other rail components. A coordinated decision to increase the use, and therefore the production, of transportation vehicles could offer opportunities to convert some of Detroit's excess capacity to produce private transportation into public transportation hardware production. One of the more creative Carter administration officials, Transportation Secretary Neil Goldschmidt, proposed a federal program to purchase and inventory buses. The state of New York has used its procurement power to require local assembly of mass transit vehicles as part of a jobs and economic development strategy. It would also be possible, as the congressional Joint Economic Committee has shown, to develop a coordinated system of high-speed "bullet trains" like those in Japan and France.[20] This would reflect a national society-shaping commitment like that of the highway programs of the 1950s. The 1950s decision was ad hoc, creating urban sprawl, excessive reliance on the automobile, energy waste, and other unforeseen consequences. A *planned* decision to upgrade and expand the nonauto transportation sectors would now appropriately be made as part of an overall investment strategy involving judgments on trade (for example, rail and port expansion), energy conservation, land use (including, for instance, urban-suburban design to alter present commuting patterns), etc.

The elements of a serious national-local investment and conversion strategy for firms like Chrysler would add up to the deliberate creation, with public capital, of a new industry. It could produce not only buses, but also trains, freight vehicles, new energy-related hardware, and so forth. It would recondition railroad beds and construct new high-speed tracks. In the era of energy scarcity, the industry created could help regenerate national economic development in the late 1980s and 1990s, just as autos, television, and computers did in other decades of the twentieth century, and, in effect, the railroad itself did in the nineteenth century.

Periods of increased economic growth and dramatically expanded employment have often been stimulated by the arrival of a major new industry. More often than not, such industries have been encouraged by government spending in peace and in war. Barge canals, railroads, and the telegraph in the nineteenth century, and military hardware and electronics in the twentieth century, were all aided by the federal government. The automobile industry was given major support by large-scale public investment in roads, highways, traffic controls, etc. The massive public investment in World Wars I and II provided much of the impetus for years of prosperity that followed.

In the new economic era, we have the power consciously to create the next lead industry, or industries, and begin planning the next as well. The choices for the next Youngstown or the next Detroit could be much wider. We have the power to stimulate new high-technology areas rather than bail out dying firms and to maintain productive full employment—a job for everyone producing goods and services that the country needs and will pay for.* We also have the power to stabilize the local economic environment in which people work and live—and thus simultaneously to build up the power of local social and political institutions as a protection against central government and as the foundation stone of a community-sustaining economics.

---

*As we shall explore in Chapter Fifteen, in the context of a comprehensive full-production plan a variety of tax, loan guarantee, procurement, and other assistance can also be brought to bear in achieving community full employment.

Part III

Only the most powerful, the most resourceful and un-
scrupulous, the hyenas of economic life, can come
through unscathed. The great mass of those who put
their trust in the traditional order, the innocent and the
unworldly, all those who do productive and useful
work, but don't know how to manipulate money, the
elderly who hoped to live on what they earned in the
past—all those are doomed to suffer. An experience of
this kind poisons the morale of a nation.   Inflation
is a tragedy that makes a whole people cynical, hard-
hearted and indifferent.

THOMAS MANN,
The Witches' Sabbath

Whether individuals, groups, or public authorities
make decisions concerning [the] distribution and the
planning of the economy, they . . . must realize their
serious obligation of seeing to it that provision is made
for the necessities of a decent life on the part of individuals and of the whole community.

POPE PAUL VI,
Gaudium et Spes

Chapter 9

THE BASIC NECESSITIES

Full-production planning aimed at community full employment addresses one side of the economic deadlock—jobs. But the equation must be solved simultaneously; sustained full production cannot be achieved or maintained unless we find a solution to inflation. So long as slow growth and periodic recession are the nation's answers to inflation, we will be trapped in endless and deepening oscillation between high prices and unemployment, wearing away our productivity and what is left of our confidence in the future. The question is: Is full employment a condition compatible with relatively stable prices? As we have seen, the answer of conventional economics, both liberal and conservative, is no. This part will explore what must be done to make that answer yes, and to do so within a framework of the principle of community appropriate to the new economic era.

We begin with conventional ideology—the idea that the primary cause of our inflation problem is big government, specifically federal deficit spending. Ronald Reagan echos newspaper editorials and Chamber of Commerce speeches all across America when he says that inflation is caused by the federal government spending more money than it is taking in.[1] The evidence has long shown that this explanation for recent inflation is a myth. For eight of the eleven years between 1971 and 1981, for instance, federal deficits as a percentage of the GNP moved *in the opposite direction* from changes in the price level. Some have argued that there is a "lagged" relationship between the two statistics—that it takes a year before the effect of the deficit on the price index is felt. Yet in only one of the eleven years, 1977, was there an acceleration of inflation the year after the relative deficit increased.[2] Ronald Reagan's first three years in office, when the budget deficit tripled but the inflation rate *dropped* from 14 percent to 4 percent, was only the most dramatic of a long string of economic lessons contradicting the conventional wisdom.

The most accurate measure of the government deficit, moreover, is the combined revenues and expenditures of *all* levels of government. And when state and local government are added in to determine the "total" public-sector deficit, any relationship between deficits and inflation becomes even harder to find. For all governments, the consolidated deficit was 0.3 percent of the GNP in 1972; it rose to a surplus of 0.6 percent in 1973, fell back to a deficit of 0.3 percent in 1974, and reached a deficit of 4.1 percent of the GNP in the recession year of 1975. Thereafter the aggregate deficit was cut progressively each year; by 1979 we had a total all-government surplus of 0.5 percent of the GNP. At the same time the rate of inflation rose steadily, to a whopping 13.3 percent in 1979.[3]

The importance of the federal debt in the economy has actually declined during the postwar period. It was slightly larger than the GNP at the end of World War II. In the late 1950s, it was about 50 percent of the GNP. Although it will increase if we do not change our economic policies, today the roughly $1 trillion national debt represents approximately 30 percent of the GNP, and it would be a lower percentage if the overall economy were not stagnating.[4] If long-term federal indebtedness is compared with the assets owned by the government, the government's "net worth" position shows regular and dramatic improvement—since the value of its land, buildings, and other physical assets has increased manyfold since the war.[5]

International comparisons reveal a similar lack of pattern. Between 1977 and 1979, for instance, government budget deficits as a percentage of the Gross National Product were 0.1 percent in the United States, 2.7 percent in West Germany, and 4.8 percent in Japan. And both West Germany and Japan had lower inflation rates than the United States.[6]

This is not to deny that specific government policies can incite inflation. For example, the fast buildup of military spending for the Vietnam War without a corresponding tax increase clearly sparked higher prices in the late 1960s and early 1970s. Sudden increases in military spending in peacetime can also selectively overheat particular industries and sectors, creating bottlenecks. And over the long run, military spending diverts technological resources from civilian work, thereby reducing productivity. The most creative scientists and engineers in Japan are working on new products and cost-saving technologies to make that country more competitive commercially. Ours are working on weapons in an environment that encourages "gold plating" and cost *un*consciousness. Government subsidies have also helped maintain high price levels in agriculture, transportation, and several other sectors. But the evidence simply does not support the proposition that federal deficits have been the cause of our inflation.

The "monetarist" variations of the deficit theory hold that it is not the deficits per se that cause inflation, but whether they are monetized —that is, whether the Federal Reserve Board permits an increase in the nation's credit supply to accommodate additional federal borrowing in the capital markets that a deficit necessitates. The evidence that money supply increases are the major cause of inflation is extraordinarily weak. In fact, throughout the decade of the 1970s, increases in the two major measures of the money supply (so-called M_1 and M_2) fluctuated *inversely* with the increases in the price level.[7] This, too, has led to complex arguments that the effect of an increase in the money supply takes time to be translated into prices and that therefore there is always a statistical lag. Yet throughout the period prices and money supply continued to go up and down in such opposition to each other that the "lag" theory has become increasingly difficult to defend. If one statistic consistently goes up while the other consistently goes down, which is lagging behind which? Are increases in prices causing an increase in the money supply as people borrow more to pay the higher prices, or vice versa? In recent decades, as Harvard financial specialist Professor Benjamin M. Friedman points out, the "observed relationship between money and prices had all but collapsed." Inflation averaged 1.7 percent *less* than the money growth rate between 1960 and 1972, yet 2.9 percent *more* between 1973 and 1981.[8]

Both the deficit and the monetarist theories of inflation are closer to reality under certain circumstances—primarily in conditions of full employment when, since the economy cannot produce more, an increase in money and credit is translated into higher prices. However, when the economy is operating at less than full capacity—as it mostly has since World War II—an increase in credit is normally accompanied by an increase in real production rather than in prices. And, in fact, there is a closer statistical fit between money supply and production than between money supply and prices.[9] It is true that increases in production will not occur when rising credit is siphoned off into speculation and nonproductive activities. But in that case, the root cause of inflation is not in the increase in money supply but in the diversion of capital to nonproductive uses.

The statistics themselves are also a problem. A decade ago there was general agreement that the money supply could be defined as actual currency in circulation plus checking accounts. The expansion of Eurodollar market loans and the development of increasingly complex domestic financial instruments, such as money market funds, has made the exact definition an elusive target, raising further doubts about almost any supposition about the impact of the money supply on inflation—or anything else.[10]

Monetarism has become a strong influence on conventional economic wisdom primarily because it seems to allow a conservative way to control the economy without *direct* government intervention in nonfinancial markets. (It does, however, require tough government *planning* of the supply of money.) Unfortunately, as we saw in Part I, conservative faith in monetarism has forced us deeper into the Phillips Curve trap. Ronald Reagan's deficits were produced by increased military spending, massive tax cuts, and decreased revenues caused by recession. Tightening credit under these conditions slowed growth further as loans were reduced to sectors of the economy already starved for cash and confidence. The impact on inflation derived not from some magic in the amount of money and credit in circulation, but from the resultant high unemployment and lower incomes. Monetarism, as diagnosis or prescription, leaves us still hung up without a way to stabilize prices at the same time the economy is put fully to work.

Neither is our modern inflation caused primarily by the people who are getting rich out of it.

Inflation certainly does have its winners and its losers. The cost to you of an increase in the price of hamburger does not simply disappear into the air. It shows up in the pockets of people all along the train of transactions who bred, raised, and slaughtered the steer, butchered, packaged, and distributed it, and finally sold it to you. For the most part, the winners and losers in inflation tend to be those who already control more economic power than other people, and who stand in the path of transactions in which prices are rising fastest. If you were in the oil business during the 1970s, you were doing a lot better than if you were selling large, fuel-inefficient automobiles. Conventional economic theory holds that the poor actually are the major *beneficiaries* of inflation. This is supposed to occur because inflation has been historically associated with periods of high employment and because the poor are traditionally supposed to be debtors who pay off their debts with cheaper money than they borrow. Like other conventions of classical economic wisdom, this has proven less relevant to the inflation of the new era. First, inflation is no longer so clearly associated with low unemployment rates; rising prices in the 1970s have been accompanied by rising unemployment. Second, in a modern, complex economy, rich people do not simply squirrel their money away in savings banks or lend it to the poor. They invest it more effectively than poor and middle-income people because the rich can hire the accountants, tax lawyers, and other specialists who find paths to high investment returns. High interest rates have also increased the disparity between investors and those whose incomes come from their wages. Finally, the pattern of inflation in recent years repeatedly has been concentrated in the basic necessities of life, such as food, fuel, housing, and medical care—things that make up a larger proportion of the family budget for low-income people than they do for high-income people.

In any event, whether the well-off do better than the less-well-off in itself tells us little about the causes and cures for inflation. Other than during revolutions, the rich are always better able to weather economic crises and the high cost of living than the poor are—whatever the "relative" impact of price increases. Since the distribution of income and wealth did not change significantly between the noninflationary 1950s and the inflationary 1970s, inequality of income and wealth is a condition of the new inflation rather than a cause. It is always possible that there was a sudden increase in the greed of people with market power, but in all probability the intensity of avarice among them remains roughly constant as well as high.

Neither can the new inflation be explained as the product of an increase in the "selfishness" of the general population—a notion that seems to fascinate experts as well as editorial writers. The idea that high prices are caused by all of us "demanding" too much—more than the economy can supply—was a favorite theme of the last days of the Carter administration. And it is resurrected every day to rationalize proposals for other people's sacrifices. The comment of the comic strip character Pogo, "We have met the enemy and it is us," is a modern cliché in the inflation debate. The theory is part moral and part economic. The former suggests that inflation is America's retribution for overindulging our appetites—the wrath of God on twentieth-century Sodom and Gomorrah. There is no doubt that waste, greed, and moral decadence are found in abundance in America. But again, there is little evidence that their strength or our supply of these sins suddenly took a leap forward in 1968, again in 1972, again in the winter of 1973–74, and then again in 1979.

The selfishness theory also does not conform to our historical experience. If it were true that inflation was a result of us all "demanding" more goods and services than the economy could produce, we would by definition be experiencing excess demand—an overheating of the economy. But throughout most of the recent inflationary period the economy has been operating at substantially less than full capacity. Even during the Vietnam War years unemployment rates in the United States were roughly double what they were in Japan and most of Western Europe.

THE NEW INFLATION

If we turn away from abstract theories of inflation and look instead at what actually happened to incite the price spiral of the past decade, we find some very specific causes. They are directly rooted in the conditions of the new economic era, and it is therefore not surprising that they do not conform to the conventional wisdom. The most important cause of our inflation problem has been a series of price "jolts," the effects of which spiral thereafter through the economy in higher prices, interest rates, and wages. The new "jolt and spiral" pattern began with the sudden, unplanned surge in Vietnam War spending in the mid-1960s. The surge rippled through the economy to the point where Richard Nixon invoked wage-price controls in 1971 in response to a Consumer Price Index that was rising at what at the time was deemed to be a politically unacceptable annual rate of 6 percent.

War and inflation are old associates, of course, and the jolt and spiral from Vietnam would eventually have subsided. But beginning in 1973, a new, more chronic source of jolts than the Vietnam War appeared on the world scene: the growing instability of two basic resources for economic survival—food and energy.

In 1973, simultaneous poor harvests in several parts of the world (especially in the Soviet Union) led to heavy demands on U.S. grain supplies. Because the United States—unlike virtually every other major industrialized country—did not have a serious policy of insulating the domestic food economy from the effects of short-term world shortages, U.S. food prices rose 20 percent between 1972 and 1973. In 1973–74 the Organization of Petroleum Exporting Countries quadrupled crude-oil prices and sent U.S. energy inflation from 2.8 percent in 1972 to 21.6 percent in 1974.[11]

The food and energy jolts each started a chain reaction of markups, higher wage demands, interest-rate reactions, and increased expectations of still further price increases. At the same time, the entire system was becoming more sensitive to the impact of such jolts because of the spread of wage and price rigidities, monopolies and semimonopolies, and the long-term decline in U.S. productivity. The 1975 recession—in part an indirect response to the price jolts—moderated that portion of inflation attributable to the cycle of wages chasing prices chasing wages, but the momentum of inflation continued. It was supplemented by further jolts in the last years of the decade, when energy and food prices were again major contributors. Energy prices rose 37 percent in 1979—and an additional 18 percent in 1980—while food prices rose 21 percent between 1978 and 1980.

The predominant pattern of recent inflation has been made up of three distinct stages. The first stage is brought on by one or more jolts. The second stage is the transmission of the jolts into higher prices, wages, and interest rates throughout the economy. Finally, there is subsequent low productivity stemming from sluggish growth that makes the economy less productive and even more vulnerable to the next inflationary jolt.

Orthodox economic analyses concentrate on the second stage of this sequence: the transmission of "jolts" into more general inflation through the *price-* wage spiral. Ironically, economists often refer to the resulting higher wages in relationship to productivity as the "underlying rate of inflation," despite the fact that the root cause has been outside the system. It is rather like trying to explain the plot of a three-act play by ignoring the first and last acts, or attempting to understand an unfolding movie by freezing one frame in a sequence and trying to explore the ongoing action by studying a single snapshot.

The obsession of economic policymakers with the second act of the inflationary drama is part of what has kept us prisoners of the Phillips Curve. Defining the problem primarily as one of keeping the lid on generalized inflation *once it is kicked off* leads first to the inaccurate proposition that the economy is overheated and must be "deflated" with high interest rates and/or deep government spending reductions. It also leads to a stress on high wage costs, even though historically prices have led wages in the upward spiral. As Walter Heller observes: "The statistical evidence is . . . incontestable: prices went into orbit first in the mid-1970s, and wages gradually followed. And again, in 1979 and 1980, when the cost of living was rising well over 10 percent per year, the rise in average hourly earnings held steady at about 8.5 percent a year."[12]

Since wages and salaries are the largest claims against output and profits, for business-oriented administrations, moderate or extreme—from Nixon, Ford, and Carter to Reagan—restraining or reducing wages has been a major policy objective. This is also an objective behind Paul Volcker's determination that the standard of living of the average American must fall. And it is why the engineered Reagan/ Volcker recession, which forced widespread labor "givebacks," has been hailed as a success by business.

The significance of the food and fuel jolts goes beyond the simple statistical fact of higher prices for specific items we buy at the store. Housing prices, for instance, rose during the 1970s because of speculation in the new general inflationary atmosphere initiated by the jolts. Demographic factors—especially the entry of the baby boom generation into the housing market, and the increase in the number of individuals living alone—also played a major role. The cost of owning a new home increased 134 percent from 1972 to 1980. For owners of existing structures, property taxes soared along with prices. Rents were up 65 percent over the same period, making the possibility of renting a cheap apartment to save for a new house increasingly a thing of the past.[13] High interest rates caused by the monetarist response to inflation have also been major contributors to rising shelter costs. Very high mortgage interest rates may temporarily hold down demand and thus reduce the *price* to the seller. But they massively increase the monthly—and thus the total—cost of home ownership. In any longer-term perspective they intensify underlying supply and demand problems by reducing the production of housing, thus storing up inflationary dynamite for the future.

A fourth sector that has made a major independent contribution to modern inflation is medical care, the cost of which rose 123 percent between 1972 and 1980.[14] Health care costs now constitute nearly 10 percent of the U.S. GNP; they rose from 6.0 percent of the GNP in 1965 to 9.4 percent in 1980. The cost of health care per capita rose from $332 in 1970 to $1,017 in 1980.[15] The overall U.S. health care bill more than doubled after 1973, to $247 billion in 1981—$1 in every $9 the average American worker earns. Health care is the nation's second largest industry, having replaced national defense in 1975. In ten years the cost for hospital rooms has risen by 234 percent, prescription drugs by 76 percent, and doctor services by 149 percent (in 1970 the average income for an M.D. was $41,800; in 1982 it was just under $100,000). The rapid rise in medical care costs has not been specifically jolt-related. With or without the dramatic shifts of the new economic era, medical care prices would have increased, and they will continue to increase as long as we maintain our present obsolete, inefficient, and wholly inadequate system of providing health care, an issue we will address in Chapter Twelve.

THE NECESSITIES PERSPECTIVE

The fact that our recent inflation was largely initiated by, and concentrated in, the four key sectors we have just reviewed is not in significant dispute. The statistical facts stand for themselves. With some reservations about precisely how the housing component of the Consumer Price Index should be calculated, economists of every political persuasion have recognized this reality.[16] They have also observed that the good luck of temporary food surpluses and oil gluts, and a housing sales slump, have helped Ronald Reagan hold down inflation. Yet in the conventional conservative-liberal analysis of the general inflationary issue, the observed reality of the "sectoral" pattern of inflation is systematically neglected.

It is not that conventional economics is ignorant of the sectors; it is rather that the new reality does not fit conventional *theory*.[17] Received theory, in fact, has very little to say about the price of a shopping bag full of groceries doubling, so long as it is offset by a decrease in the price of vacation homes or quadraphonic tape players. The ordinary citizen has no trouble with the notion of "food price inflation" or "energy price inflation." But for *economists*, a rise in he price of just one good—say, imported oil—is in fact *not* considered "inflationary." Prices rise and fall in a market economy all the time. This is supposed to produce the "efficient" allocation of resources. Economic theory, shared by liberals, conservatives, and reindustrializers, is quite consciously agnostic as to what the economy produces.

For monetarists, in fact, inflation is not defined primarily by rising prices but by rises in the money supply. According to monetarist theory, the 1,000 percent rise in oil prices in the decade of the 1970s led to inflation only because the Federal Reserve Board allowed the money supply to rise. It was the rise in the money supply that caused the inflation, not the rise in oil prices. This view holds that when the price of oil rises, consumers must react in one of two ways. To the extent that oil is not a necessity, they should use proportionately less, in which case the demand for oil will drop and bring the price back down again. To the extent that it is a necessity, consumers should pay the higher prices and decrease their demand for other goods, lowering prices of the latter and thus offsetting the high price of oil. The *average* price level, *theoretically*, should not change.

The theory is based on a set of "simplifying assumptions" that all markets are purely competitive and that all transactions occur instantaneously—that is, that there are no time lapses between one event and another. In the real world, however, markets are not purely competitive, nor do the transactions take place instantaneously or without costs. For the large number of goods sold in less-than-competitive markets, reduced demand results not in lowering prices but in lowering production and in maintaining—often raising—prices to sustain profits. This is one reason why, defying the classical laws of supply and demand, auto prices can go up while sales go down. Moreover, in the real world, people cannot easily substitute one commodity for another. It can take years, for example, before it is economical to buy a new furnace and switch from oil to gas. And in the real world the future is uncertain, so major decisions are simply held off. So, too, is financing difficult: it might make sense for the poor to invest in insulation—*if* they could get a loan. For all these reasons, when the price of imported oil is suddenly raised, it may remain high, with far less reduction of demand than expected by theory. Neither does the reduction in demand for other goods create offsetting price decreases; some prices may decline a little but the typical response of the corporate sector is to maintain prices by reducing output. It is employment that falls.

Something else happens as well: Consumers and businesses suddenly faced with higher costs of production and higher costs of living go to the bank to borrow money to maintain their purchases of both energy and nonenergy goods. The increase in bank loans adds to the supply of money in circulation. Since there is now more money chasing the same amount of goods, it satisfies the economists' definition of inflation as a monetary phenomenon. And because the government "permits" the banks to expand credit, it satisfies the conservative definition of inflation as a monetary phenomenon caused by government.

Perspective in economics is as important as it is in art. The perspective of conventional inflation theory is dominated by the abstract assumptions of the competitive model and the obsession with seeing inflation solely as a phenomenon of aggregates—the general price level. The sectoral pattern of inflation is recognized but dismissed as an oddity because it does not conform to theory. The function of theory is, of course, to simplify, to avoid the messiness of the real world in order to concentrate on the important issues. But to recall Thomas Kuhn's insight into the destructive power of obsolete ideologies, there comes a time when the messy anomalies become too important to ignore. When theory departs from reality to the extent that it is no longer useful in solving the problem (in this case, a solution to inflation that does not result in the suffering and waste of unemployment), then it is time to search for another theory, or at least abandon one that doesn't work.

A first requirement for dismantling the inflationary barrier that restrains efforts to achieve sustained full production is that we examine the messy, theoretically untidy, and highly specific concrete, sectoral realities.[18] In our search for a solution to the inflation puzzle we will, therefore, reverse the usual order of conventional analysis by focusing first on the "anomalies" that confound traditional theory. At the outset we will review measures to deal with sectoral problems that are likely to recur throughout the remainder of the 1980s and 1990s. We shall return thereafter to the secondary effects of such inflation—the fact that, once initiated, it has an impact on wage demands and the subsequent, "follow on" general inflation that ripples through the economy. As we shall see, because of temporary surpluses in global oil and food markets (in part the result of weather, in part of world recession), the first half of the 1980s is a particularly opportune time for a new approach.

The importance of the four prime inflating-initiating sectors goes beyond the direct contribution that they make to the rise in living costs and to jolting us into economic instability. They have a political and social dimension that also offer a key to the fundamental problem of drawing up a new social contract. Broadly speaking, the specific items that make up the energy, food, housing, and medical-care sectors are in modern Western culture *necessities of life.* When jolts come in the form of drastically rising prices for, say, plastic and steel, and therefore appliances and automobiles, the total impact of inflation on the average American is much less. Such items are postponable, repairable, and often substitutable. But necessities are not. A family can decide to postpone the purchase of a new car or video recorder without major damage to its standard of living, its health, or its self-respect. But it cannot for long postpone buying food if it is to live, or paying for gasoline if it drives to work, or paying the electric company.

The special importance of the price of basic commodities for political and economic stability has in fact long been recognized. From biblical times, the price of grain was a major determinant of the rise and fall of empires. And in modern America the price of food is still a major factor in the citizen/consumer's sense of well-being. Pat Caddell, Jimmy Carter's pollster, warned him as early as December 1976 that food and fuel prices would be a primary determinant of consumer/voter well-being. "It is also important to realize," he wrote, "that the consumer is far more sensitive to price change for small, frequently purchased items like food and gasoline than for larger, less frequently purchased items such as durables. For the consumer it is the small items that are purchased which signal inflation. . . ."[19]

The wife in a blue-collar family in Boston puts it more directly: "We used to have biscuits and doughnuts and eggs and sausages and a big pot of coffee on Sunday mornings. We just can't afford it any more. We can't afford extras. . . . What we hoped for has turned into something else. It's like the beauty has been taken out of life. It's like it's all on the wrong speed."[20]

When food and fuel prices rise they help create an immediate personal sense of economic disarray. The ring of the cash register and the rapid ping of the gasoline pump feed the impression that Americans are slipping behind in the world. They put a more intense edge on demands by workers for wage increases to keep up with the cost of living. This is particularly true among lower-paid workers, who spend a bigger share of their paycheck for these items. Since a large number of low-wage workers are employed in the service industries—industries with historically low rates of productivity—such wage increases are more likely to be passed on to the consumer, further increasing inflation. To the extent that workers are not successful in gaining wage increases to match the increase in their cost of living, the sense of their alienation from the rest of society accelerates.

The other two necessities are also particularly potent contributors to the psychology of inflation. Like food and fuel, payments for the rent or the mortgage are relatively nonpostponable. And in the short run there is nothing consumers can substitute for their present housing. Increases in cost simply must be paid. But housing is more than just a commodity; it is for most Americans the tangible symbol of the American Dream. It involves the sense of personal security, independence, and roots that is traditionally associated with owning one's own home. Not to have a house is to be a tenant, subject to the whim of the landlord; always there is the danger that one will be turned out, that one will become a fugitive. Access to decent housing at affordable prices is a foundation for personal security and a sense of neighborhood and community.

Medical care, too, plays a special role in family life. To the citizen of a modern industrial society it is a major symbol of security. Fear of being sick without being able to afford care is pervasive. It is the reason why almost all the industrialized nations in the world have some form of national health insurance or socialized medicine. In the United States the medical establishment has successfully resisted a formalized national health plan but has had to accept an expanding federal presence in the health-care industry through Medicare, Medicaid, hospital and medical school subsidies, and so forth. The present wasteful and unnecessarily bureaucratic medical-care system in America is a monument to broker state politics. At the same time it reflects the strong sentiments that health care is a basic right of the citizen.

Increases in the real costs of life's necessities during the 1970s helped erode our national consensus and sense of community. For the first time since the Depression, a large and growing number of Americans became uncertain whether they could continue to have the essential elements that make up the traditional American standard of living. Distortions of the new era also allowed a substantial minority at the top of the income and wealth distribution to profit from unproductive speculation and the costly overbureaucratization of the production system. More real-estate brokers, lawyers, accountants, high-paid medical specialists, etc., than the economy needs to be efficient were one result. Sales of expensive, high-quality goods and services—designer clothing, luxury autos, vacations, a degree from Harvard Business School—continued strong throughout the stagflation of the 1970s. Sales of lower-priced goods have also done well as middle-income people have had to step down their expectations. It is the middle-range market that was hurt the most, reflecting a deterioration in the purchasing power of the middle class. The result is what sociologist Paul Blumberg calls "class divergence"—or a widening gap in income and life-style between upper and lower classes.[21]

Relative stability in the prices of necessities is a necessary (but not sufficient) condition of establishing the financial and psychological stability without which neither a sustained full-production economy nor a comprehensive social contract can be achieved. Distinctions between necessity and luxury, between fair and unfair, are also extremely important in developing willingness to sacrifice. We are more likely to accept sacrifices in order that our neighbors and their children have adequate food, a roof over their head, and a doctor when they need one than we are to sacrifice so that they can buy a videotape recorder or get tickets to the World Series or buy a new car. Finally, such distinctions begin to suggest the principle that production for need rather than for ever higher profit is important in a decent society.

In studies of American buying habits, the U.S. Bureau of Labor Statistics has developed low, medium, and high budgets reflecting living standards for typical urban worker families. The low budget (which in 1980 required a gross income of $14,044 for a family of four) does not reflect a notion of bare minimum subsistence but is probably close to what the typical American would think of as the minimum that ought to be available to a consumer in return for working a forty-hour week. For example, the budget assumes that the family buys a six-year-old car, keeps it four years (until it is ten years old), and then trades it in and buys another six-year-old car. The wife in the family buys an inexpensive overcoat once every 4.8 years. The family goes to the movies 8.2 times per year. They rent their apartment. They spend 38 percent of their total consumer expenditures on food, 24 percent on housing, and 11 percent on medical care.[22]

Information of this kind permits us to begin a serious dialogue about where precisely to draw the line as to minimal standards of necessities. Economics, psychology, and common sense also tell us that consumers first buy what they consider to be necessities and then with additional income purchase other, less important goods and services. Therefore, people who have high incomes spend proportionally less on the necessities. We also know that people have roughly similar notions of what necessities are—food, electricity and fuel, rent or mortgage payments, medical care, and clothing. Beyond food and fuel, of course, the categories become quite broad. Some people use their incomes to buy more expensive housing and clothing. The statistics do not adequately break out luxury levels from necessity levels. But the pattern and logic are clear.

Any definition of necessities obviously leaves considerable room for debate, particularly within the broad categories we have discussed. It is relatively easy to say that owning two homes for personal use is not a necessity. But where do we draw the line between a house that is a necessity and one that is a luxury? Is hamburger a necessity and filet mignon a luxury even though they come from the same steer? Is a plastic hip a necessity and cosmetic nose surgery a luxury? Should clothing be included or excluded? These are difficult problems. *But they do not disappear when we refuse to take responsibility for them.* They merely get decided in a haphazard way with great damage to the social fabric—and continue to create a climate of fear, anxiety, and "every man for himself," which is the antithesis of community and of the personal values we must encourage in the new economic era.

In the abstractions of conventional economic theory, it makes little difference that the jolts that triggered recent inflation were centered in two of the most important items in the average American's shopping basket, or that housing and health care are of special significance to American family life. But, in fact, some things *are* more important than others. The "value-free" economic paradigms of both the neo-Keynesian liberals and the neoclassical conservatives allow for no public distinctions among goods. A piece of bread for a starving child has no more value than an after-dinner mint for an overfed gourmet. As economist E. Ray Canterbery observes of orthodox economics:

The distribution of personal incomes is a "given" and therefore a household's income relative to that of a second household plays no role in the choice among multitudinous goods and services. If the rich purchase caviar rather than chicken eggs, it is because persons who happen to be wealthy *prefer* caviar and the tastes of the poor run in favor of fried chicken eggs.[23]

In a world of income and wealth equality we would not bother to make distinctions between luxuries and necessities. If everyone had the same income, individual taste alone would account for choices in the marketplace and thereby govern what is produced. But the America with which a new strategy must begin is not such a world, and such a view is little more than sophistry. This is not to say that every consumer choice should be a matter of public policy; it simply means that national decisions in the new era must be made in a way that is relevant to the economic reality faced by the large majority of Americans.

Chapter 10

ENERGY: STABILITY AND COMMUNITY

The worldwide recession of the early 1980s, together with conservation, cut world demand for oil considerably, and prices stabilized and dropped back. Still, oil prices in the spring of 1983 were eight times what they were ten years before. Since we are examining whether a full-production economy is compatible with relatively stable prices, the question before us is what is likely to happen when and if we were to stimulate sustained economic growth. The answer is that on our present course we will be right back where we were in the 1970s, when any significant disruption of world oil supplies could shake the whole U.S. economy.

The Middle East could erupt at any time, cutting off supplies to importing countries—as it has done three separate times in the past decade. Contingencies include the Soviet threat, regional fighting, internal upheavals, terrorism, the festering Arab-Israeli issue, and a sudden shift in the production and pricing policy of one or more OPEC countries. It is nearly certain that we will have to cope with one or even several of these in the years ahead. Observes oil expert Walter Levy:

> The overriding conclusion is thus inevitable. Even in the short-to-medium term no firm reliance can safely be placed on the future availability of the required volumes of Middle East oil at manageable prices. If nothing else, the experience of the 1970s should have taught us this. In spite of the present world oil glut, the outlook for most of the 1980s still looks to be highly precarious and, accordingly, it would be extremely imprudent if oil importers were to base their planning for the future on current market conditions.[1]

The key to the Middle East is Saudi Arabia, with its giant production capacity. U.S. policy rests strongly on military aid. Yet the ease with which dissidents assassinated President Anwar Sadat of Egypt in 1981 was a dramatic reminder of the fragility of this approach in the extraordinarily vulnerable Middle East. Instead of undertaking a thoroughgoing review of broker state assumptions after the assassination, however, the Reagan administration intensified traditional policy by a show of military air power. Given the experience with America's previous bulwark of "stability"—Iran—the question is just how long the fourteenth-century monarchy that rules Saudi Arabia can last before a really telling blowup occurs.

PLANNING FOR INSTABILITY

The present broker state energy plan is a collection of deals among interests, none of which alone dominate the game. But it is a plan nonetheless. With relatively minor modifications and considerable refinement, in its essentials the plan has remained intact through four political administrations. It was Nixon's. It was Ford's. It was Carter's. And it is Reagan's. Carter urged somewhat more conservation, Reagan more reliance on nuclear power. But they were in agreement on the central elements: (1) high but *unstable* prices for energy; (2) the subsidization of the so-called hard path to energy independence—concentration on coal and exotic nuclear technologies such as fusion and the breeder reactor; and (3) a military commitment to the Saudi Arabian ruling class.

High energy prices should not be confused with the workings of a free market. No industry is more vociferous in denouncing government interference in the marketplace than the oil industry. Yet throughout its history, the industry has relied on government to protect it against the marketplace. For a half century the oil companies succeeded in getting the Texas Railroad Commission (half or more of U.S. oil production came from Texas for much of our history) to restrict production in order to maintain prices higher than the competitive market. In the 1950s, most Texas wells were allowed by law to be pumped only nineteen days or less a month.[2]

When the oil industry expanded its drilling and production in the Middle East, the cost of getting a barrel of high-quality crude oil out of the ground was reckoned in pennies. Competition in the free market would have completely undercut the protected price structure in the United States. So the large oil companies pressured the Eisenhower administration to establish import quotas on crude oil and during the 1960s squashed efforts by smaller independent companies to build oil refineries in the United States, and supply them with imported oil.*

Only *after* OPEC drove prices sky high did the oil companies want freedom from government interference. The government had imposed price ceilings as part of the Nixon wage-price controls, but after the oil lobbyists went to work, controls were gradually abolished—first by Carter, then, in only a slight speeding up of the timetable, by Reagan. By 1981 they were completely gone. Profits soared during the 1970s. The companies spread control over competitive fuels such as coal and nuclear power, and this broadened their financial base outside the energy industry. From 1978 to 1980 oil company profits increased 115 percent, compared with an average of 10 percent for all other companies. Oil companies spent more than twice as much for acquisitions of competing firms and nonpetroleum companies as they did on exploration and production of domestic oil and gas.[3] Oil company profits in early 1981 constituted one third of *all* corporate profits in the United States.[4] Their return on equity was 53 percent greater than the rest of U.S. industry. Even the windfall profits tax passed with great struggle and billed as a triumph of populism—can itself be deducted from income when calculating income taxes, and thus on average probably takes less than 25 percent of windfall revenues.[5]

Profits are only a partial measure of the oil industry's prosperity. Without their owners lifting a finger, oil properties rose enormously in value through the combined effect of OPEC and price decontrol. "There may never have been so sick a sweepstake in American history," Daniel Yergin and Roger Stobaugh write, "for the OPEC price revolution of 1973 and 1974 increased the world market value of proved U.S. reserves of oil and gas alone by $800 billion. The second shock increased their value by another trillion dollars." Since most oil companies own substantial coal, uranium, and other reserves, when the *general price* of energy rises, these resources also enjoy a windfall increase.[6]

An alternative energy plan should begin with the fact that the cost of producing a barrel of oil has little to do with its price in the rigged domestic and international markets. Middle Eastern oil costs far less

*The natural-gas industry, which was largely owned and controlled by the oil companies, also abhorred the free market. The Federal Power Commission—filled with people with close ties to the oil industry—saw its highest mission throughout the decades of the 1950s and 1960s to be the maintenance of *above-market prices* for the industry. So far as industry was concerned, when demand was greater than supply, the government's role was to allow prices to rise competitively. When supply was greater than demand, government was to intervene to keep prices high. It was supposed to work in only one direction—higher prices. The fight in the early 1980s over deregulation of natural-gas prices followed tradition.

than a dollar per barrel to produce. A recent industry study estimates that the cost of exploring for, developing, and producing new oil within the United States is about fifteen to sixteen dollars per barrel. The world price in mid-1983 was twenty-nine dollars per barrel.

The United States imports only part of its oil needs and a very small fraction of its overall energy requirements. Oil makes up only 43 percent of overall U.S. energy consumption (1982). We import roughly 28 percent of this; hence our dependence on external oil sources constitutes only about *12* percent of *total* U.S. energy requirements. The remainder of our energy is supplied by domestic oil, natural gas, coal, water, nuclear, solar, wood, geothermal, and other resources. We import just under one million barrels of oil a day from the unstable Middle East. We thus remain hostage to a region of the world that supplies us with less than *6* percent of our total oil and only just over 2 percent of our *total* overall national energy mix. The U.S. economy is a very large dog being wagged by a very small tail.[7]

Our interest is not simply to prevent future upward price explosions but also to reduce overall economic instability. The oil market reflects haphazard special-interest planning—the broker state elevated to the international economy. There is enough collusion to affect the market, but the mix of governments and oil companies do not have the power to maintain stability in the face of their own different interests and the ebb and flow of world oil demand. As a result we get the worst of both worlds—prices that are higher than the market demands but also extremely volatile.

Since 1973 oil prices have risen and fallen in three complete cycles, adding large doses of risk to private investment decisions, turning energy conservation into a gamble, and threatening the entire structure of the international economic order.[8] After rising spectacularly in 1973–74, for instance, the price of industrial fuel oil fell 15 percent between August 1975 and August 1978, leading many to believe that the oil crisis had been a one-shot event and that—as Milton Friedman had predicted in 1973—the OPEC cartel would soon collapse. Interest in energy conservation began to wane.[9] But suddenly OPEC was very much back in business, and prices more than doubled in the space of two years. Prices softened again in the spring of 1981, when Saudi Arabia deliberately maintained a high rate of production in the face of recession-induced demand declines to show its OPEC partners that *it* had the power to maintain prices—in this case at thirty-two dollars per barrel. Prices of gasoline in the United States began to drop, filling the popular media once again with stories about the end of the oil crisis and the breakup of OPEC. Businessmen and consumers who had invested in conservation began to wonder whether they had been fooled. Car dealers—even in the midst of recession—began to report more consumer interest in heavier, more comfortable, and more fuel-inefficient autos. Investor interest in solar and renewable-energy industries waned. The final breakup of OPEC seemed imminent. But by the following year OPEC had agreed on production controls and successfully defined the world price at thirty-four dollars per barrel, and once again the price on the gas pump rose. Then in the spring of 1983 a price war broke out among OPEC members, tumbling prices once again. Western banks, their loans already in trouble because of the recession, were thrown into a crisis when countries such as Mexico and Nigeria, which had been lent billions on the strength of future oil revenues, threatened to default. Some domestic banks that had invested heavily in energy companies also faced bankruptcy as oil drilling and equipment markets suddenly dried up. Even the federal government's own long-term budget planning—which counted on large increases in tax revenues from the oil windfall tax—was disrupted as oil prices fell.

A sensible energy plan must seek to separate the positive contribution that rising prices can make to encouraging conservation from the volatility that poses such a threat to economic stability and conservation. This requires taking the initiative for setting domestic U.S. prices away from the OPEC/oil company combine and making oil prices a part of overall government economic policies. One of the earliest proponents of such a strategy was Thornton Bradshaw, now president of RCA. In 1977, Bradshaw was the head of Atlantic Richfield Oil Company. Bradshaw was an independent thinker, but a bona fide member of the oil industry establishment. The analysis he made remains accurate:

> To set the basic crude oil price, we can depend on the marketplace, on OPEC, or on the federal government. . . .
>
> The first choice is impossible. The free-market mechanism never has worked for oil because there has always been too much oil or too little. In a period of world glut, a free market does not provide the incentive to search for future supplies. If there were a free market today (including for OPEC oil), the newly posted price of crude would fall from $12.09 per barrel to $3 or $4. Every drilling rig in the world would be stacked because oil cannot be found and produced profitably at that price.
>
> The second alternative, letting OPEC set U.S. oil prices, is tantamount to handing over control of our national future to other nations. It is obvious that OPEC's objectives can never be the same as our own.

Therefore, I am reluctantly drawn to the third alternative—the permanent management of crude-oil prices by the U.S. government. . . .[10]

PLANNING FOR STABILITY

Our situation in the international oil market is like that of any businessperson or corporation in a marketplace that is reliant on a small number of powerful and possibly uncertain suppliers. The appropriate strategy can be found in almost any business school textbook. First, we should expand our inventories so we are not vulnerable to short-term shortages. Second, we should be bargaining with our present suppliers as effectively as possible, with as much cunning, flexibility, and toughness as our position permits. Third, we should be developing other sources of supply as quickly and as forcefully as possible. It would be best if these sources were friendly, but the mere fact of more diversity can enhance our security. Finally, we need a clear guideline—within the context of this strategy—to govern the management of overall price policy.

The most obvious of the steps to achieve greater stability is a more rapid rebuilding of our strategic reserves to permit greater flexibility in moments of tight oil supplies. The temporary global surpluses of the early 1980s offer an extraordinary opportunity. The salt caverns in Louisiana and Texas that now hold our strategic petroleum reserve held approximately 293 million barrels in the winter of 1982. The mandated capacity of the reserve is 750 million barrels, and when it is filled we will be able to absorb a daily loss of 2 million barrels of imported oil—twice as much as we now import from the Persian Gulf —for a year.[11] The Carter administration, largely because of its political dependence on the Saudis and because of opposition by the oil companies, built up reserves very reluctantly; the Reagan administration initially began to speed the process a bit but then cut back. If we are serious, a high rate of expansion of buffer stocks should be a national priority.

A second step is to improve our ability to bargain. Presently there is no way for the United States as a sovereign nation to negotiate with the rest of the world because the U.S. government lacks the necessary authority. Negotiations between the United States as a whole—its consumers and businesses that need oil—and the OPEC nations, together or individually, are carried on for "us" mainly by the major international oil companies. One need not have a devil theory of oil company behavior to recognize that their interests are different from those of the United States as a whole. Oil companies' financial gains have, in fact, been directly related to financial losses of the consumer and other businesses. The oil companies themselves openly acknowledge the commonality of interest in high prices between themselves and the oil-exporting countries; in 1974 the president of Gulf Oil cheerfully admitted he thought the formation of OPEC a "good thing," that it had "done us a favor by forcing up the price of oil as it did." Another oil executive told *Newsweek:* "In the Middle East we carry the enemy flag."[12]

The inadequacy of the major oil companies as bargaining agents for the American economy is aggravated by the fact that increasingly it is other nations with whom the oil companies are bargaining. The 1960s and 1970s have seen producer nations demanding not just higher prices but also increasing ownership and control of drilling, production, pricing, and marketing to the point that many such functions are carried out entirely by government-owned and -operated oil companies. Practically all the oil reserves in the major oil-producing countries —except the United States—are nationalized, as are a growing share of production and refining facilities. Saudi Arabia and other Arab countries now regularly make the sale of a share of their oil contingent upon oil company help in building refineries in those countries and training government workers to run them. The next step involves transportation: OPEC countries are now also putting together fleets of tankers to carry oil to their customers; the Organization of Arab Petroleum Exporters has a goal of shipping 50 percent of all exports in its own tankers by 1985.

Because of the clear divergence between their interests and the interests of the major oil multinationals, virtually all of the industrialized nations have moved to put their oil business more under government control. West Germany, France, Britain, Japan, Canada, the Scandinavian countries, and Italy all have oil companies in which the government has substantial or complete ownership. One result is that other Western governments have created their own national instruments to bargain in the oil market (e.g., Canada's Petro Canada; see Chapter Fifteen); they increasingly undercut the strength of private multinationals. And as the bargaining power of *both* producing and other importing nations thereby increases, the power of the United States—which alone relies exclusively on the multinationals to "protect" its interests—decreases. At the very least, the United States should make the function of importing oil a public responsibility. Unless we establish our own national capacity, we are likely to end up unprotected and helpless as other nations force concessions from the oil companies that must come at the expense of the American consumer. Like any business facing uncertainty of supply, the United States should negotiate contracts that require supplier nations to provide a certain amount of oil for the next five to ten years.

With the government as sole importer of crude oil we could help soften world oil prices by allowing access to U.S. oil markets only by competitive bidding. One method, proposed by MIT oil economist M. A. Adelman, would involve auctioning rights to sell in the U.S. market to the lowest bidder. Each month import-authorization tickets would be printed based on an estimate of U.S. oil demand. The tickets would be sold at auction by sealed bid; no oil could be imported without a ticket. Foreign countries would pay a small fee for the right to sell in the United States. The cartel would, of course, attempt to get members to submit uniform fixed bids. But it already finds it extremely difficult to police its members, and the temptation to cheat—to sell oil at beneath the OPEC price—would be high. A system of competitive bidding would weaken OPEC's price structure by encouraging countries with urgent needs for foreign exchange to undersell world prices. It is a common and conventional use of the market.

An additional but separate step would be to create a full-fledged publicly-owned oil and gas corporation to provide the government with a direct ability to increase competition, to judge the real costs of producing gas and oil, and to implement national and international energy strategy free from the narrow interests of major oil companies. Legislation to establish a Federal Energy Corporation modeled on the TVA was originally introduced by Senators Magnuson and Stevenson in 1974. It would have combined both importing and domestic functions. It could also have exploited energy resources on public lands (including offshore tracts), where 14 percent of all oil and 28 percent of all natural-gas drilling already takes place and where the vast majority of new discoveries are likely to take place. This additional function could also allow a public utilitylike entity to serve as a "yardstick" for private producers. It would involve little change in a basic factor, since *the public already owns most of the nation's energy reserves—an estimated 50 percent of all remaining oil, gas, shale oil, and uranium.* They are on public lands that were previously and historically "nationalized." We currently lease access to national reserves to private oil companies—on terms that are extremely favorable to the oil companies.[13]

Expanding world supply in non-OPEC areas is obviously in the U.S. interest; it alters the context of world shortage in which the cartel operates best. But this is not always in the interest of "American" oil companies. It is a matter of historical record that they have resisted major efforts to diversify foreign U.S. oil supplies. To a large extent this is because most oil companies are so locked into the Middle East, and consequently the OPEC cartel, that they fear any move on their part to diversify substantially will tamper with the profitable arrangements that keep prices and profits high. The point was acknowledged in testimony before a U.S. Senate Committee when a former Exxon official was asked why his company turned down a chance to develop a ten-billion-barrel oil deposit in Oman. "I'm sure there is a ten-billion-barrel oil field there," the executive replied, "and I'm absolutely sure we don't want to go into it. I might put some money into it *if I was sure we weren't going to get some oil,* but not if we are going to get oil because we are liable to lose the Aramco concession."[14] Despite the obvious strategic benefit to the United States, the Carter administration watered down World Bank energy investment programs that would have expanded supplies in Third World nations—and the Reagan administration has strongly opposed such efforts.

A Federal Oil and Gas Corporation could enter into partnership agreements for oil exploration in areas where the multinationals refuse to go for fear of offending their partners. Diversification of production brings no guarantees, of course. Reserve estimates are not the same as oil pumped out of the ground, and political instability is not limited to the OPEC nations, but diversification would increase supplies, weaken the cartel, and generally reduce the risks faced by the U.S. economy.

The final element in a price stability strategy requires standby authority for *direct* management of crude oil prices. Standby authority for controls was approved by Congress in 1981 but vetoed by President Reagan. To increase long-term stability the goal should not simply be emergency authority, but power to manage prices within a moderate range as necessary. The target should be a small but *steady* rise in price to spur long-term conversion to more energy-efficient technologies and conservation—a price that increases slowly and predictably so that consumers and investors can count on it and therefore plan for it. This aims at something quite different from the controls of the past: when world prices are temporarily low, the government should impose a variable tax* on oil to maintain a "conservation price." In time of high prices, reserves should be released to dampen domestic market

---

*As distinct from an import *fee,* which allows high windfall gains to domestic producers.

volatility. Standby rationing should be used in real emergencies. The ideal price should be a bit above the increase in the general price level in order to assure that the real price of oil rises, and below a price that includes the cost of carrying inventory so that oil companies have no incentive to hoard oil for higher prices later. Specific taxes on luxury uses of energy can sharpen the distinction between necessities and non-necessities. Proceeds from all energy taxes should be used for conservation efforts, to compensate for the effects of higher prices on the poor, and for stockpiling oil in the strategic petroleum reserve.

CONSERVATION AND COMMUNITY

To the degree that the United States reduces the amount of foreign oil we use to even lower percentages of domestic requirements, managing energy planning in accord with a coherent overall economic strategy means "filling in" with ever smaller quantities. Reducing imports also reduces the risk of being drawn into an unnecessary Middle East war. By most estimates about half the reduction in U.S. energy use since 1973 has been as a result of conservation (the other half was because of economic stagnation). But the U.S. economy remains substantially energy-inefficient. A United States Solar Energy Research Institute (SERI) study commissioned by the U.S. Department of Energy in 1979 concluded that "through efficiency, the U.S. can achieve a full employment economy and increase worker productivity, while reducing national energy consumption by nearly 25 percent." Some 20 to 30 percent of the remaining demand could be supplied by renewable resources.[15]

The SERI study did not assume that the United States must endure freezing homes, stalled traffic, or massive unemployment. It made optimistic assumptions about both social well-being and economic growth. Per-capita income, for example, is assumed to increase by 45 percent over the next twenty years. Unemployment is assumed to fall to 4.0 percent by 1985 and remain at that level through the year 2000.[16] Moreover, only modest price increases were projected; it was assumed that by 2000, the price of oil (in 1978 dollars) would reach $40 per barrel—only a little over the price actually achieved in late 1979. (The finding suggests that in combination with an aggressive conservation plan, the managed "conservation price" need not be excessively high.)

The SERI study estimated that the equivalent of almost fourteen million barrels of oil a day could be saved through improved construction methods, insulation, storm windows, and more efficient furnaces in residences and businesses. The cost of such upgrading in 1980 dollars was estimated at between $105 and $210 billion, with an annual saving of $35 billion in oil bills (based on 1980 prices). "Retrofitting" would easily pay for itself.[17] Raising average auto gas mileage to fifty-five miles per hour by 2000 would save another three million barrels a day, even with projected increases in population and in miles driven per person. More efficient appliances would save three million barrels a day; improved industrial efficiency, five million barrels a day; and more efficient trains, one million barrels a day.[18]

The SERI study estimated the total investment cost of all its proposed improvements at approximately $37 billion–$40 billion per year for a total of $750 billion–$800 billion over twenty years (1981–2000). Since the total energy bill in 1980 alone was $360 billion, and since the improvements would save about 25 percent of energy costs ($80 billion), they obviously make sense financially. Moreover, all of the investment would be spent in America (as opposed to paying for foreign oil), and as part of an overall investment and jobs strategy for sustained full production could generate additional income and therefore public and private savings to Americans.[19]

A full-throttle conservation effort could eliminate virtually all oil imports, allowing us further savings by reducing the amount needed to devote to military spending to protect Middle Eastern oil. The United States will spend roughly $25 billion between 1981 and 1985 for a rapid deployment force whose primary purpose is to fight in the Middle East on short notice.[20] Since there is great doubt that American troops can protect easily sabotaged oil installations in politically volatile countries seven thousand miles away, were we to allocate even a portion of this budget to conservation, our energy position would in all probability be more secure.

COSTS, BENEFITS, AND IDEOLOGY

Although study after study has demonstrated the enormous benefits of conservation investments,[21] from 1973 to 1981 only 4 percent of the federal energy budget was devoted to conservation and only 9 percent to solar projects.[22] Ronald Reagan slashed these efforts even further, cutting conservation spending and solar projects. Research into ocean thermal energy conversion has been suspended, and work on passive solar design in both buildings and wind turbines has been reduced substantially, as was research into solar collectors, photovoltaics, and alcohol fuels.[23]

As the SERI study makes clear, with proper planning, conservation investments can stimulate economic growth. Conservation has also been resisted because of ideological objections to "wasteful" government spending and to planning. Again, however, a conservation strategy makes sense only on the basis of a comprehensive public balance sheet accounting of the real costs and benefits of alternatives. The total cost of electricity from nuclear power, for example, obviously includes the expense of disposing of nuclear waste. But we do not have a solution for its disposal, so it is not included in the calculation of electric rates. Therefore, nuclear power for the moment *appears*—and *is*—cheaper for the individual, but it is more expensive for the country (and the individual taxpayer), which will ultimately have to pay enormous sums for nuclear disposal.*

Nor can such a public balance sheet accounting be separated from planning questions. For the individual, for instance, it makes sense to invest in an automobile and pay the price of gasoline—since there is very limited or faulty mass transportation and rail service available. The energy costs of the combined *auto-road system* are very high. Even when gasoline taxes are used to help pay for higher expenses, however, no thorough calculation is made that compares the *total* dollar and *total* energy cost of the system to *both* the individual and the public with a serious alternative that expands mass transit and rail. The disjuncture between private and public decision-making is also a major obstacle to considering such apparently sensible options as using methanol to fuel cars. The strategy requires a national "system" both to convert auto engines to methanol use *and to produce and distribute methanol*—in short, a *plan*, not simply a tax here or there.

A dramatic illustration of our lack of comprehensive planning and accounting is provided in a study of New York's Long Island by James Benson. Benson examined two alternatives for the 900,000-household region, estimating the costs and benefits of conservation and solar energy–related strategies compared with nuclear power. The first was the proposed construction of two 1,150-megawatt nuclear plants; the second, the implementation of a conservation and solar package for each household. The conclusions were astounding. The conservation package, at a total cost of $6 billion, would have created energy savings of $32 billion—*for a net saving of $25 billion*. It would also have produced thirty jobs per $1 million of expenditures and saved the

---

*Similar considerations apply to coal, where the costs of "acid rain" and other forms of environmental degradation must be brought into the calculation.

equivalent of 310 million barrels of oil. The nuclear package would have cost $7 billion, employed 10 people per $1 million of expenditures, and resulted in total *additional cost* to the households in the region of $17 billion over a 30-year period.[24]

Let us assume that Benson's comparison between the costs and benefits of nuclear and soft-path technologies (conservation and solar) is correct (its conclusions would stand even if the calculations were substantially reduced).[25] In today's world, however, it is essentially *irrelevant:* The private corporate energy decision-making system, backed by the broker state, is simply not asking the question Benson asks. *It is mainly concerned with whether $7 billion should be invested in increased nuclear capacity.* At best it deals with solar energy and conservation as "token" alternatives. The planning question—how to provide Long Island with the energy it needs—requires an explicit and comprehensive planning institution to ask it. It requires a locus of power and authority that can decide to put $1 billion into conservation and solar energy *or* nuclear power. In *practice,* there is no such institution. Except in limited instances the only possible institution—the legislature—has taken itself out of the picture. In *practice,* it maintains a broker state mentality that its job is to hand out benefits to oil squeaky wheels and leave important decisions and the initiative in general to the private sector.

It is not surprising that we make uneconomic energy choices given the ideological confusion that surrounds the debate. Free-enterprise rhetoric is the smoke screen for subsidized broker state planning. Nuclear power, for instance, was once touted by the industry and its captive advocates in the federal government as being "too cheap to meter." The free market was also upheld as sacrosanct. But the cost of one accident—a relatively minor one in which no one was killed or directly injured—at Three Mile Island was enough to bankrupt, financially if not legally, an entire utility and will cost customers and taxpayers a minimum of $1.5 billion.[26] And as to free enterprise and risk-taking, it was the nuclear industry itself that demanded passage of the Price-Anderson Act, which sets specific limits on the liability of any company for nuclear damages. This extraordinary and classic bit of broker state legislation limits in advance the damages private citizens can collect in the case of a major accident and subsidizes insurance on liability up to the limit to boot.[27] No private firm would have invested in nuclear energy on its own. Similarly in 1978, Congress established a Synthetic Fuels Corporation to provide up to $88 billion in price supports, loan guarantees, and purchase agreements to nurture the industry. Another $5 billion was pledged in the Defense Production Act to stimulate synfuels production for military use. Soon the Western landscape was dotted with shale oil projects complete with boomtowns and shale mines. Of the more than a dozen oil shale projects that had begun in the same area, however, only one was operating in the summer of 1982. Other massive government loan guarantees, price guarantees, and tax provisions undergird the whole panoply of fusion, fission, and synfuel components of the so-called energy hard-path.[28]

Obsession with ideology is not confined to the hard-path advocates. In a typical study, for instance, physicists Mark Ross and Robert Williams (of Princeton University and the University of Michigan, respectively) review the economic advantages of solar and other "soft-path" technologies for two hundred pages. They then conclude with a sixty-page diatribe against centralized government planning, replete with constant references to the straw man of Stalinist Eastern European models (but none to West German, Swedish, French, or Japanese energy planning). "We recommend a market-oriented policy because central planning is neither desirable, necessary, nor adequate for fostering the development of fuel-conservation technologies." But many soft-path technologies are already the least expensive, yet the market does not choose them.[29] Morover this "market-oriented" strategy turns out to be planning by another name. It has three parts: first, a general government tax on fuels. Second, some two dozen government programs, regulations, and rules, ranging from federally financed research and development to the setting of performance standards for rental housing units. Third, a proposal for joint university-industry projects for development and commercialization of new energy technologies. *This* "market-oriented" strategy involves *more* interference in the market, but led by a *university*-business alliance rather than a *government*-business alliance![30]

Many soft-path exponents have also ignored issues of overall economic stability and equity in objecting to any interference with market-determined prices on the grounds that this theoretically might reduce conservation. Both hard-path and soft-path advocates join in publicly denouncing government in the headlines while *calling for more subsidies for their side in the small print.* Again, the point is not that the public sector should not subsidize private activity when it is in the public's interest. The problem is that by ideologically denying the need for planning, planning becomes covert, and subsidies become selective and irrational. Popular debate over public policy becomes self-indulgent, fashionably conservative, and completely misleading to the average citizen.

COMMUNITY

Government planning at the local level, where it is closest to the people, has made the most promising strides in conservation and renewable-resource systems. During the 1970s grass-roots efforts throughout the nation developed cheaper, more efficient, and more environmentally benign ways to produce and use energy. To a large extent, these were promoted and fostered by local governmental and quasigovernmental institutions such as rural electrification agencies, community action agencies, and nonprofit cooperatives. The projects and activities vary—like the diverse activities of the soft path. They include recycling centers, weatherization of homes for the poor and elderly, installation of simple solar collectors, windmills, the restoration of dams, housing codes that require more energy efficiency, and so forth.

Take the example of the city of Seattle, Washington. For years Seattle received low-cost electricity from its own hydroelectric plant on the Skagit River. In 1975, the City Light Company, the municipally owned utility, asked the City Council for approval to buy 10 percent participation in new nuclear plants to accommodate what it estimated would be Seattle's need for electricity by 1990. The request met with opposition from environmentalists and others who questioned both the growth projections and the low-cost assumptions of the utility. The City Council appointed a citizen task force headed by a nuclear engineer to study the city's need for electricity. Hundreds of volunteers spent hours studying, gathering, and analyzing data. They concluded that from *a comprehensive planning perspective,* the extra electricity Seattle needed should be "generated" from conservation. After a long, open debate, the City Council voted for the overall alternative plan instead of nuclear power; and it passed a new energy code, required insulation in any building switching to electric heat, emphasized more efficient land-use planning, and provided free downtown bus service to reduce automobile use. The city expects to exceed its 230-megawatt saving goal for 1990 substantially.[31]

The progress in Seattle was not without struggle—a political fight between democratic government and industry experts. Even though it was publicly owned, the management of the utility, wedded to the industry syndrome of growth and the nuclear industry's claim of cheap power, opposed the conservation effort. With the victory of the City Council's plan, the utility's framework shifted: it now supports conservation and provides aid to homeowners and businesses who want to reduce energy costs. It is also examining possibilities for biomass production, small-scale hydroelectric power, co-generation, geothermal, and new solar technologies.[32]

In the city of Davis, California, we find another example of local government planning for soft-path alternatives. With the onset of the energy crisis, a group of student architects from the local branch of the University of California came to the City Council with an analysis of how much energy could be saved by properly designed and located housing (for example, housing built on a north–south axis was warmer in the winter and cooler in the summer). The city then established a building code that set maximum heat-loss standards for all new buildings. Contractors had a variety of tools for achieving the required standards—location and exposure, insulation, amount of glass used, shading, ventilation, etc. Builders at first opposed the law, but several years after its enactment, three local builders appeared before the California legislature and voiced support for the codes. Said one of the builders:

> First of all, I was opposed to the Ordinance when it was adopted because I felt the estimated added cost to meet the requirements would not result in a like amount of energy saved. I also felt that after having built several hundred homes during the past 16 years I know how to build energy-conserving homes better than the young men who proposed the Ordinance. I was wrong and now I believe the Davis Energy Ordinance should be a model for all homes being built.[33]

Added another:

> I'd like to make one other comment. We have found that we have been able to sell about 70 percent of our houses without air conditioners, and this was unheard of through the '60s and early '70s.[34]

Another part of the housing code requires that older buildings must be inspected for minimum energy efficiency standards before they are sold, just as automobiles must pass safety inspection before they are sold in many states. In addition, the city of Davis is experimenting with solar housing and has established recycling centers, planted shade trees in front of houses to reduce summer heat, loosened zoning restrictions against people working out of their homes, prohibited developers from banning the use of clotheslines, and created an elaborate system of bikeways to wean people from automobiles.

The results are impressive. Just two years after the city began to enforce its building codes, electricity use per capita dropped by 12 percent. (At the same time, electricity use nationally was increasing by more than 6 percent.)[35] The experiences of Seattle and Davis are exceptional but not unique. David Morris, James Ridgeway, and others have found similar efforts going on in such diverse places as Clayton, New Mexico; Hartford, Connecticut; Northglenn, Colorado; Ames, Iowa; Burlington, Vermont; and Greensboro, North Carolina. They represent modest but real examples of democratic government taking the lead in pursuing a least-cost strategy through local planning.

Widespread participation is an important ingredient of the most successful efforts. During an energy conservation competition among towns in the six New England states and the five provinces of eastern Canada, for instance, public awareness of the need for conservation, as well as local enthusiasm, cut up to 17.5 percent from energy bills.[36] Schools, churches, radio stations, and labor unions were drawn into the competition. Other studies have also underscored the importance of cooperation.[37] Local planning possibilities are not restricted to small cities. An official New York City study estimated that $2.4 billion per year—fully 25 percent of its energy bill—could be saved with simple, low-cost measures that would pay for themselves in two years. They included such measures as more efficient radiator valves, night temperature reduction, insulation, more efficient air conditioner and appliance standards, and improved utilization of mass transit.[38]

Building on the experience of successful conservation efforts, a federal strategy to encourage the acceleration of community-based conservation could reward municipalities that—*as a community*—exceed national conservation norms (adjusted locally for variations in climate, population growth, etc.). Payments per barrel of oil (or its equivalent) saved above the norm could be made to reward successful local efforts. Each community could in turn decide what share of its payments to allocate to tax reduction, to individual homeowners, to small business, or to mass transportation and to public conservation education efforts.

If we are serious about traditional values of locality and individual responsibility in the energy area especially, we must get beyond the simpleminded formula that equates "free enterprise" with individual freedom. The conditions needed to sustain individual responsibility are not mysterious or bound up in deep secrets of human nature. We know, for example, that one of the most important elements in individual, voluntary energy conservation—feedback (the continuous reminder of how you are doing)—is more important than any other single factor. Three Princeton psychology professors, Darley, Seligman, and Becker, studying the town of Twin Rivers, New Jersey, showed that even financial incentives were only half as effective as visible measures of how well the family is accomplishing its conservation goals, or routine visits by members of the research team. Studies in Kansas City, Baltimore, and other cities have reached similar conclusions; all are consistent with general psychological research showing that when people are regularly provided with measures of how they are doing on a job, their performance improves.

The reciprocal relationship between individuals and their neighbors can thus be both energy-efficient and supportive of voluntary choices in the public interest. It provides a foundation for an enduring, more fundamental sense of community. In a study of community conservation efforts in areas as diverse as the rural San Luis Valley of Colorado and New York City, SERI concluded:

> In all instances the team found that community energy projects promoted a series of activity that bred community cohesion and cooperation. Solar energy was seen as a means to improve the spirit of cooperation and community action because solar related projects often inspired other projects aimed at providing housing and day care centers or growth of food. Success builds upon success.[39]

The experience of the past ten years from communities and neighborhoods all over the nation has shown that a sense of community is thus in no way abstract—it makes a substantial, concrete contribution to reducing energy waste.[40] It helps build the "small daily acts of self-denial" that de Tocqueville understood as essential to the effective functioning of democracy. But the spirit of community is undermined by indifferent, if not hostile, national policies reflecting commercialized values of waste and extravagance. When jobs and profits are pitted against an ethic of conservation and prudence, exhortations to save energy become political window dressing. A sustainable energy strategy requires us to nurture community stability and the local institutions upon which energy efficiency ultimately depends.

Chapter II

FOOD

For most of history the price of grain has been a rough measure of the standard of living for the world's people. For many of the less-developed Fourth World nations, it still is. Even after the Industrial Revolution in the West, corn prices were a determinant of economic progress. The classical British economists (Adam Smith, David Ricardo, Thomas Malthus, Alfred Marshall) who created the intellectual framework for the theory of capitalism all agreed that the price of labor depended in large part on the price of food necessary to maintain a worker in good health. Since England's ability to export goods depended on low wages, maintaining low food prices was a major objective of public policy. The conflict over the Corn Laws—between the industrial capitalists who wanted to maintain cheap grain imports and the landed farmers who wanted to keep grain prices up through high tariffs—was a central economic conflict as Great Britain industrialized at the beginning of the nineteenth century.

Given the abundance of productive farmland in the United States, high food prices have not been quite so central a concern here. For the past half century economists have looked upon grain and other foods as simply another group of commodities produced by politically powerful interests that jockey for subsidies in the familiar give-and-take of broker state politics. As the vise of the new economic era squeezes tighter, however, food prices have become a cause of economic instability. Between 1970 and 1980, they rose almost 40 percent faster than family income,[1] jolting the price level upward and contributing to the overall disruptions of the decade. After having fallen steadily for most of the postwar period, the proportion of the consumer's budget spent on food (another classic measure of a nation's living standard) stopped declining, and as the 1970s ended began to rise.[2] As we have seen, the pressure of rising food prices on the family budget was a major factor in rising wage demands in the decade. To an extent, food inflation helped weaken America's overall export position as wage costs in turn helped fuel industrial costs in world competition.

The fundamental reason food prices jolted the economy during the 1970s—and are likely to do so again—is the growing long-term global imbalance of supply of and demand for food, especially grain. The world supply of and demand for food was in favorable balance for most of the years of the postwar boom. But sometime in the 1970s, the precarious balance took a turn for the worse. In any given period, food production can increase sharply with good weather, and demand can fall due to global recession; prices may then slip temporarily, as they did in the first two years of the Reagan Administration. But it is an error to take this for granted. The longer-term trend of the final decades of the century is toward a tightening of world markets—and periodic *severe* shortages. A U.S. Agriculture Department study concludes: "For agriculture, the 1980s will be far more similar to the turbulent middle and late 1970s than to the first 25 years of the postwar period. . . . The gaps between supply and demand will continue to widen in the 1980s—possibly at twice the rate of the 1950s and 1960s, and only slightly slower than the record pace of the 1970s."[3]

One underlying factor is the number of mouths to feed. Between 1970 and 1980 world population jumped almost 20 percent, to 4.4 billion people. Reliable estimates are that in 20 years the population is likely to rise more than 40 percent, to 6.35 billion![4] In many Third World and Fourth World countries population is racing well ahead of increases in agricultural productivity. Most of the population growth, moreover, is occurring in the urban areas of the world's less-developed countries. By the year 2000, Mexico City will have a population of over thirty million people. Calcutta will have twenty million; Bombay, Cairo, Jakarta, and Seoul will have more than fifteen million each.[5]

When people move to the city, they become meat eaters with a vengeance. And it takes five times as much acreage to produce a pound of protein in meat as it does in cereals, ten times more for meat than for legumes (beans, peas, lentils), and fifteen times more than for leafy vegetables. "To imagine what this means in practical everyday terms," nutritionist Frances Moore Lappé writes, "simply seat yourself at a restaurant in front of an eight ounce steak, and then imagine the room filled with 45–50 people with empty bowls in front of them. For the 'food cost' of your steak, each bowl could be filled with a full cup of cooked cereal grains."[6]

The long-term pressure on global grain prices has been aggravated by the deliberate creation of markets for more expensive U.S.-produced grain and foodstuffs. In his book *The Merchants of Grain*, Dan

Morgan shows how the initial humanitarian intentions of Public Law 480 became adapted as a typical broker state program—pushed by grain corporations and farmers—to subsidize the shipping of grain to impoverished nations as a strategy to help sell off excessive U.S. food inventories. In 1959, four of five dollars' worth of grain exports and nine of ten dollars' worth of soybean and oil exports were financed by the U.S. government. The effect was to wean many nations away from traditional self-sufficiency based on native cereals. Once the target countries had abandoned their old tastes and were "hooked" on wheat, the big grain dealers took over the trade and raised prices.[7]

Food is not like oil for the United States. We are the world's largest and most efficient food producer—a surplus nation, supplying more than 50 percent of the world's trade in the most important category of foodstuffs. The United States is more important to the world market for grain than Saudi Arabia is to the world market for oil! Yet during the inflationary years of the 1970s food prices in the United States rose faster than they did in most other industrial countries—including our two chief industrial rivals, West Germany and Japan, which have comparatively much less significant agricultural sectors and in difficult years must import a substantial amount of their food. Between 1975 and 1980 food prices rose 45 percent in the United States as compared with 18 percent in West Germany and 30 percent in Japan.

The reason for this economic contradiction lies in the operations of the U.S. food marketing system, which has been a direct transmission belt to higher domestic prices, and to follow-up price-wage inflation. We are extremely vulnerable not only to the world market in general but also to manipulation by other nations. Take 1972, for example: The Soviets entered the world market for grain after several major crop failures. Operating through dummy trading companies, the Soviets easily bought most of the grain they needed at moderate prices before word of their massive purchases got out. Grain prices then skyrocketed in America along with prices for bakery products, cooking oils, meats, poultry, dairy, and other products with substantial grain components. The *American* consumer paid for the Soviet grain failure. The impact on meat prices—beef in particular—continued for several years. Squeezed by high feed costs, cattle producers sold off livestock, causing beef prices to drop temporarily. But the depletion of the herds guaranteed extraordinarily high subsequent prices for beef and beef substitutes (for example, pork, lamb, poultry, fish, cheese). Then, just as the cycle seemed to be working itself out, grain prices shot up again in 1980 as a result of the severe drought in North America and a new grain deal—this time with China. Prices rose some 40 percent in 1980, only to fall again over the next two years.

The initial price increases were translated into increases in farm incomes, which rose 44 percent in 1973. Sensing an opportunity to cash in on world food shortages and high prices, farmers—particularly young farmers—went into the market for land, bidding up prices.[8] At the same time, mortgage interest rates were rising. Along with established operators who overexpanded, a whole generation of young farmers took on huge amounts of debt on the assumption of continued rising prices for their crops. When prices fell, large numbers of farmers were unable to make their payments and were squeezed off their land. Following broker state tradition, they then demanded more subsidies. The American Agricultural Movement was formed and thousands of farmers descended on Washington, demonstrating and holding up traffic with parades of huge tractors. They did not get their full demands, but government subsidies did rise. The system ratcheted up the floor under food prices, locking inflation in.

The full impact of collapsing consumer incomes in the deep recessions of 1980–83 hit the farm economy at the same time that good weather had built up massive surpluses. The overvalued dollar also raised U.S. grain prices. The Reagan administration, hardly pausing for the customary bow to free-market ideology, launched a new double-barreled broker state plan: It threatened European competitors with U.S. government subsidies for American farm exports (and provided them for flour sales to Egypt); and, in a program that idled more than a third of all U.S. cropland, it handed over massive amounts of commodities to farmers who agreed to stop producing corn, wheat, rice, and cotton. The goal of the costly payment-in-kind (PIK) plan was to reduce available supplies in order to raise farm income by raising consumer prices. By comparison the famous Chrysler bailout was minuscule. The price tag was $21 billion, more than the total net farm income in 1983. Moreover, the plan reduced reserves just as drought hit many areas of the country, guaranteeing future price rises.[9]

Unless the current U.S. agricultural planning system is drastically restructured, the pattern is likely to get worse over time. Moreover, when food prices rise again and are combined with Reagan-style cutbacks in aid for the needy, we could well see a return of hunger to the United States. Surveys made in the late 1960s showed that a large number of poor people—particularly the very young and the very old —suffered from malnutrition and hunger in the midst of an affluent society. The nation's newspapers ran grisly stories of old people starving to death, hungry dogs in ghetto apartments attacking weakened children, poor schoolchildren suffering malnutrition. As a result—and with the active support of the farm lobby (which wanted to get rid of its surpluses)—the federal government started providing such things as meals for children in schools in low-income areas, "meals on wheels" for the shut-in elderly, and supplemental nutrition and food stamps for pregnant, low-income women. The programs worked: they virtually eliminated hunger from the United States and generally were run efficiently. The new cutbacks, however, are already causing health problems.[10]

THE CONTRADICTIONS OF EXISTING PLANNING

One reason world food supplies were more than adequate for so long after World War II was the tremendous productivity gains of American agriculture—which, unfortunately, are unlikely to be repeated over the next two decades. The U.S. Department of Agriculture's historic effort to increase the productivity of the American farm is one of the major success stories of government intervention. The agriculture extension service, the soil and conservation service, the cooperative service, the research and development work of the land-grant colleges, and a wide range of farm and rural development finance programs established during the New Deal produced a burst of productivity in the 1940s and 1950s. Franklin Roosevelt's Department of Agriculture was at the same time the most practical and the most radical of the cabinet agencies. It was filled with young rural idealists who believed in saving both the soil and the family farm from the destruction of the market. Irrigation, crop rotation, windbreaks, cover crops, rural electrification, disease control, and access to credit created a revolution on the American farm. Total farm productivity (the productivity of land, labor, and machinery) rose 18 percent in each of the decades of the 1930s and 1940s, and an astounding 26 percent in the 1950s.

In the 1960s, however, the rate of agricultural productivity growth dropped to half that of the previous decade. And although the 1970s saw some improvement, agricultural productivity trends remain far below the accomplishments of the three decades after the New Deal.[11] A substantial portion of initial productivity increases derived from the intensive use of chemical fertilizers. But energy-based fertilizers have become increasingly expensive and seem also to have reached a point of diminishing returns. Immediately after World War II, when little nitrogen fertilizer was used, average corn yields were fifty bushels per acre. An increase of about a hundred thousand tons of nitrogen raised average yields to about seventy bushels by 1958. But the application of another four hundred thousand tons of nitrogen by 1965 resulted in an increased yield of only another twenty bushels per acre.[12] Under pressure to produce more for less, in the 1970s farmers not only poured chemical stimulants into the soil at accelerating rates but also brought more land into production and worked it more intensively—abandoning crop rotation, contour plowing, and other soil-conservation practices. The result has not been encouraging: There has been an alarming decrease in the quality of American farm soil. The U.S. Department of Agriculture estimates that the inherent productivity of 30 percent of U.S. cropland is actually declining through the excessive loss of topsoil; cropland and topsoil losses are now almost five tons per acre on average. In Iowa the average is nine tons and in some places sixteen to twenty tons. It is a vicious circle; soil erosion causes a decline in productivity, which is then made up for by increasing applications of commercial fertilizers, which in turn erode the soil even further. Substantial reductions in the soil conservation programs by the Reagan administration will exacerbate the long-run erosion problem.[13]

The substitution of machinery for labor is also reaching its limits. The farm population of the United States is now 20 percent of what it was in the 1920s, and agricultural workers represent a mere 2½ percent of the U.S. labor force.[14] Some 235 million of us—to say nothing of additional tens of millions of people around the world—consume the output of 3 million farmers and farm workers.[15] Further displacement of labor is obviously more and more difficult. New technology now involves not so much the substitution of machinery for labor, but the substitution of expensive machines by even more expensive machines. Between 1960 and 1980, farm machinery prices tripled. High interest rates to finance new equipment have added further to the cost of farm production.[16]

Finally, self-defeating patterns of technological change that *seem* efficient for the individual farmer but that are inefficient for the farm industry have also intensified. For example, cattle used to be raised efficiently on diversified farms where animals were fed largely from grain and grass raised on the same relatively small unit. But the livestock business has become increasingly specialized; cattle, hogs, and chickens are raised in large feedlots and temperature-controlled barns. Over the last decade and a half, the percentage of cattle raised in feedlots with a capacity for more than a thousand head doubled, to 72 percent. As *Business Week* points out: "Unlike diversified farm operations, those producers must purchase all the grain they need in the nation's volatile and increasingly expensive markets, often bidding against giant export firms."[17] The result both adds to price pressures and increases environmental problems due to run-off from feedlot operations.

The complex series of broker state agricultural price subsidy programs compound such sources of cost increases and environmental degradation. There is some logic in subsidizing farm income to preserve a degree of food self-sufficiency, and all industrialized countries do it. Unlike industrial goods, farm production cannot be planned very well. But the *way* in which this is done in America is not very sensible. The most efficient means of maintaining farm income when prices temporarily fall is to send the farmer a check for the difference between what he earns when prices are low and what he needs to earn a decent income. This permits the subsidy to go where it is aimed—to farmers' income—and allows the public and the policymakers to calculate the cost of the subsidy at any given level of price and farmers' returns so as to judge whether it is worth it. It also allows targeting on both equity and efficiency grounds to smaller producers.[18] But despite its use in some areas, this kind of direct subsidy has been opposed as a general principle by the farm bloc in Congress as "socialist." The government check is too much like welfare!

Conservative ideology instead has resulted in a complicated, costly system of government-induced, artificially high prices as the central means of maintaining farm income in bad years. Like the pre-OPEC broker state oil strategies, this "supply side" program is also designed not to increase but to reduce supply. And it often ends up encouraging farmers to destroy fruits, vegetables, and even livestock while consumers go hungry. Some eight to ten billion dollars per year are regularly spent to raise food prices some 15 percent above what they would otherwise be. The programs also feed an army of speculators, brokers, and bureaucrats, the first two of whom are given incentives to manipulate the system, and the last to prevent its manipulation.[19]

This wasteful "free market" planning continued under Ronald Reagan. Well before the massive 1983 "PIK" bailout, the basic structure of the broker state agricultural system was affirmed as the fundamental strategy of the new administration. With only a few well-publicized exceptions and modifications the key farm programs were not eliminated, but quietly continued. Notorious sugar import quotas were also approved, and the government continued some forty-eight "marketing orders"—government regulations and plans that require farmers to destroy fruit, nuts, and other products to create shortages and maintain high prices. In 1984 the administration approved a new program to pay dairy farmers to reduce milk production. When Reagan's Agriculture Secretary, John R. Block, announced the early 1982 continuation of "set aside" programs that require farmers to curtail acreage planted in wheat, corn, rice, and cotton if they wish to remain eligible for loans and subsidies, he said that of course he would have preferred not having to do so: "But we're in a price problem right now, and the quickest way to get out of it is to reduce the supply from this summer's crops. . . ." Asked how the policy squared with President Reagan's insistence on free enterprise and market-oriented farm programs, Mr. Block replied: "This does cause me some philosophical problems, but the problems with low grain prices are much greater."[20]

PRICE STABILITY

America is virtually the only industrial nation that eats its grain at the world price. Most other industrial countries provide a buffer system between domestic prices and export prices to ensure greater stability. Producers and consumers therefore face a more reliable environment in which to make their own production and consumption decisions. In the European community, for example, long-term target prices are established that provide farmers with incentives for production. When world prices are low, governments buy from their farmers at or just below the target prices and resell to domestic users, taking a loss. When world market prices rise, an "export levy" is put on raw food exports, reducing the incentive to export. (To the extent that there is a domestic surplus, export levies are reduced.) The farmer gets a long-term commitment that his real income will be maintained (through setting of target domestic prices), and the consumer and the domestic food industry get a commitment that they will be protected against large fluctuations in world prices. Canada—which, like the United States, is a major food exporter—and Japan, in more limited ways, have similar systems.

Since the United States is the only major food exporting country whose domestic market is fully open, protective mechanisms among other producer nations increase pressure on U.S. domestic prices. It is very much like the oil system, where we increasingly face other national government-industry systems in international trade rather than the free market. European, Canadian, and Japanese consumers have much better protection. The U.S. consumer, however, pays not only a world price that is higher than a free-market price, but also one that is pushed even higher because other nations do not reduce consumption as much, since their prices are artificially low. The handful of giant U.S. grain export companies make large profits, while the American consumer also pays the longer-run cost in the depletion of U.S. soils in order to be the major grain reserve for the rest of the world.

We are thus left with the worst of both systems: the instability, inflationary jolts, and resource waste of capitalism, and the rigidity and bureaucratic waste of socialism. One answer, in theory, is to return to the market, dismantle the subsidies, and entirely "free" the farmers and consumers to take their chances. This, of course, is fantasy. First, the modern world of food production and distribution, like the rest of the economic world, demands some stability. The farmer is dependent on the weather; forcing him to sell his goods in the open market while requiring him to buy in a market dominated by corporate-administered pricing practices is to doom him. Second, we have a national interest in maintaining a diversified, ecologically sustainable farm production system and the productivity and resourcefulness of the individual farmer-operator. The best source of productivity is still the shadow of the individual farmer-owner on his own land. Third, the free market will not happen. Those who think the government will truly "get out of agriculture" for the long haul are ignorant of the forces at work that have created the system. Despite fifty years of rhetoric by farm organizations, rural congressmen, etc., on the virtues of the free market, the agricultural price subsidy system remains. It is not the product of liberal bureaucrats. It is not the product of urban liberals in Congress. It is the product of the farm bloc and their political representatives. If the farmers wanted the free market, they would have it.

The remaining option, which other nations have explicitly recognized, is a cooperative arrangement in which consumers and farmers are both assured stability and reasonable prices which, together with greater reliance on direct paymetns, are high enough to maintain real farm income (that is, the costs of production and a reasonable return on investment). The European system is not without difficulties, and the limited use of supply reduction programs is inevitable in periods of surplus production (in part to encourage conservation; in part to supplement direct-payment income-maintenance strategies). But the need for such efforts is greatly reduced in the environment of generally lower prices and improved consumer demand of a full-production

economy. Farmers, of course, will always want high prices, and consumers will always want low ones. But a policy of planned, *explicitly
shared agreements,* as opposed to the crazy-quilt politics of separate,
uncoordinated, and increasingly unaffordable broker state handouts to
consumers and producers, is the only logical way to create a framework that recognizes that commonality of interests.

A public balance sheet estimate of costs and benefits of food stabilization policies would measure the positive impact of this sector's contribution to overall economic stability. The "order of magnitude"
potential output and tax revenue gains of undisrupted full production
are, as we have seen, measured in the hundreds of billions of dollars.
The cost of reducing the food sector source of disruption would be far
less.

Managing a sustainable compromise between American producers
and consumers of food requires that the farm income program be
integrated with policies to expand reserves and regulate the flow of
exports to stabilize domestic prices in times of shortage. As with oil,
temporary global surpluses offer an unusual opportunity to deal with
the reserve issue. An institution accountable to the public and geared
not simply to the farmers' interests but to overall economic goals
should be established. "The wisdom of continuing to emphasize public
policies of export expansion," writes agricultural expert E. Philip Le-
Veen, "must be challenged in light of the adverse effects of resulting
instability on the domestic economy."[21] In years of high world prices,
excess revenues from export sales licensed by (or directly handled by)
a National Grain Board (together with direct government payments)
could be used to provide farmers with "deficiency" payments needed
to maintain incomes. In particularly good years, revenues might be
returned to consumers through tax reductions (or even a cash rebate
proportional to food purchased at the grocery store). This would be
a visible demonstration to consumers of their benefit from the "deal"
to stabilize prices between themselves and producers. A study by an
agricultural consulting firm, Schnittker Associates, suggests that if
such a system had been in effect from 1972 to 1978—*and other aspects
of a four-part basic necessities anti-inflationary strategy had also been
implemented*—"real" food prices would have declined by 9 percent, in
contrast to the 12 percent increase that actually occurred. This would
have saved consumers some $85 billion (in 1972 dollars). At the same
time, farm income would have been maintained in step with increases
in nonfarm income, and $19 billion could have been accumulated in
a public cash reserve. Land prices would have risen at an annual rate
of 5 to 6 percent, as opposed to their actual rate of 16 percent.[22]

Any system of export management tends, in time of shortage, to intensify world price rises. As a result, in the absence of appropriate offsetting balances, other nations, particularly poor ones, can experience higher costs. But *the present system makes it all but impossible to create a sensible international approach to the long-term world food crisis.* First, it leaves export strategy to those who have no incentive to assist the world's poorest people. Second, the increases in effective demand —the jolts—have come from countries such as the Soviet Union and India, which have the resources and technology to increase agricultural productivity but which have given priority to other investments. The U.S. consumer in effect pays for *their* grain reserves (and disproportionately for European reserves as well), which frees their resources for other uses. This not only relieves them of the obligation to put their own food production house in order, but also allows them to permit, if not to encourage, accelerating meat consumption beyond their own capacity to support it. Ironically, our willingness to be the open grain reserve for the Soviet Union also increases its ability to spend resources on weapons, thus adding to pressures on the United States to put more resources into our own weapons.

In the near term, special bilateral agreements to assure poor nations (and others) access to food supplies at fair prices in shortage years are absolutely essential. It also makes eminent sense to press forcefully for a large-scale international reserve system. Such a reserve would be much more efficient and less expensive than national reserves. But so long as the United States is willing to be an open reserve for the benefit of the richer industrialized nations, the latter have little incentive to create a meaningful international system. If the United States were to restrict open access to U.S. stores, making it more expensive and difficult for other industrialized nations to maintain stable prices and supplies, Japan, Europe, India, and others would be forced to bend to the task of creating a new reserve.

The permanent elimination of world hunger as we move from temporary food surpluses into more difficult times depends on steps taken in individual nations to improve agricultural self-sufficiency and create a more equitable distribution of income. World food difficulties are not caused by an absolute shortage of arable land. The potentially arable land in the world is at least double that of all land that has been in cultivation over the past few decades and at least triple the land actually being harvested at any given time.[23] The problem is the economic and social structures in underdeveloped countries that prevent the people from feeding themselves.

Above all, meaningful land reform is required—and policies that reduce the burden of military spending in poor nations and that give agriculture priority over manufacturing. One of the most important ingredients in a long-term solution to the world agricultural problem is a shift in American foreign policy—away from support of right-wing governing groups that, because they rely upon landed elites, often have an interest in preventing agricultural reform. Continued U.S. support of landowner-backed governments in El Salvador after they gutted even the modest reforms of the centrist parties is simply the latest case in a long and dreary record of U.S. policies that are both insensitive and ultimately contrary to our own interests.

Free-market theorists like to argue that unrestricted world prices will stimulate Third World and Fourth World production. But what has repeatedly happened is that high prices have stimulated *some kinds* of increased Third World and Fourth World production *for export,* further reducing food produced for home consumption! Land in Mexico has shifted from beans for home consumption to strawberries for American consumption; in Brazil to greater coffee and tea exports; throughout Central America to flower production for U.S. markets. As Richard Barnet observes: "Rich and generally well-fed countries are now importing more and more of their food from countries with a high rate of malnutrition."[24]

THE FOOD INDUSTRY

In the long run, many more basic changes will have to be made in our own food system if inflationary costs are to be reduced. The increasingly concentrated and centralized structure of corporate control in food processing and distribution contributes to rising prices all down the line. Ninety percent of all the canned soup sold in America is produced by one firm. Eighty-one percent of flour is sold by the top three. The top three account for 82 percent of all the breakfast cereals, 79 percent of all the peanut butter, 98 percent of all the marshmallows, and 81 percent of all the nuts. In most U.S. cities, four or fewer supermarket chains control a majority of local grocery sales, and in eleven major cities, the four leading supermarkets control between 75 and 90 percent of the business. Safeway, the biggest grocery chain in the world, is bigger than Shell Oil and U.S. Steel.[25]

Concentration contributes to excessive food prices through higher profits, managerial salaries, and advertising expenses than would prevail in competitive markets. FTC economist Russell Parker and Department of Agriculture economist John M. Conner estimated that monopoly power in the food industry cost consumers ten to fifteen billion dollars in 1975, 5 to 8 percent of what they spent in that year for food. Between 1970 and 1979, the *share* of the consumer food dollar going to corporate profits rose by one third as corporate profits nearly tripled.[26]

One answer is to apply to the food industry the provisions of a bill proposed by the late Senator Philip Hart of Michigan. Hart's proposal —the Industrial Reorganization Act—would have required divestiture if four or fewer companies accounted for 50 percent or more of sales in any line of commerce in any year out of the three preceding the complaint—if there was no price competition within an industry, or if the average rate of return of a company exceeded 15 percent for five of seven preceding years. In the same spirit, the Clayton Act—which prohibits monopoly control of markets—should be amended to prohibit mergers of firms in the food industry that separately account for 15 percent or more of industry sales.[27]

There is also enormous scope for expanding smaller human-scale institutions. Over the past ten to fifteen years, a rich variety of local experiments, often supported by innovative state governments (Pennsylvania and Massachusetts have been leaders), have provided a realistic basis for a "development decade" in this area. These institutions include various forms of "direct" marketing, including selling by farmers directly to consumers at farmers' markets; through nonprofit food stores; and to institutions such as schools and hospitals. Alternative marketing efforts also include consumer food cooperatives and food-buying clubs. Food co-ops, including the Consumers Cooperative of Berkeley, with about eighty million dollars' worth of business per year, offer savings ranging up to 40 percent.[28] Although token federal funds have been used to support these activities since 1976, the support has been inadequate relative to the potential that exists.

To save transportation energy, we will also have to move toward greater regional self-sufficiency in the production of certain commodities: We now truck vegetables an average of two thousand miles to market![29] State programs to rebuild truck gardening have had considerable success recently. We can also further this goal through the use of vacant urban land for cooperative community gardens. With better planning and the use of organic approaches and appropriate technology, food production as a whole could be a net producer of energy for the rest of society, rather than the large consumer it now is.[30] More local production combined with the restoration of healthy, locally based processing firms such as bakeries and canneries contribute not only to stable and lower food prices but also to stable communities.

Chapter 12

HEALTH AND HOUSING

STABILIZING HEALTH COSTS

America's health-care system is the broker state gone haywire, with all of the disadvantages of the public and the private sectors combined. We have created a system that gives the doctor every incentive to increase services and none to reduce costs. "Fee for service" medicine regularly stands the market on its head. It is an engine of inflation.

People in physical pain and fear of sickness do not quibble over the doctor's fee. Nor do they question the need for elaborate tests, excessive use of expensive medical technologies, return visits, specialist referrals, expensive prescriptions, and even operations that may not be necessary. Because the system is greased by third-party insurance, there is little incentive to cut such waste. As in military production, the higher the expense, the greater the profit.

The coverage of services is also irrational. Blue Cross, for example, will pay for a hospital visit in many instances, but not for a visit to the doctor's office—which means that the doctor will often unnecessarily admit a patient for an expensive hospital stay rather than treat him or her in the office, thereby adding to the cost of medical services. Congressional hearings reveal innumerable similar cases in which the system forces physicians to order expensive services because insurance will not pay for the inexpensive ones. For example, Senator Edward Kennedy tells the story of a woman in Boston who needed an X ray but could not get to the hospital by herself. The insurance would not pay for a $3 or $4 taxicab ride. So the doctor ordered an ambulance —at a cost of some $70—to pick her up. But the ambulance could be ordered only if she was going to be hospitalized, so she had to be admitted to the hospital. So the health-care system had to pay $350 for a $35 X ray. And yet everyone was satisfied—the woman received her

X ray, the doctor had treated his patient, the hospital got the business, and the insurance company raised its rates.

The money to be made out of this system has brought increasing numbers of private corporations into the once largely public and non-profit hospital area. Some private hospitals have taken the "cream" of the medical population (those with nonchronic illness who have money or insurance to pay), while other institutions, often in poor areas, overburdened and underfinanced, have been forced to close. There is also the huge drug industry, which currently spends thousands of dollars per physician to sell a bewildering array of concoctions —some useful, many useless, and some dangerous to the patient's health. Predictably, the piling on of unnecessary costs and shoddy care has gone beyond the legal bounds of the lax system. The 1970s saw a parade of scandals in cities and towns all across the nation as fast-buck operators set up nursing homes and exploited Medicare and Medicaid programs to bilk the federal government. Legislative hearings uncovered case after case of elderly patients suffering neglect, cruelty, infections, poisoning, unnecessary illness, excessive drugging, and death from fire.[1]

The Medicare and Medicaid programs, the heart of the government part of the system, are typical broker state products—compromises between the rising political demand for national health insurance and the economic interests of the medical-care industry. The government covers costs for the politically important segments of the market that are not profitable for the private sector (the elderly because they have more need for health-care services, and the poor because they cannot pay for them); the medical-industrial complex is paid off with opportunities to make plenty of money providing services on an expanded cost-plus basis. This political deal has helped produce the specific form of medical-sector inflation we have been burdened with for more than two decades. The amount of private and public dollars going to health care more than tripled in ten years, rising from $332 per person in 1970 to $1,017 in 1980, with the share of total GNP devoted to health care rising from 4.4 percent in 1950 to 9.8 percent in 1982.[2]

There is nothing wrong with increasing the amount of national income going to health care. In fact, we would expect an affluent country whose population is aging to be devoting more of its resources to extending life and making it more physically comfortable. The problem is that the rising share of national income does not appear to be associated with appreciably better national health. Not only is health care in America tremendously expensive, but it is also gradually becoming less and less effective relative to health care in the rest of the world. The United States ranks below over forty other countries in preventing deaths from cancer; over fifty other countries have a lower death rate from circulatory disease; seventeen others have lower infant mortality rates. Men live longer in seventeen countries, and women live longer in eight![3]

The present system in the United States is hopelessly biased toward continuing high costs. Doctors play a unique role in society. They are regarded as being capable of bestowing life and causing death; they have awesome power in the marketplace. In the days when a doctor's life and work were rooted in a surrounding community, he worked under a set of mutual obligations to his neighbors and was rewarded with respect and a decent income. Price gouging was not unknown, but it was rare and universally condemned. In the evolution from family physician to miniconglomerate, these constraints have been broken. Doctors no longer perform in the context of community but in the context of the marketplace; health-care fees increasingly become the price for life itself. Armed with such power, medical care as a business is an economic monster threatening to gobble up more and more resources. We cannot solve the problem of health-care inflation until we restore a framework of community to the health-care system.

The doctor is only the most obvious overloaded circuit at the center of an increasingly obsolete general system. Dr. Quentin Young, chairman of medicine at Cook County Hospital in Chicago, points out that in the case of many patients, "Their real troubles are in their workplace, in their community, troubles with the wife or husband, or trouble with the kids—everyday problems that might be solved by working with a union, club, a political party, or some similar involvement. Instead, these troubles are brought to the doctor, who has of late replaced the traditional counselors like the wise old family member, the recognized community leader, or the priest. The doctor, ill equipped for this responsibility and short of time in the bargain, often responds with a prescription for tranquilizers."[4]

Physicians will always be the central figures in the technical and clinical process of curing the sick. But it does not follow that they should dominate almost entirely the entrepreneurial, managerial, and public-policy functions of medicine as well. The system is stuck on the notion of the doctor as a unit of private competitive enterprise. Yet by and large, we do not want doctors to compete; *we want them to cooperate.* Medical knowledge is too limited and the problems of illness are too complex for physicians to shave the quality of their services, to

waste their time on cute marketing gimmicks, etc. The buyer of medical care often has no second chance. It is one thing to buy a "lemon"
at a used-car lot; it is another to buy one on the operating table.
Moreover, the atomistic "fee for service" market in which you pay a
physician for curing you rather than for keeping up your health ignores the crucial role of prevention in health care. Study after study
has shown that personal prevention—which mainly means following
common health habits—can add years to our lives and eliminate painful and costly disease. Yet for the physician, prevention is intellectually
dull, emotionally unrewarding, and financially unremunerative.

Creating a publicly accountable health-care system appropriate to
American culture involves a vast reorganization of the medical sector
of the economy. Even under the best of political circumstances this is
a difficult task, and it will take time to evolve new attitudes, behaviors,
and institutions. The first step, however, is to be clear about the basic
elements necessary for a new system.

One essential near-term feature is comprehensive health insurance
for all Americans. The threat to individual security of doing without
health insurance is such that this anxiety overrides any general consid-
eration of cost in the public mind. The current broker state mix of
partial coverage by private insurers, Medicare for the elderly, and
Medicaid for the poor is not only inefficient but also unfair: some 22
percent of Americans have no health insurance at all![5] Three quarters
of those who lack any health insurance are in families earning less than
fifteen thousand dollars a year. A large proportion are working people
in jobs which do not provide insurance but who are ineligible for
public medical-care programs. The system also penalizes the employee
who works for a small company or low-profit firm that refuses to offer
health insurance—particularly in the high-turnover service industries.
In times of recession, matters are worse for the millions of people who
lose their insurance when they lose their jobs.

There is no technical reason we should not follow the lead of almost
all other Western countries and institute a system of national insurance
that covers everyone for the full range of in- and outpatient care,
doctor visits, lab tests, X rays, etc., and that provides services for
catastrophic illness. The basic necessity of medical care should be a
fundamental right of every American.

A comprehensive public-insurance system would limit doctors and
hospitals in advance to set fees (with some regional variations) and
would not permit them to charge more than the insurance pays. With
universal medical insurance the government would not have to get into

the business of regulating each purchase of equipment for each individual hospital. Cost regulation would be controlled primarily by fixing fees and therefore limiting incomes of hospitals and doctors. Next door in Canada we have a demonstration that government-organized comprehensive health care can be provided at reasonable cost.

A combination of universal health coverage and cost containment was embodied in the original Kennedy-Corman bill, introduced several years ago in Congress. After Jimmy Carter backed away from his campaign promise to support national health insurance, Kennedy scaled down his own bill to permit private insurers to get the government-subsidized premiums. Even this more expensive version was estimated to cost some $31 billion less than the total national health bill by 1985.[6]

But as long as the system revolves around a fee-for-service basis, responsive health care at reasonable cost will continue to elude us. Moreover, any comprehensive health-care system ought to be decentralized and community-based. Flexibility, individual attention, the involvement of family and other volunteers, and the planned use of paraprofessionals to substitute for routine tasks traditionally performed by physicians can create more effective treatment. Only in small, non-bureaucratized settings is such flexibility possible.

In the Health Maintenance Organization (HMO) we have an embryonic model of a health delivery system that begins to eliminate the distortions of the private-practice, fee-for-service system. A steady, purposeful expansion of the approach, under increasingly local community control, should be a second feature of a new system.

Doctors who work in a Health Maintenance Organization are on salary, and members receive all services for a fixed per-person or per-family fee. Because fee-for-service payments are eliminated, neither doctors nor hospitals lose money by preventing illness, nor do they gain by providing unnecessary treatment.[7] Even in its more limited form it provides the consumer with the benefits of teamwork, integrating the skills of different doctors and better use of paraprofessionals. In its more extended form it can be a locally accountable, consumer-oriented health-care system that emphasizes prevention as well as cure and maximizes the involvement of the patient and his or her family in the treatment of illness.

HMOs have had impressive results in reducing inflation costs. Members of the MedCenter Health Plan, a Minneapolis–St. Paul HMO, receive service that would cost 15–20 percent more under conventional health insurance. Nationally, total costs (premium and out-ofpocket) for HMO members are 10 to 40 percent lower than those for comparable health insurance. Overall, hospitalization rates are about 30 percent lower than for people covered by fee-for-service insurance.[8]

Dr. Jack Resnick, an internist with a New York City HMO, has described additional advantages:

> For one thing, I don't have to put patients in the hospital just for tests or X rays. We do them here. For another, if I come across something that's not in my field, all I have to do is walk down the hall and ask someone who knows. You can't get that kind of feedback in private practice.
>
> The politicians say that HMOs are good for patients. I say they are good for doctors.[9]

Imbedded as they are in a surrounding fee-for-service *system*, HMOs have limited potential as individual institutions. Because doctors have the option of returning to the more lucrative private practice, HMOs must provide nearly comparable incomes or risk losing them. Existing HMOs also rarely own their own hospitals and so must pay the going rate in the private sector. Any attempt to expand HMO membership runs into the problem that present hospital capacity, which is already excessive, cannot be put under HMO control without buying it out —which would add additional capital costs to the HMO budget without increasing services to patients. Outside the major cities there is also strong opposition to HMOs on the part of the local medical establishment. In 1980, HMOs still had enrolled only 9.4 million people, 4.3 percent of the population, a large number of which were for-profit companies organized by doctors into what is little more than prepaid group practice.

In short, although HMOs could represent a potential model of a local consumer-controlled system of health-care delivery that minimizes costs, over time the system as a whole must be expanded and restructured if they are to become a significant feature of a new approach. To the extent that the consumer is not directly represented in HMO policymaking, the model runs the danger of being overly concerned with cutting costs (in order to be more attractive to employers, who pay the membership fee in lieu of insurance premiums) at the expense of quality medical care.* Strong consumer participation in the management of the HMO is thus a basic requirement of a balanced system. Ultimately we need a national health service in which doctors

---

*This is a feature that Reagan administration proposals to tax health-care benefits to increase price competition would exacerbate.

and all health workers are salaried employees and care is delivered in community-controlled HMOs. The concept is embodied in at least one legislative proposal before Congress—the Health Service Act, introduced by Congressman Ron Dellums of California.[10] Under this proposal, a combined national-local health-care system would be democratically controlled by community health boards comprised of both health-care users and providers. Several communities would join together to form districts to support jointly facilities that are too expensive for one community. The health service would provide for adequate health care while allowing the flexibility that local, accountable management allows

The average physician's net income in 1982 was $100,000,[11] and it is frequently objected even by those who would otherwise support the idea of a national health service that doctors are too independent and/or too greedy to submit to a system that limits their income. They cite the numerous doctors from other countries who come to the United States in search of more lucrative practices, which conjures up the fear of a mass exodus of medical professionals from the United States. The fear is excessive: national health services, insurance systems, and associated constraints now prevail in most other Western countries. Moreover, since a large number of otherwise qualified people are prevented from going to medical school because of cost, a policy of tuition-free medical education in exchange for specified service could increase the number of medical school graduates oriented to a new program. Such an approach would also eliminate the need for doctors to charge high fees to pay debts incurred in medical school.

An embryonic national health service already exists in the National Health Service Corps (some doctors are still forgiven part of their student loans in return for working a specified number of months in doctor-short rural and urban areas).[12] The corps should be expanded as the basis for a longer-term transition to a full-scale health service. Doctors who have already graduated should be given the option of having their debts paid by the government in return for service.

With HMOs and a national health service as vehicles of change, the transition to a community-based system can be started within the framework of comprehensive national health-plan insurance. Individual consumers who join certified HMOs could simply have the federal government pay the equivalent of their insurance premiums as the membership fee. Corporations and state and local governments experimenting with competition for medical services could be given incentives to phase into such a system. Given the greater efficiencies of

HMOs, they should prosper relative to conventional systems; as long as premiums are equivalent to the benefit payout going to private hospitals and doctors, the HMOs should develop the capital they need to grow. With additional loans and other assistance, over time the HMO could become an expanding part of the health-care system. Requirements for community participation can be built into the agreement by which HMOs are certified to receive premiums from the federal government. Existing public hospitals and neighborhood clinics should be strengthened rather than reduced as additional components of a new system.

Overall expenditure decisions for a new health-care system should be made within the framework of a total "public balance sheet" accounting that weighs the costs of specific treatment alternatives against the costs of tougher environmental and health and safety regulations, and/or more effective personal health education programs.[13]

HOUSING AND COMMUNITY

The cost of housing—symbol and foundation of American middle-class life-styles—exploded during the 1970s. Between 1972 and 1981, the average price of a new single-family house went from $38,000 to $83,100. The average selling price of a used home went from $33,000 to $78,000.[14]

Most families spend more of their income on shelter than on any other single category in their budget. It takes more than a fifth of the average family's income. Among renters, a quarter pay more than 50 percent of their income for rent.[15] When costs rise, the family budget is squeezed, and pressures for increased wages grow. Those just entering the market, particularly young families aspiring to the middle-class life-style they were brought up to expect, feel cheated. As one bewildered young wife complained on television: "My mother had a house. His mother had a house. My older sister had a house. We work as hard as they do. Why can't we afford one?"

The tremors that shook the foundations of the housing market—and with temporary interruptions will continue for some time—run along four economic fault lines. The first cause of cost increases was new era inflation itself, which led to a bidding up of the price of housing, both as a hedge against future inflation and as a speculative investment.

Real-estate speculation, aided by tax subsidies, became something of an obsession for upper-middle-class America in the 1970s. The decade saw a tripling of mortgage credit, from $474 billion in 1970 to $1.4 trillion in 1980. Yet the number of new houses produced in the 1970s was only about 20 percent above the number produced in the 1960s. The huge increase in mortgages did not go primarily to build houses but to buy up old ones, drawing prices up to dizzying heights, which put the American Dream farther and farther away from the next generation.[16]

A second major factor, which caused monthly housing costs to rise, was high interest rates generated in part by fear of inflation and in part by the Federal Reserve Board's tight money policies. In the nine years between 1972 and 1980, average mortgage interest rates almost doubled. For example, at 7.5 percent in 1972, the buyer of a $60,000 home on a thirty-year mortgage paid $150,000. At 15 percent in 1981, the same house cost $273,000 over thirty years.[17]

As interest rates rose, housing starts also dropped. Despite generally accepted estimates that the country needs to build new housing at a rate of about 2.7 million units a year for the decade of the 1980s, construction fell to a little over one million units per year in 1980 and 1981.[18, 19] Growing supply shortages were masked by the high interest rates, which dampened demand in the early 1980s. They are storing up inflationary dynamite for any future time when interest rates fall and demand resumes. As we have seen, the dwindling stop-start pattern of housing construction in response to interest-rate cycles also increased housing costs by discouraging investment in efficient production machinery that must periodically stand idle and by forcing construction workers to seek higher wages to compensate for long periods of unemployment. (It is important to note, however, that although wages have increased, labor's *share* of housing costs has fallen steadily over the postwar years, from 33 percent in 1949 to 16 percent in 1980.)[20]

Pressure on housing prices has also increased because of an acceleration in the growth of the number of households. By the 1970s the children of the postwar baby boom were setting up their own homes, and their parents were getting divorced and separated in droves. New "liberated" life-styles accelerated housing demand. The 1980 census reported that while the number of married couples living together rose 8 percent over the decade (to 48 million), the number of persons living alone rose 65 percent (to 18 million) and the number of unmarried couples living together rose 200 percent (to 1.5 million).[21] The number of separate households was increasing 50 percent faster than the rate that prevailed in the decades after the Second World War. Household formation rates are expected to continue to grow rapidly throughout the 1980s.

The fourth major factor is the growing shortage of "developable" land in and around metropolitan areas where population is expanding. The random, helter-skelter nature of industrial and commercial growth brings with it demands for residential housing in areas inadequately prepared for it. Lack of sewers and roads and in some cases a simple lack of physically suitable land prevent supply from accommodating the new demand. Added limitations have come from the discovery by upper-middle-class suburban residents that exclusionary zoning can keep the social problems of urban America at bay and at the same time increase property values. From 1950 to 1980 the cost of developable land—purchase costs and necessary site improvements—rose from 10 percent to 23 percent of the cost of a new home.[22] As we noted in Part II, overall national geographic investment patterns have also shifted jobs and families to areas of shortage where new housing must be built, even though housing surpluses exist in abandoned communities.

To the list of housing cost factors, we must add property taxes, which have also grown because localities have had to bear a heavier share of the national tax burden.

For all these reasons, not only has the hope of owning one's own home faded for young families, but also the availability of houses and apartments at affordable rents has shrunk. Capital is simply not available for the construction of less profitable apartment buildings for low- and moderate-income families. Such investment cannot compete with other opportunities generated by spending of the more affluent sector of the population. A decent apartment for a family of four where both husband and wife work to bring home $20,000 per year cannot offer the high returns of building ski lodges for the rich. The shift in the housing market for low-income people during the 1970s was particularly dramatic. In 1970, there were 9.3 million renting families with incomes below $5,000. In that year there were 10 million rental units renting at less than $105 per month, or 25 percent of the income of someone making $5,000 per year. By 1980, the number of families making $5,000 or less had shrunk to 7.5 million, but the number of rental units going for $105 or less had shrunk to less than 2 million![23]

One response to the escalating costs of rents in a number of areas around the country has been rent control or rent stabilization. New York City; Washington, D.C.; Baltimore; Los Angeles; Santa Monica; and San Francisco have all passed rent-control or rent-stabilization laws, as have over a hundred towns and cities in New Jersey. Ordinances range from limitations on how often and how much landlords can raise rents (in Los Angeles) to a freeze and rollback provision in Santa Monica. Most rent-control programs are designed to regulate the frequency and amount by which landlords can raise rents and to provide protection for renters.[24]

In the short run, rent control or rent stabilization can stabilize neighborhoods and prevent rent gouging by landlords. But they cannot add to the supply of rental housing unless accompanied by policies to increase supply and/or competition. This means putting more investment into housing production.

The haphazard housing policies of the broker state that were designed to expand housing production have both alleviated and aggravated inflation. By far the most important way the federal government helps shift capital by subsidizing the housing market is through tax expenditures—primarily homeowner deductions for mortgage interest and property taxes. Tax expenditures are an engine of inequity and of inflation. First, they go primarily to upper-income homeowners: About 95 percent of housing-related tax deductions go to families with incomes above the median; 60 percent of the benefits go to those in the top 10 percent of the income distribution. In turn, the generous federal benefits to upper-income homeowners have created a powerful incentive to buy much bigger and more expensive housing than needed *as a speculative investment,* which raises housing prices generally. Taking advantage of tax expenditures and the overall market, the investor who bought an average house in 1970 with a 20 percent down payment was able to make about a 900 percent return on his money by 1980. In contrast, a purchaser of an industrial bond would have seen his asset drop 53 percent in real value.[25]

One related result has been the widespread conversion of rental apartments to condominiums or cooperatives, which gives the individual apartment owner the tax advantages of home ownership. But these advantages, again, are available mostly to people with high incomes, so the process typically converts low- and moderate-priced rental housing into high-priced housing for the rich, further reducing the supply of rental housing for the majority of Americans.

The federal government also subsidizes housing by guaranteeing bank mortgages for moderate-priced housing, and it creates a national market for such mortgages so that the banks can resell them to get cash to make new loans.

Finally, the federal government provides direct construction and operating mortgage interest subsidies for homes for a modest number of low-income families and the elderly. But *these* programs are far smaller than tax expenditures. The U.S. Treasury reports that in 1982 tax spending was *five times* that directly spent for housing programs. This is not the result of Reagan's cuts alone. The federal budget has financed fewer and fewer low- and moderate-income houses each year since 1976. Jimmy Carter's budget request for 1982 provided for less than half the number of federally assisted houses than did the Ford budget of 1978.[26]

The record of the combined broker state programs for housing is far from perfect, but by and large the programs worked. When financing was made available, homes got built, lived in, and paid for. Taken together, they literally changed the face of America. Since 1949, the insured loans of the Federal Housing Administration, the Farmers Home Administration, and the Veterans Administration helped provide millions of American families with decent homes they would not otherwise have been able to afford.[27] They took a generation out of overcrowded urban slums and gave them a patch of lawn and enough rooms into which to fit a family; they made Americans by far the best and most comfortably housed people in the working world.

Yet our system of housing finance cannot continue to work in the future without a major overhaul. It absorbs too much of the nation's savings for the shelter it does produce, and it aggravates housing inflation. There is, in fact, no comprehensive cost accounting or coherent plan for housing. The amount of capital made available for housing is not established on the basis of housing need but is mostly the leftover result of other decisions made about the economy concerning monetary policy, tax policy, investment in new skyscrapers, military expenditures, etc. Nor does the Secretary of Housing and Urban Development have much say over the manner in which housing is distributed. Congress and congressional committees, in broker state fashion, create wasteful "Christmas tree" housing budgets—something for every congressional district and special real-estate interests.

The first major girder upon which a serious housing program must rest is a direct plan to stabilize the initiating sources of the new inflation; the roots of speculative investment in housing must be cut. In the context of such a plan, a sustained full-production economy can with tax reform reduce long-term deficits and permit a responsible monetary policy that lowers interest rates—a second essential element to undergird specific housing "programs." It is then a matter of public choice what share of the nation's capital to invest in housing.

Within this framework, common sense tells us that housing planning should begin first with target goals for regions, states, cities, and neighborhoods. Even with the inadequacies of broker state housing programs, we have developed a set of institutions that—if there were a will—could reasonably turn out the components of a national housing plan. These include the local and state housing authorities that have been engaged in producing such estimates to satisfy the legal requirements of the Housing Act, and the host of nonprofit community organizations that have developed housing expertise. There is also sufficient apparatus at the local level to identify the present and expected supply and demand conditions in housing markets in practically every part of the country.

A commonsense housing plan would also discriminate between those needs it is reasonable to assist and those that are not. Obviously, expensive housing, vacation, and luxury homes do not require special subsidies. Sensible planning would concentrate scarce resources on low- and moderate-income housing, which is in short supply. A number of housing planners have suggested that subsidies should be limited to homes costing less than 125 percent of the median selling price. This would not prohibit the building of luxury and vacation homes; it would simply stop the use of public monies for people who do not need a subsidy.

Changing the IRS code could turn the present mortgage interest deduction into a straight tax credit of 25 percent of mortgage interest payments, with a ceiling of five thousand dollars. This would still permit homeowners to shelter up to twenty thousand dollars in mortgage interest payments, but for the year 1982 we would have made over $4 billion available to subsidize low- and moderate-income housing. A lower cap—say, twenty-five hundred dollars—and/or extending the idea to property tax deductions would capture even more.[28]

The next step would be to target programs to the people who need them. Two obvious categories are:

- New housing to satisfy young families with steady jobs just coming into the housing market, the key to stabilizing the social structure of our communities.
- Housing for those who cannot work, or—although working—cannot earn enough to maintain decent housing at 25 percent of their income. These are the nonworking and working poor, largely residents of urban slums and permanently depressed rural areas, and the elderly.

The first need can be addressed by extending and modernizing the direct approaches that proved successful in the first two decades after World War II. For example, the public sector provides a certain portion of the front-end cost of getting a new family into their first home. This financing usually need not represent a loss to the Treasury. As we saw in Chapter Seven, mortgage subsidy costs, especially for middle-income families, are small relative to the investment they leverage and the new jobs and taxes they generate. In the past they have paid the government back severalfold.[29] With provisions for recapture of public subsidies upon resale, the public return could be even greater.

Another approach involves the building and rehabilitation of cooperative apartments in cities, a change in ownership structure that addresses the way in which housing is owned, managed, and traded. There are approximately 450,000 cooperatively owned apartment houses in the United States today.[30] Co-ops offer benefits both in stabilizing housing markets and in developing a sense of community. Co-ops contribute less to speculation than individually owned condominium apartments, which are easily sold and resold, each time increasing the price. Individual co-op units turn over, but they do so in most areas less easily and have a much smaller impact on the market. The cooperative system itself also tends to keep costs down by encouraging collective self-help and reducing vandalism and deterioration of property. Cooperatives, finally, have smaller development profits built into the price and have the advantages of group financing.

What of those whose incomes cannot support decent housing? Again, there is no great mystery about what to do, assuming that we are serious about the goal. For example, the present program operated under Section 8 of the Housing Act provides flexible subsidies to increase the supply of housing specifically for low- and moderate-income people. The program has been subject to escalating costs, largely because of the forces operating in the housing market in general, but also as a result of the expensive "incentives" the program msut pay out to investors, developers, and landlords.

One answer is nonprofit-sponsored housing, in which a local community institution—a church, a labor union—becomes the developer. Since the nonprofit sponsor is operating on a broader balance sheet than the private developer, it can elect to forgo part of its profit in return for, say, better housing for its membership, an upgrading of the neighborhood, an increase in jobs, a reduction in crime. Moreover, by forgoing part of the profit, costs to the Treasury are lower. On a project of, say, a million dollars sponsored by an inexperienced nonprofit sponsor, costs might be higher than those of a more experienced private developer. But the indirect tax subsidies to profit-making sponsors are likely to run far more.

Nonprofit sponsorship has often been opposed by major banks and homebuilder lobbies in Washington. The only reason that it has continued at all has been that for the most part, profit-making developers do not themselves want to serve low-income people in low-income neighborhoods. Yet, once they have gained experience, it is the small-scale, local nonprofit sponsors who have been most creative in lowering building costs by using volunteers or training workers through government programs, by obtaining land through donations for tax purposes, and by using existing government housing as the basis for upgrading the overall environment of the community. Los Sures, a New York City housing group, for instance, in 1980 managed eight city-owned buildings, eleven absentee-owned buildings through city contracts, and, with other neighborhood groups, nearly sixty thousand apartments in the Hispanic Williamsburgh section of Brooklyn It also renovated several hundred more units to be sold to tenant groups or neighborhood groups. In South Bend, Indiana, a similar small organization, Renew, Inc., was helping restore empty houses for low-income residents with average income of eight thousand dollars through an unusual rent/land contract program that prepares families for the costs of home ownership while enabling them to establish a credit record with the banks.[31]

The experience with nonprofit housing sponsors has not been uniformly successful by any means. Particularly at the beginning, nonprofits tend to be unsophisticated and unsure of their role. Like the development of any organization—profit or nonprofit—patience is required. The broker state's lack of interest in encouraging community has mostly discouraged nonprofit sponsorship. A serious housing commitment by the federal government would give encouragement and adequate technical aid to community groups sponsoring housing projects. It would create standards for performances along with penalties and rewards for failure and success.

The simplest, most direct and efficient way of providing subsidized housing for low-income people—particularly in the cities—is public housing. Until the late 1940s, public housing in America was a small program for white, stable, working-class families in large cities who could not otherwise afford decent housing at reasonable prices. Public housing units were attractive, in demand, and the concept was politically popular. With the coming of the postwar boom and the creation of tax and mortgage insurance subsidies that allowed the white working class to own their own homes in the suburbs, the tenants in public housing projects changed color and income class. Public housing became a poor people's program, and in the calculus of the broker state, it had low priority. It was designed in huge, ugly, and alienating high-rise blocks—massive warehouses for welfare cases, filled with children with no place to go and old people terrified to go anywhere. The Pruitt-Igo project in St. Louis became the media image of public housing—a series of stark, high-rise tombs that became so mauled by vandalism, crime, and disorder that they were demolished by the city after being open for only sixteen years.[32]

But the stereotype is misleading. Eighty percent of public housing units in the United States are low-rise garden apartments or single-family houses. Seventy percent are in cities of less than five hundred thousand people, and 30 percent are in communities smaller than twenty-five thousand. In the 1960s local public officials were freed to buy smaller parcels or lease existing housing; small projects of less than a hundred units are now feasible. Public housing authorities have also begun encouraging private cooperative ownership by tenants and generally have become more responsive to tenants' needs through regular meetings and provisions that allow tenants to become members of governing boards. In St. Louis, the scene of the Pruitt-Igo disaster, tenants of the Cochran Gardens public housing project now manage their own building through a contract with the city and have taken responsibility for renovating their own apartment complex.

Public housing is cheaper than standard subsidized housing programs because there is no need to provide financiers with expensive incentives. Direct subsidies for a two-bedroom apartment for a family of four are 60 percent lower than those for Section 8 rental housing over a five-year period, and 45 percent lower over a ten-year period.[33]

The past two decades of housing programs have taught us that participatory and community-enhancing arrangements also produce cost savings; people have a strong desire for decent housing and are willing to do much of the work themselves. Do-it-yourself is not simply a concept for the middle class. Sweat equity—in which people make their down payment (usually on an abandoned building) through their own work—has also proven effective in reducing the costs of rehabilitating multifamily housing. In New York City, where the city already owns some ten thousand abandoned apartment houses, sweat equity projects have reduced rehabilitation costs by as much as 50 percent.[34]

Over the long run, housing policy and the problem of adequate supply cannot be divorced from other community planning considerations. In the years ahead, housing density will have to be increased gradually to prevent further energy- and land-wasting suburban sprawl. Planning to locate jobs and homes closer to each other can increase efficiency at reduced overall costs. We will also need to plan for adequate capacity in critical building-materials industries to reduce bottlenecks to higher levels of production, and we will have to coordinate public employment and training programs to develop marketable skills in housing construction and solar energy retrofitting. These are not difficult aims to imagine achieving in the context of a coherent plan, but existing broker state policies are not doing, and cannot do, any of these things well.

Another longer-range question concerns the cost of land. Land prices have been the fastest increasing component of new-home prices. Some increase in land prices is inevitable and necessary for the efficient allocation of resources, but it is important to eliminate unnecessary increases due to speculation and to capture gains for public use.

There are three ways to do this. One is through taxing the speculative profits from land development—an old American idea dating from nineteenth-century economist Henry George. George held that land values—as opposed to the value of improvements—rose because of population and other outside forces that derived from social decisions and therefore were not created by any productive investment of the landowner. He proposed that all of the increment in land values be taxed at a rate of 100 percent. A modern, modified version of such a tax on land speculation was enacted by the state of Vermont in 1973. Under this law, anyone buying or selling land within a period of six years must pay a capital gains tax on the profits at different rates, depending on how long the land was held. If land is bought and sold at a higher price within six months, the state tax is 70 percent. Each year the rate declines, reaching zero after six years.

A second approach is for the state to buy the development rights to land. Under our legal system, property is a "bundle" of rights—to use land, to sell it, to keep other people off it, to develop it. To a large degree, returns from speculation depend on only one of these rights —development. The idea is to separate development rights from the rest of the bundle and permit the public to buy control of them, while allowing a private market the right to use property within certain restrictions.

The third alternative is outright public ownership. For the first time in modern American history, the question of public ownership of land as a tool for urban development was seriously advocated by several authorities during the 1970s. Even banker David Rockefeller proposed a national development land bank to use public powers to condemn and accumulate land for private new-town developers. Former HUD Secretary Robert C. Wood has observed:

> Fundamentally, we are at the point where public ownership and public planning are probably the essential components for a genuine land reform program.
>
> Certain levels of density no longer make tolerable private ownership and development even though zoning and planning requirements are available to affect them directly. Only a general plan with land ownership and control being the decisive forces in critical areas can do the job.[35]

Public land ownership is common in Europe. In 1946 Britain created public development corporations to build fifteen new communities, each with a population of sixty thousand. In Sweden in recent years, 80 percent of the housing underwritten by the central government has been built on municipally owned land that is either sold or leased to the builders. In the Netherlands, the public acquisition of land and its lease or sale to developers dates back to 1902. Amsterdam leases all land except for industrial sites, while Rotterdam leases industrial sites and sells land for all other uses. British and Scandinavian experience with public ownership also suggests that local planning authorities can play a useful part in public development. In Sweden, for example, local communities prepare a master plan for long-range development and a detailed plan that controls current development. The detailed plan, once approved by the town council, requires the town to purchase land in areas that are marked for dense economic activity.[36]

The American Institute of Architects offered a proposal in 1972 for the joint federal, state, and local acquisition and development of one million acres of land in selected urban-fringe areas of the country. The AIA estimated that one million acres could accommodate one third of the nation's growth over the next thirty years at the relatively low average density of twenty-five persons per acre. "The appreciating value of this land," said the AIA, "—realized by lease and sale over the next thirty years—would be enough to cover its original cost plus a large proportion of the cost of preparing the land for development."[37]

Public ownership of land and/or its development rights will not occur overnight in the United States. They threaten not only special private interests, but also an American obsession with land speculation. But we are in a new era: the vast majority of Americans cannot get rich speculating in land, and the force of land speculation that drives families out of inflated housing is becoming increasingly more destructive of community. It is the responsibility of public policy gradually to extract from the simple act of buying a home the commodity speculation that both poisons our neighborhoods and undermines individual security.

But there can be no fundamental solution to many housing and land shortage problems unless planning for community economic stability targets jobs and industries to areas that already have excess housing rather than to areas that already have shortages. "Throwaway cities" throw away housing. A serious plan makes sense only within the broader context of a community-sustaining economics.

Chapter 13

BREAKING THE INFLATION BARRIER

Addressing the main initiating cause of recent inflation opens the way to sustained full production—the key, as we saw in Chapter Six, to the higher rates of productivity growth without which no longer-term approach to price stability is possible. Restructuring our energy and food markets to avoid further jolts protects us from a recurrence of sudden, destabilizing price increases. Rationalizing our housing and medical-care systems undermines expanding price pressures in those areas resulting from market failures. Reducing excessive military expenditures is another necessary step.

But there remain other structural problems in the system. A comprehensive effort must expand education and training, undertake advance planning to eliminate potential production bottlenecks, target jobs to areas of labor surplus, and reduce wage pressures. We are also blocked from reaching high levels of employment by the army of restrictions, monopolies, subsidies, special protections, and the like that have created an economy increasingly inflation-prone on its own terms. To deal with these problems, a number of advanced nations (for example, Japan, West Germany, Austria, Sweden, and Switzerland) have been experimenting with "income policies"—informal and formal agreements among government, large corporations, and labor unions—not to increase their share of national income when rising economic growth gives them a special advantage. The techniques have varied with the planning styles of the countries involved, but the goal is common to all; in exchange for government pledges to promote generally higher profits and full employment, business and labor agree to make price and wage increases dependent on gains in productivity.

The greater success, relative to the United States, of some of these countries in balancing employment growth and price stability during the 1970s was in part a reflection of the existence of such policies. Income policies in Austria, for example, are based on its system of "social partnership," which includes unions and employers in virtually all major aspects of economic policy. The specific determination of wages and prices occurs through joint commissions but is set in the context of broader negotiations on sectoral, social, fiscal, and other policy matters. As the OECD observes: "In many important fields . . . it is inconceivable that the government would take decisions without prior agreement. . . ."[1] Austria's inflation record was well below that of both Western Europe in general and America during the 1970s: 7.2 percent from 1971 to 1976; 4.8 percent from 1977 to 1980. All the while it maintained an annual growth rate of 5 percent, with unemployment normally in the 2 percent range.[2]

A step in the direction of incomes policies was first taken by the Kennedy administration in 1962.[3] It asked business and labor to limit voluntarily their price and wage increases to increases in productivity. The violation of the guidelines by U.S. Steel brought a dramatic public confrontation between Kennedy and Roger Blough, then chairman of U.S. Steel. Blough backed down publicly, but several months later he was able to get practically all he wanted in a series of unpublicized price increases.

A more elaborate set of guidelines was promulgated by Jimmy Carter. His formula called for complicated calculations based on productivity and previous wage and price history, and it included a number of exceptions and amendments. Although Carter avoided Kennedy-like confrontations, Carter did back up the guidelines by announcing that government contracts would not be awarded to those who violated them. Faced with the more inflationary world of the 1970s, Carter's guidelines were, however, woefully inadequate to the task. Moreover, as labor pointed out with justification, the guidelines were much more effective in restraining wages than prices: the government could easily monitor wages through a central source, but business had to be monitored by having access to price information on thousands of different products, an almost impossible task. Thus, when the nonlabor energy and food jolts hit, wage earners were squeezed both by the guidelines and by the rising cost of necessities.

A major problem with voluntary controls is that they are perceived as unfair to those who comply. Because they are voluntary, people do not believe that others will abide. America is not a small community where people can judge others' actions for themselves. Our ability to win or to lose in the race to maintain our standard of living depends in such a situation on the voluntary compliance of millions of total strangers—in a culture where getting ahead of one's neighbor is the highest social goal. And, as we have seen, management and labor in America are much less organized than in other industrial nations, so there is no one who can speak and make agreements on behalf of either group and command a consensus.

The failure of voluntary guidelines led the Carter administration to propose tax incentives to induce wage-price stability. The heart of the plan for so-called real wage insurance was a federal tax credit to be paid to workers who voluntarily kept their wage increases below a certain percentage if inflation continued. In Carter's proposal it was 7 percent; the worker could take a tax credit on the difference between his increase and the actual inflation rate. The proposal (which was not enacted) would have covered the first twenty thousand dollars of a worker's wages up to a 10 percent inflation rate. The tax credits were to be reduced in steps over time.[4]

A tax-based incentive program has the advantage of reinforcing wage restraint with tangible rewards and is therefore an improvement over a strictly voluntary plan.[5] But it has several important drawbacks. First, there is little in it for the worker who has the clout to demand a higher than average wage increase. Second, the tax credit is normally only a one-time benefit, while wage increases extend indefinitely. Third, workers who are likely to be most affected by it are those who cannot easily get higher wages on the basis of their bargaining power in any event. In this case, the tax incentive plan becomes a massive— and costly—subsidy to employees (and employers to the extent that they can justify slightly lower wages because of the subsidy). Fourth, there is no direct *price* restraint. Even if labor costs are slowed, there is little to prevent employers from keeping their prices up, particularly at a time when the government is pumping large amounts of money into the economy in the form of tax credits.[6]

To be effective, measures to restrain prices and wages must be mandatory or involve very steep penalties.* Ironically, our experience with peacetime controls was provided by Republican President Rich-

*To the extent that tax-based systems penalize violators rather than offer incentives to voluntary compliance they become increasingly difficult to distinguish from mandatory control systems.

ard Nixon, who imposed them in August 1971 when the Consumer Price Index was rising at an annual rate of 6 percent. Nixon's wage-price controls had several purposes. One was to strengthen the international position of the dollar, which had been falling against Western European and Japanese currencies. Suppressing prices also permitted the administration to pursue an expansionist fiscal and monetary policy to raise employment in time for the 1972 elections; it enabled Nixon to hold the lid on the kettle while turning up the heat.

Contrary to conventional economic wisdom, the evidence is that wage-price controls worked, if not perfectly. When they were applied in a universal way, they stopped inflation. A detailed analysis of the "Phase II" experience by economists Lanzillotti, Hamilton, and Roberts estimated that consumer and wholesale prices were considerably lower than they would otherwise have been.[7] Under the best of circumstances, however, wage-price controls are a temporary expedient. Although concentrated economic power has decreased the effectiveness of competition, price signals are important for producers and consumers. And the subjugation of the entire economy to rigid controls would over the long run distort investment priorities and transform inflation into a different form, such as black markets or a deterioration in the quality of goods. Moreover, wage-price controls by themselves are full of inequities: they tend to freeze relative wages and prices to the relationships that exist at the time controls are introduced.

Applying controls after the price-wage spiral has begun, moreover, is like closing the barn door after the horse has escaped. If food prices skyrocket and wages are then held down, the "lid" is applied in a way that forces real wages between a rock and a hard place. As one of the administrators of Nixon's control program commented, it had the effect of "zapping" labor. This is one factor that often makes labor union leaders more wary of controls than businessmen: Controls tend to freeze the action before labor can regain what it has lost. It is also one of the reasons why wage demands accelerate when controls are removed, as they did at the end of the Nixon administration's "Phase II."

Average *real* weekly earnings (measured in 1977 dollars) were $198 in 1972, but *fell* all the way to $172 by the end of the decade—a reverse march of real income back to a level reached originally in 1962![8] Reflecting upon the failures of the incomes policy he helped administer during the Carter administration—when *both* energy and food costs exploded—Barry Bosworth clarified the central dilemma of all incomes policies: "It is unreasonable to emphasize wage restraint unless government is willing to act against the strong increases in the prices of goods, such as food and energy, that are central determinants of basic living standards."[9]

The key to *sustainable* incomes policy, one that is not transformed into a machine to squeeze the average wage earner, is that it be *comprehensive*—that it move beyond the narrow question of wages and prices to include the main factors affecting the real income of American families.

This requires that an explicit planning accord be negotiated that recognizes the major interests of labor, business, and government. For labor, full employment, rising real income, and health and safety protections at the workplace; for business, labor peace, a cost structure that remains competitive, a reduction in uncertainty, and higher sales and therefore higher profit growth; and for government, stable, steady growth to provide growing revenue. The underlying reality of any understanding must be an assumption that no party will be as well off on its own as it will be if it enters a collective agreement.

The principle that only increases in productivity can support increases in living standards must be reflected in the determination of wages and prices. Roughly speaking this means that wages cannot rise much beyond average gains in output per worker. Here is a place where controls can play a useful role. A period of mandatory controls can prevent a resumption of the old spiral when economic stimulation begins to take the slack out of labor markets. Controls should continue thereafter as a standby mechanism, to be used if needed in the future.[10, 11]

It is not necessary that the government have power to establish controls in every market, only over those markets in which corporations can restrict supply or otherwise raise prices well beyond the point justified by market conditions—or where labor unions have extraordinary power to impose wage settlements on weak, disorganized employers. Whether a specific market is subject to the domination of one or more corporations that "administer" prices rather than respond to market forces is difficult, but not impossible, to determine. Such conditions prevail when the number of corporations in a market is small enough for them to know each other well and to know what each other is doing. Roughly speaking, if 40 percent of the market is controlled by four or fewer corporate sellers, it can generally be assumed that some ability exists to set prices over and above the natural market level. By and large, strong labor unions tend to be associated with industries with a fair degree of concentration, so that for the most part we are talking about the same people, unions, and firms.

Initially, a less than perfect but serviceable policy might simply cover the top two thousand corporations.[12, 13] The two thousand largest corporations constitute roughly half the GNP. They establish the pattern for wage-price increases that, typically, set terms of reference for less concentrated parts of the economy. They have sophisticated accounting and personnel departments. As a practical matter, planning wages and prices in the large corporation amounts to setting the general direction of wages and prices throughout the economy.

All incomes policies have administrative difficulties and weaknesses. Their claim to superiority is that in any comprehensive public balance sheet accounting they are less rigid than permanent controls, and they avoid the alternative of recession; they permit "large order" hundred-billion-dollar gains from full employment and higher productivity as an offset to "small order" inefficiency losses within specific labor and product markets. But the problem of freezing inequities remains. A sense of fairness and equity among individuals is essential for the functioning of a huge, interdependent economic system. Given the small percentage of the labor force covered, collective bargaining agreements are simply not sufficient to do this. Higher levels of labor demand tend to narrow the differential between those at the bottom of the scale and those higher up. However, over the longer run, equity can be assured only by additional direct measures.

Of all the advanced non-Communist countries (with the possible exception of France), the United States has the most uneven distribution of income and wealth. Before taxes, the top 20 percent in America gets 12 times the lowest 20 percent; with income taxes included, the difference is 9.5 to 1. In West Germany, the ratios are 7.9 to 1 and 7 to 1; in Japan, 5.6 to 1 and 5.2 to 1. Most of the other OECD countries *start* with a more equal income distribution than the United States *ends* with after taxes and then proceed to move their incomes still closer to equity.[14]

The comparison between the United States and other countries is even more striking when we consider that most of the other countries also have extensive social welfare systems that provide greater real benefits to those at the low end of the economic ladder than show up in the income distribution numbers.

In 1977, fully employed American white males in the highest 20 percent of the income distribution earned on average five times those in the lowest 20 percent. Among other members of the work force the ratio was twenty-seven to one. Lester Thurow has made the reasonable suggestion that a longer-range goal should be to make the distribution of income among all Americans the same as that which now exists for fully employed white males. Since this group by definition has sufficient incentive to work, such a standard cannot be said to undermine the country's present incentive system.[15]

Among all *families* the income distribution ratios were eight to one.[16] As we have seen, family income was sustained during the 1970s (even as *individual* real earnings fell) in part by transfer programs and in part by more women going to work—the housewife in effect paid for the failures of the policymakers! Both of these factors, however, are of declining importance. As government transfer payments are reduced, those at the bottom will fall farther behind. And a significant proportion of the women who can most easily enter the labor force have already done so: between 1960 and 1980 the percentage of women with children ages six to seventeen in the labor force rose from 39 percent to 61.8 percent, while those with very young children (under six) shot up from 18.6 percent to 45 percent.[17] For such reasons, without a fundamental change in the way we run our economy, the experience of inflation in the future for most families is likely to be one of much greater economic burden, loss, and pain. This not only will exacerbate social tensions but also is likely to be translated into tougher wage demands to maintain real family income, which will further undermine attempts to make incomes policies work.

Confronting the issue of inequity requires that a comprehensive incomes policy also include tax reform. By this time there is little need to argue the case that the tax system is unfair, irrational, and wasteful. The simple, most direct, and most equitable solution is to tax all income regardless of its source at a progressive rate designed to reduce income and wealth inequities further. One approach that could simultaneously also help bring down prices would be to reduce both employers' and employees' Social Security payments, perhaps by half. This should be offset by general revenue contributions to the Social Security trust funds (financed in turn by loophole closing and other reforms discussed in Chapter Seven).* In terms of both equity and incentives, we should also consider a progressive wealth tax. As numerous observers have recognized, the transfer of wealth from one generation to another has set up a growing class of people who do not

---

*It would also make sense to enact a progressive "windfall benefit" tax to recapture gains that upper-income groups might derive from government efforts to stabilize necessity prices.

have to work for a living yet exercise huge amounts of economic power. Even before the Reagan reductions, inheritance taxes were ineffectual. They amounted in 1979 to .2 percent of total net worth.[18]

This leaves that part of the population that cannot work—the elderly, the handicapped, and those otherwise incapacitated. A full-production economy would generate tax revenues and reduce the welfare load. The richest nation in history could appropriately then set certain minimal physical standards necessary to sustain individuals who cannot work at a threshold living standard—so much food, so much space, so much warmth, and so forth. Over the years opinion survey research suggests that people define a fair welfare level at a little over half of what the average family currently spends to maintain its own standard of living.[19]

MONETARY POLICY

Monetary policy has carried the recent burden of fighting inflation, partly because of the political power of rigid monetary theorists but above all because we have had no real alternative strategy for curing inflation. High interest rates also add to the cost of government and the deficit: Federal interest payments more than doubled between 1978 and 1982, rising from roughly $44 billion a year to approximately $110 billion.*[20]

To the degree that full-production planning raises productivity and stabilizes inflation *directly,* interest rates no longer have to carry the burden—especially as the tax flows of full production narrow the deficit. Ironically, this paves the way for achieving the legitimate long-term goal of the monetarists—a stable increase in the money supply that is not bloated by price inflation. If inflation is handled through nonmonetary solutions, the nagging problem of money market "expectations"—in which increases in the money supply result in higher

---

*A good share of those payments go to institutions and the wealthy, who in turn deposit the money, making it once more available for investment. This is an important point that weakens the oft-repeated argument that government spending inevitably "crowds out" private investment. The Reagan administration's ambassador to France, investment banker Evan Galbraith, has pointed out, moreover, that since depreciation allowances have been large compared with actual investments in recent years (in part because investment has fallen; in part because equipment costs have not risen as fast as expected), *gross* private savings are much larger than the *net* private savings estimates often cited. Galbraith notes that business investment for 1983 was projected at $315 billion, or $45 billion less than 1982's depreciation. The total credit demand for 1983, private and government, was estimated to be $515 billion, "an amount well below (by at least $100 billion) the total of our cash flow, net foreign inflow, and government money returned to the market."[21]

interest rates because investors *fear* that such increases signal more inflation—can also be alleviated.

Two fundamental reforms of the Federal Reserve System are appropriate in this context. The first is to expand the technical authority of the system over all forms of money and credit. The Federal Reserve Board regulates the money supply by raising and lowering the "rediscount" rate—the price it charges for money lent to private banks—and through the buying and selling of Treasury securities. When the Fed sells securities to banks it absorbs their reserves and thus reduces their lending ability; when it buys securities, bank reserves and opportunities to lend expand. The creation of new techniques and new forms of money has seriously weakened the Fed's ability to control credit. The creation of bank holding companies that can issue their own largely unregulated credit is another way around the Fed's money control. The development of financial "futures" markets, money market accounts, variable interest rates, and the rapidly changing nature of electronic financial transfer has also altered the nature of the money supply's "velocity"—the speed with which it turns over. Perhaps the most important weakness in the Fed's ability to manage the money supply is that America's largest corporations are able to borrow money in the huge Eurodollar money market, which is beyond the limits of the Fed's control.

To ensure that the Federal Reserve Board actually does have the power to expand, contract, and allocate the level of money and credit, any institution in the business of extending credit and lending money should be included in the system. The Federal Reserve Board should have the power to regulate reserves of insurance companies, finance companies, and other nonbank domestic lenders as well as to control the overseas borrowing of American companies. The Federal Reserve Board (and other central banks abroad) should also enact reserve requirements and reporting regulations for U.S. branch banks operating in Eurocurrency markets.[22]

If the Fed's power over monetary flows should be expanded, its independence—which has made it a force for instability—should be diminished. Pulling and tugging against the economic policies of the administration in office, to a narrow interest group, increasingly unable to make its monetary goals stick, taking on responsibility for avoiding depression as well as inflation, the Fed has flipped back and forth between restrictive and expansionary policies, sometimes cooperating behind the scenes, sometimes "hanging tough," sometimes buckling to pressure in an increasingly bewildering and publicly unaccountable fashion. Moreover, the bankers who run the Federal Reserve have used the system more and more to protect their own commercial class interests in periods of economic stress. The Fed's willingness to bail out mismanaged banks and to absorb the costs of bad loans and excessive speculation has created a new permissiveness among bankers; many know that the Federal Reserve will save them and their institutions when they get into trouble. The bailout of the Franklin National Bank—and the shameless rescue of the Hunt brothers from their own self-destructive speculation a few years later—signaled that if the deal were large enough there would be little penalty for financial recklessness.

The argument for an independent Federal Reserve is rooted in a distrust of democracy. Talk to a banker and he will tell you that Presidents and Congress will always be inclined to knuckle under to pressure to keep money relatively cheap. Yet the President and members of Congress must face the public and account for their decisions in elections. The Fed's governors can continue to make mistakes for fourteen years before there is any way for the public or its representatives to sack them. As writer-lawyer Philip Stern has commented, the separation of the elected government and the Federal Reserve Board "is like vesting the captain of the ship with total responsibility for the safety of his craft, and giving him full control over everything on board except the engine room. He can call for full steam ahead, but if the engine room fails to respond, there's little he can do other than cajole and negotiate."[23] Moreover, if the chief engineer makes a profit on every gallon of diesel fuel he uses, or benefits every time he makes repairs, or otherwise responds to a different set of incentives from those of the captain, antagonism, tension, and chaos are built into the system.

A first step would be to cut the terms of office for the members of the board in half and to make the term of the chair coterminous with that of the President.[24] Another step would be to expand representation on the board from a closed circle of bankers and financial economists to a broader economic policy group, which would include representatives of labor, consumer groups, small business, and the public at large. Finally, the open market committee—a group of bankers who control the Federal Reserve's buying and selling of government securities—should become advisory and eventually be abolished. Within the context of full-production planning, the Federal Reserve Board, like the central banks of many other countries, should be made part of the executive branch of government, preferably as a subdivision of the Treasury Department. Clearly, if the President of the United

States is entrusted with the ability to obliterate the entire world, he can be trusted to regulate the domestic supply of credit.[25]

Effective arrangements for limiting income are possible only in the context of a spirit of community—and a sense that, despite class antagonisms, we are all in it together and that people will be treated fairly. Where incomes policies have been successful, it has largely been as a consequence of a broadened program of equity. Professor Leland S. Stauber notes that in Austria:

> The attitudes of wage-earners toward proposals for wage restraint are affected by how they view, not only prices, but the incomes and wealth of their more affluent fellow citizens. There is therefore an important social dimension—one not captured by thinking of "wages and prices"—to the likelihood that government calls for, and efforts to bargain about, wage restraints will be heeded. . . .[26]

That "social dimension" is the central issue. It is a dimension that establishes the *context* for all institutional and policy reforms. We are not a small nation like Austria. But in our own continent-spanning culture, we are beginning to understand that complex economic issues must be anchored in some broad, basic principles—or else their capacity to build consensus and engender sustained support is frittered away in a myriad of technicalities that leave the citizen confused and the economy floundering.

In the calculus of community, the broad principle that the basic necessities of life ought to be stabilized as a *fundamental* matter takes on an importance equal to that of *community* full employment as the anchor to full-production economic planning. Politically, a comprehensive strategy built upon this cornerstone introduces explicit values of fairness and common goals to anti-inflation policy. It expresses the community-strengthening idea that an economy should first and foremost be concerned with production for need, transforming the fight against inflation into an instrument for a new social contract.

Part IV

[The] literal restructuring and rebuilding of American society offers the only physical and intellectual challenge capable of absorbing and giving focus to the physical and intellectual resources of the country during the next generation.

WILLIAM APPLEMAN WILLIAMS,
The Great Evasion

Chapter 14

BEYOND THE BROKER STATE

No design for making economic decision-making accountable to public goals can be taken seriously unless it recognizes the problem posed by the power of the large private corporation to bend government and public opinion to its will. In his much-acclaimed study *Politics and Markets,* Yale University professor Charles Lindblom concludes:

> It has been a curious feature of democratic thought that it has not faced up to the private corporation as a peculiar organization in an ostensible democracy. Enormously large, rich in resources, the big corporations . . . command more resources than do most government units. They can also, over a broad range, insist that government meet their demands, even if these demands run counter to those of citizens. . . . Moreover, they do not disqualify themselves from playing the partisan role of a citizen—for the corporation is legally a person. And they exercise unusual veto powers. They are on all these counts disproportionately powerful. . . . The large private corporation fits oddly into democratic theory and vision. Indeed, it does not fit.[1]

What to do about the corporation's power to manipulate and control democratic government remains an unanswered question of the new era of economic planning. Adam Smith understood the tendency of business to monopolize and restrain trade, but in his world the main competing units were individual entrepreneurs, limited in their ability to grow and to absorb competitors in their own life-span. The development of the corporation over the past two hundred years transformed the competing unit into an institution that could live, accumulate, and expand forever.

Since the late nineteenth century we have elaborated a system to protect competition, regulate monopolies, and maintain minimum health and safety standards in the marketplace. The record is uneven. Regulatory agencies are notorious for being captured by the firms they regulate, often undercutting competition by restricting entry into industries and otherwise protecting businesses from each other. On the other hand, regulation has undoubtedly made for a healthier and safer society. Some poisons have been kept off the market, some children have been saved from being burned to death in flammable bedclothes, some workers have been saved from being blinded or scalded, and the worst forms of price fixing have been discouraged.

Whatever the balance between positive and negative economic effects, it is quite clear that regulation has not solved the larger political problems corporate power poses for democratic processes. Neither have efforts to prevent the accumulation of market power through antitrust law. Giant corporations have the freedom and wealth to drag antitrust cases along for years, wearing the government down or outlasting it until a more favorable administration assumes office. The number of antitrust cases that are prosecuted is tiny compared with the incidence of monopoly and oligopoly. The number of such cases that are ever brought to trial is minuscule. And the number of times a large company is actually convicted is so small that when it happens it is a major news event.

Moreover, the question of corporate size ought at least in part to be resolved by what is best for national economic efficiency. If a large corporation is useful in pursuing the national interest as defined in an accountable economic plan, it may be unwise to break it up even if it has considerable market power. Corporations that inhibit the development of new products or restrict the introduction of new technologies ought to be broken up. Serious criteria can come only out of a continuously refined planning process that defines clear objectives, not nineteenth-century theories of competition in static, idealized markets. Most important, antitrust misses the central point of *political* power, since it is focused almost exclusively on the issue of price competition in specific markets. The problem of the multinational oil companies is not simply that there is insufficient price competition for crude oil; the problem is that the oil companies have the political strength to prevent us from achieving energy independence.

Similar problems exist in approaches to corporate reform proposed by Ralph Nader and other consumer lawyers. The Federal Corporate Chartering Act, a bill that has been languishing in Congress for several years, would require giant corporations to be chartered by the federal government, much as many commercial banks now are. Corporations would have to have a full-time board of directors composed entirely of outside people—that is, those without any ties to the management of the company. Elections by shareholders would be regulated to assure democracy; disclosure of information to shareholders and employees would be mandatory; and the rights of workers, taxpayers, and consumers to file suit against corporations (and government agencies that collude with them) would be strengthened. The proposed Act would also require divestiture when four or fewer firms control more than 50 percent of any industry. Mergers or acquisitions by other companies among the largest eight in any industry would be prohibited.[2]

Strengthening protections for those who might be harmed by corporate power is obviously useful, as is more disclosure of information. But the bill still leaves the central problem largely untouched. A Twentieth Century Fund study by Professor Edward Herman of the Wharton School of Finance and Commerce concludes that the behavior of large corporations does not significantly differ no matter who is on the board. When given a choice between current management, and management that might be more beneficial to shareholders' interests, shareholders usually back the status quo.[3] Nor is it likely that adding consumer or worker representatives to boards of directors can significantly alter fundamental decisions; Chrysler's problems went well beyond what can be effected by putting a UAW president on the board.

Proposals to curb the corporation's political powers include eliminating its ability to generate political contributions and, simultaneously, public exposure of candidates' expenditures. Except in referenda elections which affect their business, corporations are prohibited from making *direct* contributions to political campaigns, but there are many well-used and abused indirect ways of funneling corporate contributions to candidates. The easiest is for executives to contribute to a candidate or to a political action committee and for the costs to be covered explicitly or implicitly in their pay. Total contributions from political action committees to congressional candidates were $55.2 million in the 1979–80 election cycle. Of this total, 64 percent came from corporate and business association PACs, compared with 24 percent from labor.[4] Stricter limits on contributions would make our system more democratic and more rational.

But even if elections were funded out of the public treasury, as they are in much of Western Europe, without a more fundamental approach corporations would still inherently dominate much economic planning and policy because they control the process of producing and distributing essential goods and services. Since the economy is organized around large corporations, it is not surprising that their care and feeding is what economic policy tends to be all about: Who else is going to build the factories? Who else is going to hire the people? Who else is going to transport the goods?

Joseph Schumpeter, the only serious conservative rival to Marx as an economic philosopher in the past century, concluded that in the end socialism was inevitable. It was the fate of the successful corporations, he believed, to move beyond individual entrepreneurship and succumb to the bureaucratic mode. In his classic work *Capitalism, Socialism, and Democracy,* he wrote:

> Since capitalist enterprise, by its very achievements, tends to automatize progress, we conclude that it tends to make itself superfluous. . . . The perfectly bureaucratized giant industrial unit not only ousts the small or medium-sized firm and expropriates its owners, but in the end it also ousts the entrepreneur and expropriates the bourgeoisie as a class which in the process stands to lose not only its income but also what is infinitely more important, its function. The true peacemakers of socialism were not the intellectuals or agitators who preached it but the Vanderbilts, Carnegies and Rockefellers.[5]

Henry C. Simons, founder of the conservative Chicago school of economics, came to believe that many corporations—*as opposed to individual entrepreneurs*—at the very least had outlived their usefulness:

> All monopoly or bargaining power implies special privilege to limit production, to restrict entry into industries or occupations, and thereby to levy tribute upon the whole country. . . .[6]
>
> In one aspect it is a matter of uncontrolled corporate imperialism and giant enterprise aggregations. The profligate dispensation of privileges under incorporation laws may have accelerated the industrialization of America. . . . But they are surely ill designed to sustain progress or tolerable operation of the economy they promoted. Turned loose with inordinate powers, corporations have vastly overorganized most industries. Having perhaps benefited briefly by corporate organization, America might now be better off if the corporate form had never been invented or never made available to private enterprise. . . .[7]

Simons clearly recognized the need for community constraints on the market, and he advocated strong laws against merger and expansion beyond a certain size.[8] His concern for localism and community made him favor public ownership of utilities, railroads, and any other industry that was not competitive. An early critic of the powerful nexus of corporate and political power concentrated in broker state regulatory schemes, this highly respected conservative teacher of Milton Friedman declared that "every industry should be either effectively competitive or socialized."[9]

PUBLIC VS. PRIVATE EFFICIENCY

The dominant role of the giant corporation in our society is buttressed by outworn ideological clichés that give excessive credit to its economic efficiency at the same time they absurdly characterize the inefficiencics of a government that itself is hobbled in its capacity to act rationally by corporate influence. This is partly because government inefficiency is easier to identify than private-sector inefficiency. Government lives in a fishbowl. The books of public agencies are open, and the media feel they have a right to information about public figures. We scrutinize every nickel of public spending and ignore rip-offs and inefficiencies in private business that cost us as much, and more, in high prices and shoddy products and services. We make jokes about the Post Office but forget about the Penn Central collapse. Exaggerated and oversimplified parodies of government replace rational assessment.

One source of bias is the structure of media control. British journalist Henry Fairlie recalls:

> A few years ago I attended one of those pompous week-long seminars at the Aspen Institute to discuss investigative reporting with a number of celebrated American editors and newspapermen. I made my point that there was an economic system that needed inquiry and at last burst out against the imperviousness of my American colleagues by saying that I would write without payment for them a series of articles to be entitled, I Have an Enemy at Chase Manhattan. But there were no takers; and Walter Ridder, the owner of Ridder newspapers, made a very funny speech on the final morning of the seminar, saying that he had tossed and turned all night wondering why we don't do what Henry asks, and attack the capitalists, and that as dawn had broken across the Rockies he had found the answer: Because I am one of them. . . .[10]

Another source of bias derives from the fact that efficiency in the public mind is identified with profitability, and we have for the most part restricted public agencies to those things that are inherently not profitable. *By definition* we have declared the public sector inefficient. Even in those areas where there is some similarity between what the private and public sectors do, we usually compare "apples and oranges."

The rise of private delivery services that can often deliver packages faster in and between major metropolitan areas is often cited as "proof" of the private sector's superiority over the public postal system. But private delivery businesses are profitable precisely because they concentrate on those parts of the business that are profitable—big-city commercial deliveries. The job that society has given the Post Office is to show up at the front door of every business and residence in America five and six days a week with whatever anyone else in the world has decided to send them. Private business lobbyists, moreover, have prevented the Post Office from fully competing for certain types of profitable delivery business and from developing certain types of technologies reserved for the private sector. The Post Office must also subsidize educational materials and books and magazines and is forced to maintain service in the most remote rural areas where the per-citizen cost is extremely high.[11] Claiming that private delivery systems are more efficient than the Post Office is like saying the football halfback is more efficient than the tackle because the former scores more touchdowns.

Despite our pervasive antigovernment ideology, the record of public agencies in economic activities is by no means so bad. During World War II the federal government created a variety of efficient businesses —such as aluminum and steel mills and the oil pipeline from Texas to the East Coast—all of which were later purchased by the private sector. Among other activities, the government currently operates civilian airports, builds ships, buys and sells real estate (managing a third of the nation's land), and efficiently administers giant pension and insurance programs. The Department of Defense owns defense production facilities leased to contractors. There are also a wide variety of quasi-public enterprises—public authorities that operate facilities such as ports and harbors, transit systems, recreation areas, bridges, and turnpikes. Typically, these are self-contained corporations operating outside the civil service with boards appointed by governors and mayors. Revenues and expenditures are separate from general taxes and expenditures; surpluses are sometimes turned over to the state, sometimes held for expansion, and deficits must normally be approved by the legislature.

The state of Wisconsin has run what appears to be the most efficient life insurance company in the nation—the State Life Fund, created by Republican populist Governor Robert LaFollette in 1917. The company is solvent and unsubsidized and sells life insurance for 10 to 40 percent less than its private competitors. It has no sales agents and does its business entirely by mail. A legacy from early midwestern populism is the state-run Bank of North Dakota. The bank is the depository for state funds and accepts individual and commercial deposits. It is prohibited from making direct loans on its own, but it does participate with private banks in making loans to businesses. The bank has operated profitably since 1919.

In addition to banking and insurance, states operate liquor stores, hotels and resorts, and lotteries. South Dakota makes and sells cement, Nebraska produces and sells hog cholera serum, and the state of Virginia has been in the limestone business.[12] The city of Portland, Maine, once was in the coal and wood fuel business, the city of Camilla, Georgia, used to sell ice to its citizens, and the city of Los Angeles once owned its own newspaper. Thousands of cities run their own water companies—silent, mundane daily testimony to the fact that public enterprise can do a solid job when it has a straightforward mandate.

A Twentieth Century Fund study of public authority operations in several states and cities found that with some exceptions, "the present system of public authories has been generally successful at producing good management and effective operations."[13] The major criticism was that public authorities were too conservative in their operations and tended to reflect the interests and the biases of businessmen who dominated their boards.

Still, public enterprise in the United States has been too scattered and idiosyncratic to make easy comparisons with private enterprise. The area where there is enough information to make some rough test of the proposition of private sector superiority is the electric utility industry, where some 20 percent of the U.S. market is served by publicly owned utilities. Even here, comparisons are not perfect. There are, for example, differences in markets: generally, private utilities serve the larger, more profitable urban areas, while public utilities and rural cooperatives serve the less profitable countryside (although a few big cities—for example, Los Angeles, Seattle, and Memphis—have their own power companies). On the other hand, public utilities in the West can take greater advantage of cheaper federal hydroelectric power projects. Public utilities do not pay local taxes and can offer investors tax-free municipal bonds. On the other hand, they do make payments to localities in lieu of taxes, and private utilities have gradually lobbied Congress to reduce their federal taxes. In fact, the law enables private utilities to charge customers for taxes that they do not have to pay. In 1980 this windfall to the 150 largest private utilities came to almost two hundred million dollars.[14]

On the surface, the public enterprises clearly have a better record.

In 1979 public power companies charged 39 percent per kilowatt hour less than private power companies.[15] The latter maintain that this differential is due to taxes and greater use of hydropower. Public power advocates argue that the advantages and disadvantages of each mode even out. But our concern is *efficiency, not the price of electricity.* If we eliminate the disputed costs of producing and distributing power and the tax factor, we can isolate the key area in which comparisons should rationally be made—the cost of administration and management per kilowatt hour. When we do this we find that the public sector consistently performs more efficiently. In 1979 private utilities spent 68 percent more per kilowatt hour on accounting and collection expenses, 75 percent more for customer service, information, and sales costs, and 75 percent more for general administration.[16] The 1979 comparison is not an anamoly. The data show greater management efficiencies for public utilities consistently year after year.

The record also shows that public utilities have been far more responsive to the need for conservation and the development of renewable resources than have investor-owned companies. Municipally owned electric companies led the way in shifting advertising from promoting sales to promoting energy conservation, while most private companies continued to resist promoting conservation because it would further depress sales.[17] Public utilities also led the fight against oil companies' efforts to charge higher prices. When the price of oil rose in 1975, for example, Union Oil Company doubled the price of geothermal energy delivered to the privately owned Pacific Gas and Electric Company. PG&E paid the increase and passed on the cost. When faced with an oil company's outrageous prices, the publicly owned utility in Jacksonville, Florida, withheld payment, took the oil company to court, and won a settlement of $1.5 million, which was promptly refunded to its customers.[18]

Public enterprise is far more common abroad. In Western Europe public enterprises account for 8–12 percent of total employment and 15–30 percent of total capital investment.[19] Six of the largest twelve and fifteen of the largest fifty of Western Europe's industrial firms are wholly or substantially owned by governments.[20] Electric utilities in most Western industrial countries are publicly owned. Coal mines in England and France are owned by the government. The West German, Canadian, French, Italian, and British governments are major shareholders in their respective oil and gas industries and have substantial ownership in iron and steel and airlines. The banking industries of West Germany, France, and Italy are largely government-owned. In 1982 the socialist government of François Mitterrand in France continued a long tradition when it included the remaining private banks and five conglomerate multinationals in the public sector.

In many countries publicly owned automobile companies compete with private firms. Renault in France (which now owns 48 percent of American Motors) and Alfa Romeo in Italy are two of the best-known examples. Forty percent of the shares in Volkswagen are owned by West German government agencies, and the British government recently acquired 78 percent of the stock in British Leyland Motor Corporation. The Swedish government is the largest single shareholder in Volvo and has some ownership in the aluminum, aircraft manufacturing, electronics, and shipbuilding sectors.[21]

Lufthansa, Air France, British Airways, Air Canada, and Air Italia are all government corporations. The Japanese government owns 46 percent of Japan Air Lines, and the Dutch government owns 70 percent of KLM. Swissair is 25 percent owned by the federal government, cantons, and various government agencies of Switzerland.[22] The Swedish government owns 25 percent of the nation's domestic timberland, and it mines 70 percent of the nation's iron ore. The Canadian provinces of Alberta, Saskatchewan, and British Columbia own large portions of the provinces' gas, coal, and timberland. Saskatchewan owns half a million acres of farmland that it leases back to young farmers who couldn't otherwise afford the investment.[23]

The experience of public enterprise in the West suggests that, contrary to the common assumption, public enterprise has *not* been as a whole less efficient than private enterprise, and in many cases has been superior. Given the wide variety of political and economic circumstances involved, it is not surprising that the behavior of public enterprises, like the behavior of private ones, has been uneven. Our concern here is not to prove the superiority of one over the other but simply to examine the widespread impression that government enterprises must by their very nature be less efficient than private ones. The evidence is that such is not the case.

Many nationalizations have been extremely successful. For example, the British government nationalized the coal industry in 1947 when it was composed of numerous small, inefficient, and often unsafe mines. The National Coal Board took over these small mines and combined them into regional groups. At the local level managers have considerable autonomy, and major capital investment decisions made at the national level are handled relatively quickly. In his study of British public enterprise, Professor William A. Robson found that within ten years after nationalization the productivity of British mines had become the highest in Europe, and safety standards had improved. Robson concluded in his study, "The truest answer that can be given to the question about the performance of the nationalized industries since they were taken over is that each one of them is undoubtedly in a better condition than it would have been under private enterprise or, as was the case with gas and electricity, divided between private and municipal ownership."[24]

A similar conclusion was reached by another British researcher, Richard Pryke, who found that between 1948 and 1968, productivity among public firms was actually higher than among private ones. There is some evidence that the productivity of public enterprises may have declined relative to private enterprises in the 1970s. In large part this seems to be a result of the greater freedom that private sector managers have to lay off workers when hard times appear. Private firms are thus more able to shift the costs of unemployment to the public sector as a whole, while public firms tend to absorb more of these costs on their own books.[25, 26] University of Michigan economist William Shepherd concluded in his own study of the British economy, "The broad experience of British public enterprises is that performance can be equal to or better than private enterprises would probably yield."[27]

Across the Channel, French public enterprises in railroads, aviation, electricity, and automobiles have been responsible for much of France's industrial innovation and, in the case of aviation and autos, a significant part of her manufacturing exports. The performance of the government-owned Renault, for example, has been successful by any market criteria. And while the joint British-French Concorde project has been an economic loser, the joint French-German-British Airbus has been a winner.

There are, of course, many examples of public enterprises losing money because of political decisions to serve unprofitable markets or to keep prices low. There are also examples of public enterprise mismanagement. But given the mystique of private enterprise and the bias against public enterprise, it is important to bear in mind that where clear comparisons can be made, public ownership has a decent history on the private sector's own ground of individual firm efficiency.

A NEW MIX FOR THE MIXED ECONOMY

Must government be *inherently* bureaucratic, wasteful, clumsy, and burdened by red tape? Must we rely forever on the giant corporation to manage all major economic activities—with all the implications this has for maintaining the power of corporate influence in the broker state? The answer to both questions is no—at least not if we choose to build upon the best experience available to us as we move through the next two decades.

"The role of the government, when one contemplates reform," writes John Kenneth Galbraith, "is a dual one."

> The government is a major part of the problem; it is also central to the remedy. It is part of the problem of unequal development, inequality in income distribution, poor distribution of public resources, environmental damage and bogus or emasculatory regulation. And it is upon the government that reliance must be placed for solution.
>
> Both roles of the government require the same remedy—that it be broken free from the control of the corporate planning system. Until the government is so emancipated, simplistic proposals for government action will be useless. . . . No one can appeal with confidence for vital therapy to the village doctor if he serves even more devotedly as the local undertaker.[28]

A new mix for the mixed economy would include greater reliance on public firms *where they are appropriate either to free public decision-making from excessive private influence, or when needed to implement the requirements of a coherent plan.* Despite the drumbeat of opposition to "big government" in America, the corporate sector has supported the establishment of one or another public enterprise or quasi-public enterprise corporations such as Comsat, Conrail, the Export-Import Bank, the "synfuel" corporation, bridge and tunnel authorities, and so forth, *when it has benefited their interests.* Relieved of ideological blinders against all public economic activity, a sensible overall policy would treat both public and private institutions as instruments to implement strategies for a more prosperous and equitable society. Private enterprise clearly has an advantage in producing and delivering goods in a truly competitive market where there is an identity between ownership and management. It would be absurd to promote the spread of public enterprise in sectors of the economy well served by small- and medium-sized businesses. As we move away from the small entrepreneur-manager, the advantage of private enterprise weakens. At the other end of the scale, the giant multinational is often as bureaucratic an institution as government, and, given the examples of successful foreign public enterprises, it is doubtful that the internal efficiencies of General Motors would be any different if, like Renault, it were wholly government-owned.

We have already proposed two public enterprises with specific planning functions—a grain board and a federal energy corporation—and we shall propose a national development bank. Another sector that might be considered is military production. Substantial military contractors dependent on government purchases are hardly enterprises operating in a classical free market. The fact that they are private firms free of the public disclosure and accountability constraints of public agencies is a major cause of the inordinate power of the military-industrial complex. *Their* plans often determine *our* national decisions; then *we* blame "government" for waste! Nationalization of a few of the largest military contractors whose work is all or overwhelmingly military could reduce at least one source of the dynamic expansion in the military budget. The cost overruns, padded bids, and corruption that are so widespread in the present system suggest that government-owned military producers could hardly do much worse.

Under almost any long-range scenario we can expect an expansion of the amount of the nation's capital investment generated by direct government investment or indirect subsidies. Whether the vehicle is a national development bank, Felix Rohatyn's proposed new Reconstruction Finance Corporation, or general "industrial policies," the taxpayer, through the federal government, will likely provide increasing amounts of equity financing (or sophisticated loan arrangements that are de facto covers for equity financing) to private industry. Common sense suggests that if government is to take the risk, it should have some say about how things are run—at the very least by having representation on boards of directors to protect the taxpayers' interest. The states of Massachusetts, Connecticut, California, and Alaska all have already established public agencies that take equity positions to help finance new enterprises in selected areas. A public holding company —a rough American equivalent of the Canadian Development Corporation (49 percent of which is owned by the Canadian government) —would afford flexibility to strategies involving federal investments in public enterprises. The aim is not to create a new bureaucracy but to establish a mechanism to help achieve overall planning goals. A four-year plan to revitalize heavy manufacturing might involve buying enough shares in U.S. Steel and Alcoa to achieve significant government influence on the board. Another four-year plan stressing health care might suggest going into the market for seats on a few pharmaceutical companies. Public investment to support a national transportation plan might include a seat on the board of a railroad car maker.

In a community-sustaining economy, a new mix is also important at the local level—especially since locally controlled firms add to stability. As we discussed in Chapter Eight, in recent years there have been a small but growing number of local efforts to create worker- and cooperatively owned firms. Since the 1920s, a significant number of worker-owned plywood companies have operated successfully in the Pacific Northwest. The first were started in the 1920s by Scandinavian immigrants who had an experience and tradition of cooperation. Although their number has been reduced by the recent housing depression, by the mid-1970s they comprised about one eighth of the U.S. plywood industry, with sales ranging from three million to twenty million dollars annually. There are at least a hundred other American firms in which rank-and-file local employees own all or substantial portions of the shares.[29] This estimate does not include the much larger number of companies in which ownership is held primarily by managers, nor the one to two thousand small craft and similar worker cooperatives. As we saw in the examples of Youngstown, Ohio, and Herkimer, New York, pressure for worker ownership has spread in response to plant closures in an environment of high unemployment. Industrial workers faced with the prospect of long-term unemployment have chosen to buy out their plant and run it themselves. The process has been aided by the employee stock ownership plan provision of the Internal Revenue Code, which permits tax-deductible contributions to employee-owned trusts. The trusts borrow money to buy company shares, and the workers use subsequent profits to pay back the bank. There are some five thousand companies currently involved in such trusts.[30]

A 1977 survey of thirty worker-owned companies by the University of Michigan's Social Research Institute concluded that such firms showed a higher level of profit than conventionally owned firms of the same size in the same industry. Since many of the companies were failing when the workers took them over, the record is even more impressive. Despite the sometimes controversial overtones of "worker ownership," the efforts have also had the strong support of local businesspeople. In Youngstown, for instance, although many were justifiably skeptical that enough money could be raised, businesses whose future was dependent upon local business conditions—banks, real estate, retail stores—supported the "Save Our Valley" effort. (In contrast, local branch managers of national manufacturing firms—particularly rival steel companies—were openly hostile.)

Worker and community ownership of plants that would otherwise be shut down is obviously no panacea. By the time a corporation is ready to close a plant, it usually has been allowed to deteriorate so far that it is difficult to re-create a competitive, viable business. And often new worker-owned enterprises must compete with a former owner who has shifted business to another factory and has maintained competitive advantages for himself. Another burden is the large amount of debt financing that is typically needed, a problem made even more difficult by high interest rates in the past few years. On top of this is the problem of beginning with an unorthodox management structure that must be built by trial and error. The plywood companies in the Pacific Northwest developed in an era of high demand for plywood —a time when it was easier to experiment, since high prices helped pay for the cost of mistakes.

More than just a few of the efforts to save jobs and help stabilize the local economy through worker/community ownership have also benefited the selling corporation more than the workers: Tax advantages and loan guarantees have given the seller a better selling price than he might have gotten on the open market. Despite the difficulties, it is clear that so long as capital is excessively mobile and threatens local community stability, such efforts will continue to grow. Since 1978 legislation has been introduced at the local, state, and federal level to require advance notice of plant closings and to aid worker- and community-owned firms as a form of local self-help that transcends old left-right categories.[31] Isolated from a coherent planning effort, legislative programs of this kind are likely to remain marginal. In the context of a serious strategy of community full employment and sustained full production, however, technical assistance, loans, and loan guarantees could steadily build up locally accountable and community-based enterprises as a way both to add stability to local economies and to increase democratic and participatory institutions at the core of a new planning system.

In such a context emphasis could also be given to another model in the institutional mosaic—the quasipublic community development corporation. The "CDC"—modeled in part on the Plymouth Colony, the country's earliest economic institution—is a product of efforts by people living in depressed urban and rural neighborhoods to generate and attract capital. The theory of the CDC is that by organizing community political and economic support for new businesses—protecting them from crime, giving them technical assistance, helping them fill out forms with bankers, and operating some support businesses directly—such community-backed efforts can help initiate growth in an economic wasteland.

Several hundred CDCs are operating in various parts of the country today, but only a handful have developed sufficient capital to make a major economic impact on their communities. The most well known is the Bedford-Stuyvesant Restoration Project in a deteriorated section of Brooklyn, New York. The project was begun by the late Robert Kennedy after he was jeered and hooted in a 1967 visit to the area by residents angry at politicians who had promised much and delivered little. Spending $63 million over a decade, the program has helped start 116 businesses, providing 3,300 jobs; placed nearly 7,000 local persons in jobs or job-training programs; renovated 3,337 home exteriors (providing jobs or training for 4,364 local people); and completed over 660 new or restored homes. In southeastern Kentucky, the Kentucky Highlands Investment Corporation has similarly provided employment for area residents, many of whom lack traditional job skills. The CDC has helped start businesses that now have annual sales of over $10 million in an area noted more for coal mining than for manufacturing. The largest, Outdoor Venture, employs over 120 area residents in its tent-making operations.[32]

Worker-owned firms and community-owned development corporations are modern variants of the cooperative model—a form of local participatory enterprise that has also expanded in response to new era economic problems. Cooperatives have, of course, always been widespread in agriculture. Some are large bureaucratized institutions; many are small and democratically managed. By the mid-1970s the 7,500 agricultural marketing, supply, and service co-ops had a business volume of $57 billion, about a third of the total agribusiness market.[33] Land O'Lakes, Sunkist, Ocean Spray, Agway, and Welch's are some of the most familiar. But it is in retail food that the greatest co-op expansion has occurred. Largely in response to stagflation, the number of food cooperatives in the United States more than quadrupled, from 227 in 1971 to 1,060 in 1977, and the number of members involved rose from 533,000 to 1.2 million. The movement helped spur the creation of the National Consumer Cooperative Bank in 1978. The bank is modeled on the Farm Credit System, which over the years allowed farmers themselves to take control of the farm credit bank as their loans were repaid. As cooperatives repay the cooperative bank's initial capitalization of $30 million, they, too, rather than the federal government, will become its owners.[34]

Like all innovative institutions, community corporations, worker cooperatives, and the Cooperative Bank have suffered from management problems and often political attack. They have been largely isolated and alone in their efforts to nurture the cooperative experi-

ence, but they represent an important element in any serious effort to
extend democracy to the economy.

At both the national and local level, reducing the power of vested
corporate interests and diversifying the institutional mix in the economy open the way to a more honest examination of government and
private decision-making. But this on its own does not resolve other
major difficulties. For example, bureaucracy creates problems of communication, coordination, and the need for incentive in both public
and private institutions. And short-term time horizons are a problem
in the public sector as well as the private. In public institutions, the
cycle of elections means that everything comes up for grabs every two
or four years. Regardless of the individual worker's performance, he
or she is subject to periodic wrenching change. In public institutions
the discontinuity problem also creates a huge gap between the interests
of the permanent civil service and the interests of elected policymakers.
The former become extremely cautious and slow to suggest new incentives. The civil servant who is too responsive to the policies of one
administration jeopardizes his standing with the next. "Presidents
come and go," is the old Washington axiom, "but I'll be here till I'm
sixty-five."

The fundamental answer to increasingly short-term time horizons
in the private sector is a coherent full-production plan which reduces
long-term investment uncertainty. Similarly, there is no way to address the public time-horizon problem seriously without recognizing
the central role of agreed-upon goals that affirm stability as a major
priority. Nor can the problem of competing interests be dealt with;
Roy Ash, who after running Litton Industries directed the U.S. Office
of Management and Budget, observes: "Just imagine yourself as chief
executive officer where your board of directors is made up of your
employees, customers, suppliers, and competitors. How would you
like to run that business and try to be effective?"[35]

Without firm guidelines to hold on to, public officials are vulnerable
to the demands of any strong constituency that wants something they
have the legal power to give. Only the existence of an explicit plan
gives government officials a way to defend themselves against the
conflicting pressures of contending interests and constituencies. The
more explicit the plan, moreover, the more an official is restrained from
exercising arbitrary power. Explicit goals also mitigate the problem of
discontinuity. A multiyear plan that overlaps two or more administrations provides a more sensible way of measuring success than the

number of projects a politician can attach his name to. A publicly announced plan can also make the bureaucracy responsive: John F. Kennedy's pledge to put a man on the moon was the driving force behind one of the most outstanding government accomplishments of the century. Only an explicit plan, finally, provides the citizen with clear criteria to judge and discipline the bureaucracy.

To the extent that a goal or a plan is the product of elite planners achieving agreement around a table—rather than of widespread public discussion and debate—its power to transcend bureaucratic problems is limited. Then special-interest policies, pork-barreling, and inefficiency must grow. Efforts to try to promulgate a consensus by institutions isolated from decision-making by popularly elected official bodies can neither discipline the government nor enlist the active support of the people. The difficult processes of democracy cannot be short-circuited. The planning by stealth and arrogance that is implicit in the planning formulas of the corporate industrializers promises neither a sense of mission nor the ongoing support necessary to sustain long-term strategies. The development of economic goals anchored in broad-based values through a process of democratic participation is preferable not simply because it conforms to democratic values; it is preferable primarily because it is the only planning mode that can work.

Chapter 15

TOWARD DEMOCRATIC PLANNING

Democratic planning means making hidden choices open and explicit. It is a reasonable assumption that this will make for better decisions. But democratic planning cannot guarantee that we will do well, *only that we will know what we are doing.* In America today, the problem of planning is the problem of democracy. The late Kalman H. Silvert observed in *The Reason for Democracy:*

> Busing, pollution, racism, violence, crime, the cities—these are not problems of democracy. They are the problems created by a lack of democracy. They are specific maladjustments in a society that has not mustered the skill, temper or power to keep itself together. The problems of democracy, however, concern instead how to permit intelligence and effectiveness to be brought to bear in the re-establishment of self-governance, self-determination, self-adjustment, and self-definition.[1]

Yet the specific problems are real and must be solved or they will unravel society. The economic planning task therefore is a dual one. We have to create institutions to solve the concrete problems that press down upon us. And we have to do so in a way that steadily increases our own capacity to make those institutions accountable to us. We must accordingly reconcile two seemingly contradictory tendencies. One is the need for *action* to get things done. This is a *centralizing* tendency. Responsibilities may be delegated, masses of people may be involved, and decisions may be made openly, but the need for action inevitably centralizes power and authority, whether in a bureaucracy or a corporation. The second force is the need for *participation.* This is a *decentralizing* tendency, and it tends to slow things down. But it also makes for longer-lasting decisions. Once decisions are made on the basis of consensus they do not have to be resold over and over to the people involved. The legitimacy of the action has been established.

Issues of decentralization and centralization involve both size and function. At one end of the spectrum of planning institutions are hierarchically structured private corporations dedicated to profit growth. Close by are public bureaucracies such as highway building agencies, the military, cancer research institutes, etc., which require more consensus than private corporations but still can achieve specific goals most efficiently when left alone. At the other end are legislatures, whose primary task is the development of consensus but who have little capacity for concrete action. Cooperatives, worker-managed private firms, and volunteer agencies fall into place in other parts of the spectrum.

The present public sector gives us the worst of both modes. With no accountability to an overall plan, action institutions representing different constituencies battle each other and work at cross purposes, undercutting each other's function. We all know, for example, that there are fundamental choices to make between economic development and environmental protection. And we are all agreed that we must reach some accommodation between these two legitimate concerns. But under piecemeal broker state planning, decisions are forced to the top of very narrow, interest-group-dominated agencies. The "trade-offs" occur through battles among giant corporations, government agencies working at cross purposes (for example, the Corps of Engineers and the Environmental Protection Agency), and nationally organized environmental groups. Each has its constituencies and its congressional allies. The struggles often lead to long-drawn-out court fights. The process of decision-making is removed from the individual citizen, whose role increasingly is to cheer from the sidelines while lawyers battle it out in court.

Nor is the present system undergirded by consensus-building goals. Without a clear commitment to maintain employment in specific communities, environmental regulations can indeed eliminate jobs, as can efforts to promote national economic efficiency by encouraging labor-saving automation. By its very nature, piecemeal planning is an attempt to impose the interests of one group or one sector on the rest of society. Quite naturally, other interests feel threatened and attempt to obstruct, leading to overall social waste and conflict. Economic planning must have a positive answer to the average citizen's reasonable question: What's in it for me? The answer cannot be that *we* will beat the Japanese to 40 percent of the world's computer business, although *you* will lose your job or your small business in the process.

WHO PLANS?

The power to define options brings with it the power to influence the choice of those options. Among the reindustrializers and corporate planners there is a clear preference for keeping this function independent of—"insulated from"—the elected government. *Business Week*, for instance, offers an unabashed, corporate-dominated planning process based on achieving a consensus of big government, big labor, and big business. The idea is a throwback to an earlier period of broker state history. But the fact is the "big three" are *all* discredited: Very few Americans buy the proposition that a small group of people representing these "institutions" should have authority to determine which industries should live and which should die, which communities will be sacrificed and which will receive the windfall bonanza of subsidized growth. Moreover, the main financing institution—a new "RFC" isolated from full production planning—is an institution *designed* (like the New York City Municipal Assistance Corporation ["Big Mac"], upon which it is modeled) to extract wage and other concessions from industries and communities in exchange for its financing. Like Volcker's dictum at the national level, such industrial planning at the community level will have the effect of reducing Americans' living standards.

A more "liberal" solution to the problem of "Who plans?" is to entrust the process to an elite corps of public servants and technocrats, on the model of MITI in Japan or the French civil servants who developed Le Plan. This would put decisions in the hands of a relatively small group of highly trained, competent technocrats who have no particular personal stake in the distribution of costs and benefits from the plan. The presumed nonpolitical objectivity of the model is attractive, and the experiences of Japan and France have something to recommend it.

In other countries technocratic elitism has a better chance of working because the elites have historically come from the same small social circles as the rest of the political and business leadership of the nation. There is also a more developed sense of public service on the part of European and Japanese bureaucracies: a career in the civil services brings with it high status and attracts the countries' most dedicated and able people, a situation that does not exist in the United States. The lack of a competent, prestigious bureaucracy whose concern is stability and caution has often led to arbitrary government by U.S. technocrats. It can be seen in the high-handed, insensitive behavior of such bureaucracies as the Corps of Engineers and the old Atomic Energy Commission. The United States does need to develop and train competent civil servants for the day-to-day operations of a planning system, but an attempt to transfer the MITI model to the United States ignores the lessons of the past thirty years: Without clearly set, publicly enforced guidance, bureaucracy tends to become unaccountable, inaccessible, and, most of all, captive to special interests.

The central problem common to both the reindustrializing corporate planners and the neoliberal technocrats is the mistaken notion that whatever the exact makeup of the planners, they can and should be kept out of the political process. This is a particular fallacy of those who see planning as primarily a problem of economic adjustment to new technologies, trade, or other narrowly defined economic forces. The technocrats give their optimum solution to the politicians, who are expected to "sell" it to the people. But if the politicians cannot deliver—and the evidence strongly suggests that in America they cannot—then the technocratic scenario collapses of its own weight and we are once again trapped in the rubble of "zero sum" politics.

Proposals to establish independent or quasi-independent coordinating "commissions" or boards suffer from a similar defect. Economist Alfred Eichner, for instance, says of planning that "choices require that a bargain be struck *at the top* among all the affected interest groups, with that bargain then ratified, as part of a 'social contract' through the subsequent actions of public officials."[2] An independent or quasi-independent planning entity seems attractive because it seems to avoid the worst give-and-take of interest-group politics. But the idea that interest groups will really look the other way as a commission decides their fate is fatuous. *There is no way to plan behind the public's back.* We cannot responsibly shift capital from one industry to another without repercussions. We cannot responsibly move it to any industry unless we specify where it is to come from—other industries, the elderly, the education budget, national defense. These are political questions that can only be settled democratically. Making the independent planning agency "advisory" fudges the issue and dumps it back onto the lap of Congress and the President. Proposals to insulate the planning process from politics are also flawed on basic organizational grounds in that they insulate planning from the core of the public sector. Effective planning must coordinate the strategic flow of capital. This is not possible if the near-trillion-dollar federal budget is not at the center of the decision-making process. To insulate planning from politics is to isolate it from reality. Rather than giving the planners authority to plan effectively, it deprives them of power and further exacerbates the irrationality of the piecemeal mode of the broker state.

We have learned from the experience of almost every large public or private institution that if the planning function is not directly tied to the power to implement, it becomes irrelevant. To the degree that planning is kept away from the daily routine of the chief executive officer, its benefits get lost. Planning separated from operations does not work. Inasmuch as economic policy will remain the central issue of American domestic politics for some time, any President will inevitably have to put his or her own stamp on economic planning. No solution is perfect, but the most sensible is to provide that the planning apparatus be maintained within the Executive Branch, and its work reviewed, "checks-and-balances" style, by an agency of Congress. Such an Executive Branch institution in effect integrates the functions of the current Council of Economic Advisors and the Office of Management and Budget. The planning agency does not have to be a large bureaucracy. Japan's MITI has only twenty-five hundred employees. The team of French civil servants that develops Le Plan is housed in a small château.[3]

The planners' job is to draw up several multiyear scenarios that provide different ways of achieving specific economic goals. The scenarios must, of course, be translated into multiyear budgets, but their content is not simply dollars. They should spell out priority areas in considerable detail—how many new homes will be built over the next four years, how much solar energy capacity will be in place, what will be the proposed ratio between doctors and population, how much military capability will we need and for what specific purposes.

If infrastructure, low- and moderate-income housing, energy conservation, new technologies, and health maintenance are taken as some of the initial lead sectors in an overall growth plan, the implications for individual industries of the economy—conceived "vertically" (for example, steel, robotics, lumber, pharmaceuticals)—need to be delineated. At the same time, considering the economy in its "horizontal" divisions, the scenarios should identify the impact of such investments on employment, prices, and wage levels. This might generate options for shortening the workweek or for a universal system of sabbaticals as automation and robotization increase.

For private-sector industries over which the government has less direct influence, the plans should identify levels of production that are consistent with the overall public goals. This will establish criteria for an early-warning system. A plan also tells us what we need know about the use of scarce resources such as capital. There is only so much to go around. Let us say, for example, that the agreed-upon economic plan for the period assumes output of 160 million tons of steel per year for the domestic market. Above that level, steel production may be less of a national priority, and tax and other incentives should be scaled back to retard capital investment for the construction of new capacity. Below that level it might be encouraged to stimulate new investment. At present the government helps out the steel industry mainly on the basis of its ability to lobby in Washington. A plan provides a way to judge whether a crisis in the steel industry is a crisis for the country.

Because it is an economic plan rather than simply a budget, the indirect effects of each option also need to be considered. Expanded housing production, for instance, might require encouragement for expansion of the lumber and construction machinery industries, aid to local governments to help resolve land use and zoning problems, and increased job training for building-trade skills. A decision to build a new weapons system might mean a sharply increased demand for scientists and engineers and thus a decline in the pool of talent available for commercial, industrial, health, and other research. Such a decision might be compatible with an increase in housing but not with a major commitment to try simultaneously to dominate the world market in robotics.

If one option calls for increased military spending to strengthen our capacity to protect oil supplies in the Middle East, another might call for spending the same amount of money to generate the equivalent supplies through conservation or building up the national oil inventory. A scenario of conversion from military to civilian production can tell us how many workers in Seattle could be shifted from building airplanes to manufacturing "bullet trains" and subway cars if we so choose.

COMMUNITY-BASED PLANNING

If democracy and planning are to be anchored in local communities, then the system must also have a way for national planning goals to be set at least in part directly by citizens deciding what they need. This requires that as the nation increases its capacity for economic planning, power is built up from below. The rule is that, if a public function can be performed at a more local level, it should be.

Building an effective and dynamic local planning dimension to the system will take time. At present cities and even states lack the authority and power over capital investment that makes economic planning relevant; they are trapped in the mutually destructive competition for business location described in Chapter Eight. But, to the extent the capacity of the national government to target investment geographically grows, localities can plan around such national commitments. If a community is assured, for example, that the town's leading firms will have enough business to hire two thousand workers over the next four years, and maintain stability beyond that period, the town can plan with some confidence for training local young people to take the new jobs; it can encourage local entrepreneurs to become suppliers and to expand retail trade; it can provide local contractors with reliable estimates for housing needs. It can also have sufficient confidence to plan longer-term transportation and bus service effectively and to develop the kinds of energy-conservation approaches that require a sustained commitment.

Fortunately, we do not have to start from scratch. Over the past two decades state and local governments have gradually expanded their general planning experience. They have made investments in technical and organizational skills that can be built upon. The overwhelming majority of cities and towns currently have dozens of different boards and commissions involved in planning. A generation of younger planners has grown up with more experience, knowledge, and flexibility than its predecessors. Advocacy planning—in which planners develop alternative plans for different constituencies, thereby making the planning process more decentralized and democratic—has added an additional dimension. Planning skills are no longer simply the province of architects and people who have gone to city-planning schools; the profession's basic function of projecting the future, creating alternatives, estimating costs, integrating social and physical variables, and debating the merits has become accessible to most citizens.

Moreover, in dozens of states, citizen commissions have authored long-range plans to guide future state government policy. Many have held extensive hearings and local meetings in which citizens have had an opportunity to think and debate such questions as "What do you want your neighborhood to look like ten (or twenty) years from now?"[4] Because most of the efforts have so far been isolated from the direct political process, by and large they have resulted in little more than some good ideas packaged in colorful reports that make a newspaper splash and then sink out of sight. Yet they are initial steps in the evolution of a longer-range *sub*national planning capacity—what author Alvin Toffler has called "anticipatory democracy."

A community-sustaining economic planning strategy can revitalize and build upon the network of people, institutions, and local planning techniques that has been established. *But this is possible only if national planning has local stability and the expansion of democracy as its aim* and if its overall goals are understood and supported at the local level. The task of slowly evolving a truly democratic form of planning is *not* simply one of creating local extensions of the national planning system so that national plans can be more effectively translated into local action. The task is rather to build up a local planning capacity and more democratic economic institutions so that national planning more and more actually reflects people's participation and their views of what they want their locality to look like.

At best the process of fitting national and local planning together will initially be "two steps forward, one step backward." The one certainty is that the process is not predictable. Yet it helps us identify the major elements involved if we begin to think through a broad scenario of how it might work.

For example, the first step might be legislation to require the President to send a national economic plan to Congress by the end of his first year in office. The elements of the first plan would cover overall goals for full employment in the nation's communities, combating inflation in the basic necessities, general environmental standards, national defense, and the promotion of new technological, scientific, and educational objectives. It would also include a comprehensive statement of the fiscal and monetary means to carry them out and any necessary government reorganization.

The four-year plan would end at the completion of the first year of the next President's term, thus requiring each new President to take some responsibility for finishing the plan of his or her predecessor and giving time to prepare his or her own plan. It would attempt to increase long-term stability by changing the frantic and inefficient way in which the economic programs of incoming Presidents are currently prepared. New people, starry-eyed and flush with political victory, now try to put their particular stamp and style on economic policy without time to understand either the workings of the system or to have their proposals properly tested and subjected to debate. Both Jimmy Carter and Ronald Reagan came into office this way, the first with hardly any preconceived notion as to what to do, the second with a group of ideologues who had spent a decade being obsessed with the notion that government can't do anything.

The planning agency would prepare at least two alternatives, making them available to both the President and the public. The President would make his final decisions and send his plan to Congress. The papers upon which the plan was based would be open to both Congress and the public so that the logic (or illogic) of the plan and its parts would be clear.* Congress would have the right to change the plan however it saw fit as long as the overall implications were made explicit and public. It would, however, have to adhere to a strict time limitation for debate and final passage. The adoption of a plan would guide the allocation of the federal budget and the activities of all federal agencies over the next four years.

After the first plan was enacted, the second phase of the system's development would go into effect—the buildup of a capacity to integrate local and state plans into the framework of the next round of national economic planning. Federal money would go into improving local planning competence and stabilizing local jobs for communities above a certain size. At the beginning, local planning would concern itself with employment goals to accommodate present expected growth, environmental stability, necessary local public investment, and health, housing, and education to support such goals.

Beyond this, planning for full production at the community level would require two analytic tools. One is an estimate of the number of jobs needed over, say, a four-year period to attain full employment— a job for every willing and able worker. This would be a straightforward statistical projection based on population, expected growth, the particular makeup of the community's unemployed (skills, education, percentage of handicapped, etc.), and known or expected near-term events, such as the completion of a rail line or the closing of a plant in a declining industry.

The second tool would be a community investment agenda—a listing of local public priorities over the same period. The process of identifying the investment agenda would obviously vary from place to place, depending on local political institutions. Planning does not do away with politics; it puts politics out in the open. Special interests are clear. Alliances between political leaders and economic interests are illuminated. Politics continues to be a realm of deals and compromises, but they are labeled so they can be judged for what they are. In this sense planning is a "truth in economics" law.

The level of detail in the local plans would obviously vary and

*The current Joint Economic Committee and the House and Senate budget committees should be brought together as the basis of a congressional planning capacity; and the current law, which requires a "reconciliation" of all program budgets in a comprehensive decision, should be expanded to stipulate that the implications of decisions be delineated in coherent scenarios.

change as time goes on. Certain items would have to be decided, such as broad land-use patterns, local factors in the cost of basic necessities, employment goals, and capital expenditures. Many details would not need to be included. With experience, each community would begin to identify those things that its own citizens wanted to decide immediately and those things they had found they could put off.

Since planning must be understood as evolutionary, in the first phase the job estimates obviously would give the national government only a rough idea of the number of new jobs needed to sustain full employment in a specific community. Once a full-scale capacity had been developed, a more interactive process could take place. This would involve estimating the number of jobs expected through normal expansion of the national economy. National and regional computer models would help provide these estimates, which would be subtracted from the total jobs needed to give an estimate of the job *deficit* or *surplus* expected in each area. Where there is a deficit, another step is needed: calculation of the local job multiplier—that is, the number of local jobs in services, retail trade, government, and other secondary areas that are generated from each new primary job created. Generally, the larger and more diversified the community economy the higher the multiplier—for example, New York City has a higher local multiplier than Herkimer, New York.

Such calculations give the economic plan initial guidance for the number of new "primary" jobs that have to be created in a community to sustain it at full employment. Upon this basis it is possible at both national and local levels to review alternative options for production and employment, and to reach a politically negotiated national decision.

Once a fully integrated local-national system is in place, we can go beyond this. In a developed system the national planning agency would be responsible for proposing two alternative plans to the President, each of which represented an integration of community and national goals. It would operate along fairly rigid time frames that assured that alternatives be drawn up and offered to Congress by a certain date. Congress would also be required to make its decision in a timely way. As with the current federal budget, after a comprehensive plan was adopted, all policies of the government would be required to conform to it, unless changes were made by specific agreement of the President and Congress. The final plan—the integration of community needs and functions that must be served at the national level—would involve two parts: first, a federal budget divided into current operating expenses; second, a capital budget that separates out those expenditures which are investments for the future.

A fundamental mechanism to guarantee that the plan meets its key goals would be a requirement that the government ensure that a job exist for everyone able to work who does not get one through the normal functions of the economy. A provision for a guaranteed job was included in the original version of the 1975 proposed Humphrey-Hawkins bill. Making the government the employer of last resort and the right to a job enforceable by law establishes a clear standard. If a person is willing and able to work and cannot find a job, the federal government as employer of last resort is forced to hire him or her to do useful work at wages commensurate with his or her experience.

A job guarantee does not mean that the government is forced to employ people who clearly cannot or do not want to work. Those with special employment problems—mental illness, alcoholism, etc.—should be offered medical and other appropriate help. The unskilled and illiterate should be offered training. But the small percentage of the population that is looking to rip off the system should not be given cushy jobs. *Only when society has a true commitment to full employment can we clearly distinguish those who do not want to pull their share of the load.* As long as we have involuntary unemployment, as long as there are not enough seats in the theater for everyone who is waiting in line, society is obligated in some way to furnish help to everyone.

CAPITAL ALLOCATION

A serious national planning process will need to reorganize and strengthen the government's capacity to encourage capital to flow into priority areas. Many tools are available: federal spending for procurement, tax incentives and penalties, a variety of business assistance loans and loan guarantees, federal restraints on the use of pension funds, investments in natural resource development, and industrial R&D. Coordinated in an overall public investment plan, such activities could be made much more effective, and the bureaucracies that administer them could be made accountable through measurement of specific outcomes.

Our capacity to implement planning can be augmented through the creation of a national development bank. One function of such a bank would be to reorganize the present lending activities of the government under one roof and to assure that they conform to the general requirements of the overall plan. A second function would be to organize needed investments that the private sector is unwilling or unable to make in certain industries and geographic areas. The bank would be capitalized by a direct appropriation of the U.S. Treasury and would then sell bonds and other securities in the nation's money markets. One important source of investment capital is workers' pension funds. In these functional aspects, the development bank would be similar to the RFC proposed by Felix Rohatyn or Senator Edward Kennedy's National Development Corporation.[5] The bank would not, however, be a free-floating institution; it would be required to make loans and equity investments in private and public projects that support the plan's goals.

Public development banks and banklike institutions have a long tradition in capitalist countries. Their primary functions are, first, to finance an adequate economic infrastructure needed to attract private capital to an area to start businesses—transportation, sewage and water supply, housing, industrial parks and so forth; and second, to provide capital at lower interest rates to designated private-sector institutions. In the United States, agencies have been set up to make loans to farmers, small businesses, home buyers, businesses in depressed areas, and a wide range of other special sectors of the economy. The states have also created a variety of narrow-purpose development finance institutions to lure businesses within their borders.* These also make low-interest loans, buy and renovate buildings and lease them out to business customers at low rates, build access roads and industrial parks, and generally act as subsidizer to new business in order to induce private investment to create more jobs and taxes. Building on such precedents, the national development bank would be decentralized in regional and local subsidaries. Each regional bank would provide financing both for infrastructure investment and for equity financing of high-risk community enterprises.†

Another way to help guide capital to priority areas is to require the reorganized Federal Reserve Board to create differential reserve requirements and rediscount rates, and otherwise, through regulation, to encourage private banks to make loans for purposes that support the plan and discourage those that waste capital in speculation, mergers, and excessive or risky overseas investing. By making some loans more

---

*In 1978, twenty-nine states had programs for state or local loans for existing plant expansion, nineteen states had loan programs for new building construction, and forty-five states had city or county general-obligation bond financing available for industrial development.[6]

†In the longer haul, such regional institutions could help form the basis for a more autonomous reorganized direct regional planning system. See p. 276.

expensive to make than others, banks and other financial institutions can decisively influence the pattern of investment. If a steel company had to pay a substantially higher interest rate for buying an existing oil company than for expanding its capacity to produce rails, it would be more likely to concentrate on the latter.

Let us say that national development planning calls for an acceleration of capital flowing into robotic engineering and new rail and mass transit systems. The development bank would make long-term funds available for such investment projects in communities in which employment growth was below the national average. The Federal Reserve Board would then encourage the private banking system to give special attention to the financing of companies expanding into robotic engineering and other high-technology industries. The federal government would increase investment in these industries through federal tax code adjustments as well as direct investments and assistance to engineering schools, technical vocational schools, etc. Within the scope of a geographically determined decision, competition for assistance would be encouraged wherever possible.

The public balance sheet would focus on community. It would estimate the cost of *not* conserving capital—that is, the cost of reproducing somewhere else the abandoned housing, factories, stores, and public facilities that would result from doing nothing in the abandoned area. The system would estimate the energy costs both of construction and of moving populations out of the compact older cities to the sprawling, transportation-intensive newer ones. These costs would represent an upper limit on the amount of public assistance that was justified in any given situation. They might also suggest that government programs to finance business, housing, sewers, roads, etc., in areas of excessive growth would be restricted or made more costly. Federal help would be conditioned on the provision of local matching resources. The federal government cannot guarantee the economic future of communities that are inherently economically unviable. But where the desire to maintain a community is particularly fierce—as evidenced both by its dedication and by its financial commitment—it should be possible to receive assistance in the face of large economic odds.

Since the development of democratic planning must obviously be understood as evolutionary, it is impossible to try to guess at the details of how it might look in a decade. Moving away from broker state planning to democratic planning will be difficult. But it is important to remember that we are not concerned with planning the entire economy. What are important are the strategic society-shaping decisions. We are looking for ways to build a society with strong structural supports and a great many local spaces for hollowing out. What must be planned and stabilized is "the setting of life, not life itself."

Chapter 16

REBUILDING AMERICA

The American economy, the wealthiest in history, is rudderless. For roughly three decades following World War II we rode a wave of prosperity. That wave is spent. Buffeted by the pressures of a new economic era and succumbing to the illusion that the widening "trade-off" between unemployment and high prices represents the only real ity, economic policy has careened between inflation and deflation, deepening stagnation and sporadic upturns.

There is no reason that hope cannot be restored to this bountiful continent. But the United States cannot recover its economic health unless the federal government becomes a more competent manager of the economy. We have argued that an extension of government is inevitable, irrespective of political ideologies. A worldwide metamorphosis is transforming the broker state into an increasingly complex, if covert, planning system. The difference between liberals and conservatives lies less in their view of the appropriate size of government than in whom government serves. To be relevant to our new condition, our political attention must shift away from ideological resistance to government and get on to such questions as: Will government management be rational or irrational—that is, planned or unplanned? If planned, who will plan? For what goals?

Economics is the social science of choices. It teaches us that the world is a finite place and that therefore everything has a cost. "There is no free lunch," goes the axiom, although it omits the important point that the diner is not always the one who pays.

Before Keynes, economics was almost exclusively the study of the behavior of individual units in the marketplace. Economics was *microeconomics*— it sought to answer the question of why firms, consumers, and workers made the choices they did when faced with changing conditions of the market. Participants in the world described by microeconomics are not so much actors as *reactors*. The world surrounding them is "given"—assumed to be beyond their power to control. Choice can only be individual, private, atomistic. This perspective makes microeconomics particularly supportive of keeping the government out of the economy.

Keynes' *macroeconomic* model, which was concerned with movement of the economy as a whole, included the government as a participant in the marketplace. Keynes showed that what for the classical economist was "given"—the total amount of consumption and investment in the system—could be changed by deliberate government action. Thus he dramatically widened the scope of economic choice. For the first time a non-Marxist economics showed that individuals did not have to be merely reactors to the marketplace; through their collective influence on government they could determine the economy's future. Recessions became less like hurricanes and more like airplane crashes. And for a brief moment economics discarded its reputation as the dismal science.

Keynesian economics was a first step toward planning, but only a first step. The critical problems of the new era were beyond his model; macroeconomics has enabled us to avoid another Great Depression but not to solve the worsening "jobs–prices" trade-off. The neoconservative reaction pushed economics backward, once again narrowing our horizons. The retreat to nineteenth-century economic ideology brought with it the ideas that choices are imposed on us and that economic life is primarily a question of reaction to forces outside our control.

There is no question that hard choices confront us. But the choices are ours, and we have the power to frame them. The statement that there is not enough soup for everyone does not necessarily justify the statement that *you* have to go without eating. At the very least you may want to know: How much is there? Might we make some more? Can't we share what we have? Is there anything else to eat? And, of course: Why me? Confronted with the prospect of going without supper, you will want to widen the horizon of the discussion—you might discover some new choices.

We have proposed choices centered around a strategy for resolving the seeming incompatibility between full employment and stable prices. It calls for regionally balanced full employment simulated by increases in domestic public investment and an anti-inflation program built around assuring access to the basic necessities of life. A commitment to sustained full production in turn can help us embark on the longer-term task of decentralizing and democratizing our economic institutions, both public and private.

The next question is obvious: What are the political prospects for the substantial changes needed to resolve our crisis? It is easy to be pessimistic about them. Money dominates politics. Those who control large amounts of private capital are resourceful, are quick to defend their prerogatives, and rarely act in other than their own short-term interest. As one labor leader said of the steel industry: "They shoot anything that moves." Neither are there as yet reasons to think that organized labor leaders, assured of at least a few seats at the planning table, will be substantially more enlightened about the process of democratic participation. And we are still in the grip of a lingering conservative ideology dominated by the myth of the impersonal market.

Still, the failures of the conservative economic program in the first years of the 1980s have undermined some major ideological and political constraints that until now have prevented us from dealing with the realities of the new economic era. Conventional conservatism has had no more success in solving our economic problems than conventional liberalism. It is apparent that neither can deliver full employment and stable prices. We may well be living through what philosopher Hannah Arendt once termed an

odd in-between period which sometimes inserts itself into historical time when not only the later historians but the actors and witnesses, the living themselves, become aware of an interval in time which is altogether determined by things that are no longer and by things that are not yet. In history, these intervals have shown more than once that they may contain the moment of truth.[1]

The New Deal and the neoconservative counterreformation are no longer. Economic planning is not yet. This present interval may well be the moment of truth for democracy.

There are reasons to believe that our new economic conditions may themselves be paving the way for political change. The inevitable expansion of government responsibility for the economy brings with it an inevitable transformation of our perception of how the economic world works. Despite its rhetoric, even the Reagan administration protected a variety of industries—autos, steel, agriculture, nuclear energy—from the free market.

As government's involvement in strategic economic decisions grows, the *way* in which it is involved must move increasingly to the forefront of awareness. To the degree that our capacity to influence the future becomes the context for political debate, the pressures for contending sides to produce practical rather than ideological answers must increase. The act of planning delineates choices and forces those involved to get specific.

When economic problems are seen as the result of immutable market forces, there is little to do but accept them. When they are seen as the result of specific decisions made by specific people, the game becomes open to everyone.

Moreover, just as literacy is essential for a functioning democracy, so an increase in economic literacy—stimulated also by economic crisis —strengthens the trend toward public accountability. During the postwar boom, economic policy was not the most important political issue to the average citizen. Over the past decade the amount of economic news has vastly expanded and along with it the level of public discussion. A more informed citizenry will not by itself produce more rational planning. In the near term it could produce a more rigid stalemate as the skills and leverage of contending parties are strengthened. Over time, however, if economic problems are not solved, simplistic nostrums quickly lose appeal. The public even now is engaged in a practical if chaotic search for the right formula. And as long as the pain continues—as it must, absent a new strategy—they are likely to change Presidents and policies until they find ones that work.

Nor are the American people nearly as conservative as conventional wisdom holds when it comes to economics. Pollsters regularly report pluralities and majorities for such ideas as government-guaranteed jobs, wage-price controls to stop high inflation, national health insurance, and gas rationing rather than high prices.[2] Large majorities regularly report they prefer smaller, stable communities as places to live and to raise their families. Neoconservative propaganda notwithstanding, the 1980 presidential election was not a clear ideological decision to move to the Right. Ronald Reagan won only 50.7 percent of the popular vote, a mere 26.7 percent of those eligible to vote.[3] The election was a political decision to throw out a bumbling Jimmy Carter, who had no strategy for the new inflation. Analyzing the results of the 1982 congressional elections two years later, pollster Pat Caddell observed that it appeared "an anxious, uneasy public may have been looking for a more drastic agenda of change—and not simply from the Right—than that which was served up by politics this year."[4]

In broader perspective, attitudes about sex, race, family life, marriage, and religion have undergone a virtual revolution in the short space of a couple of decades. The number of unmarried couples living together has more than doubled since 1975. Forty percent of all marriages now end in divorce. Fifty-three percent more adults had tried marijuana in 1979 than in 1974, and nearly 35 percent of the eighteen-to-twenty-five-year-old group currently use it. Daniel Yankelovich reports that in 1958, 80 percent of Americans believed "For a woman to remain unmarried she must be 'sick,' 'neurotic' or 'immoral.' " Twenty years later that view had shrunk to 25 percent of Americans. He also reports that for the first time in American society only a minority of people experience "discomfort" at having a friend who is homosexual. The "prototypical" American nuclear family—husband working to support a wife and children—now represents a mere 15 percent of the labor force![5]

That our ideas and values, social and economic, will stay mired in old paradigms is perhaps the least likely outcome as the new economic era unfolds.

Any time of transition brings with it deep-seated stress. The eagerness with which we have embraced our new freedoms has matched a well-documented feeling of rootlessness and purposelessness. Yankelovich has also measured an increase in what he calls a *search for community*—"an intense need to compensate for the impersonal and threatening aspects of modern life by seeking mutual identification with others based on close ethnic ties or ties of shared interests, needs, background, age or values." Yankelovich finds a "large and significant" increase, from 32 to 47 percent, of Americans involved in this search.[6]

In an age of alienating megasystems, impersonal technology, and forced mobility, whether we can expand democracy depends on the success of that search for community. The ideology that promotes greed and beggar-thy-neighbor individualism is rapidly becoming less relevant to both individual and national survival. Moreover, it is neither the case that capital creates all wealth, as conservatism holds, nor that labor is the source of all value, as Marxism argues. The fundamental source of our common economy is the broader, inclusive entity we call the community—it sustains us, gives us our traditions, nurtures us over generations with ideas, information, and technology, and allows us to exchange and cooperate with each other. Without the community there is nothing but the isolated, lonely individual scratching out little more than his or her own sustenance—if he or she is lucky. Our task is to fashion the generally recognized mutual responsibilities of individual and community into a practical ideology appropriate to the new era.

The desire for community is sometimes confused with a wistful longing for the good old days of small towns and barn raisings, of antique technology when life was simpler. As long as we root values of community in the past, however, we prevent ourselves from creating a viable politics in the present. The nineteenth-century and early-twentieth-century models are insufficient. The extended ethnic family living in a neighborhood of extended families has been destabilized by the forces of mobility, growth, and change. Neither is it enough simply to call ourselves a "community" in a continent-spanning society moving toward three hundred million citizens.

A key to achieving equilibrium between the needs of the individual and the requirements of planning in a democracy is the construction of stable, responsive, and effective mediating institutions. Many such institutions exist—corporations, labor unions, churches, chambers of commerce, farmers' organizations, and so forth. The pull of the national and international forces is so strong, however, that most take on the characteristics of central planners—headquarters in Washington, great distances between members and leadership, absorption in national abstractions. Vertical mediating institutions also tend to be *exclusive*—by definition, they represent special interests. On the other hand, horizontal mediating institutions—towns, cities, states—are inherently *inclusive.* The city council's function, if not always its performance, is to represent everyone in the city—all classes, races, industries, etc. It is open to challenge when it excludes. Moreover, unlike the board of a corporation or labor union, the council has no vested interest in centralizing economic or political power at the national level. Without romanticizing its performance it is naturally in tension with centralized planning. The same logic suggests that over the longer haul the intermediate-scale unit of the region should be given a large measure of autonomy in planning.*

The concept of community, as we have seen, must extend *over time* to the next generation. A strategy of full production and effective use of resources is not the same as undifferentiated growth that has no concern to conserve resources for future members of society. The key difference lies in the acceptance of values beyond the marketplace. Insulating houses, building solar collectors, and maintaining watersheds are logical elements of a plan that takes both jobs and the longer-term community seriously.

*This is different from administrative decentralization. A serious emphasis on the region would look to it ultimately as the long-run integrator of planning functions that in part devolve downward from the federal level but that most importantly represent an upward integration of planning based on the needs of local communities. An *initial* focus on locality thus addresses planning at the levels of both nation and region.

The concept of community also extends to other people. A strategy of sustained production is essential to the reinvigoration of the world economy that Third World and Fourth World nations so desperately need: as long as stagnation continues, they will continue to decline into decay, violence, and totalitarianism.

Overnight creation of economic planning aimed at sustaining community would be a recipe for economic and social disaster. We have neither the institutions nor the ideology to support it. Nonetheless, such planning is the only way we can hope to survive with our democracy and freedoms intact over the coming decades. Again, solving this paradox requires economic policies that deal with the immediate problems of inflation and unemployment *yet at the same time reinforce those individual values of cooperation and collective decision-making that increase our ability to plan competently.*

We have argued that only if solutions to our economic problems are anchored in shared human values can those solutions have a chance ultimately of overcoming the broker state's interest-group bickering and deal-making. Statisticians can debate national definitions of full employment, but in Youngstown the vast majority supported bold strategies for community jobs—making it impossible for major Ohio politicians, including even the conservative then governor, James Rhodes, to oppose their plan. Defining job strategies around the *local* paradigm of *community* full employment helps break the ideological deadlock around the issue of national full employment that all too easily isolates minorities and women. Similarly, emphasizing specific solutions to sectoral price problems bypasses an obsolete inflation politics that targets either social budgets, the poor, labor, or all together. Focusing on the necessities permits a principled coming together of the vast majority.*

The inflation issue is crucial; it is the Achilles' heel of Keynesianism, of the neoliberals, and of the Democratic Party. So long as there is no well-understood alternative principle that confronts the neoconservative postulate that big government and unbalanced budgets cause inflation, then a mad politics of reducing government, cutting budgets, and inducing recession *must* dominate economic policy.

Such a politics in turn devolves into implicit or explicit racism. As

---

*In the midst of the Carter inflation, a precursor of such an alliance—"Consumers Opposed to Inflation in the Necessities"—a coalition of some seventy-eight labor, elderly, consumer, environmental, and religious groups—urged such a strategy as the alternative to budget cutting and recession.

economic pain deepens, it pits the blue-collar taxpayer against the black and brown unemployed worker and welfare recipient. Issues of crime, mandatory sentencing, and capital punishment put a violent, repressive political edge to an economic strategy that inherently isolates the ghetto.

Either a political regroupment of the vast majority around the problem of *managing the system* for sustained economic health will be achieved, or intensifying animosities will continue to divide individuals and groups. It is a dangerous illusion to think that Reaganomics' demise will mean an automatic return to middle-of-the-road Democratic politics. The world is not standing still. Neither is the Right. Kevin Phillips reminds us that a crisis alliance between the populist Right and the corporate planners could become a recipe for an American form of fascism.[7]

History also suggests that in times of stress, leaders under pressure to distract attention from domestic failure all too often seek out foreign scapegoats. In the nuclear age it would be folly to imagine America as somehow immune to such pressures.

The most fundamental requirement of a politics of community is a bringing together of our public and private views of how to deal with the future. In our own lives we plan ahead, save money, educate ourselves and our children. Much of what we do concerns the future. Planning for tomorrow gives meaning to our lives today. A politics of community involves an extension of private responsibility to a concern for our neighborhoods, our cities, and the country. In the end, only if economic planning is seen as a process in which a steadily expanded capacity to plan is itself a primary product does it make sense.

"The making of a community is always an exploration," writes British social theorist Raymond Williams, "for consciousness cannot precede creation, and there is no formula for unknown experience."

> It is, in practice, for any man, a long conversion of the habitual elements of denial; a slow and deep personal acceptance of extending community. The institutions of cynicism, of denial and of division will perhaps only be thrown down when they are recognized for what they are: the deposits of practical failures to live. Failure —the jaunty hardness of the "outsider"—will lose its present glamour, as the common experience moves in a different direction.[8]

A serious strategy must walk on "two legs." One leg is the principle that true social change can come only when people's attitudes and values change. The other is the principle that institutions can help shape the values that guide the way individuals behave. The process must be reciprocal; it involves both individual accountability to the community and community accountability to the individual. It is also incremental. We are concerned here not with the creation of a Utopia, but with the messy, day-to-day business of developing the conditions for a lasting social contract. Changing institutions changes people who will in turn change institutions, and so on, "people" being ourselves. In a democratic society political economics must be hospitable to that part of our character that accepts responsibility for the common good. To the extent that we build the spirit of democracy and cooperation into our economic institutions, in the neighborhood, workplace, and community, we get *practice* on how to be democratic and cooperative. And we desperately need the practice.

At the same time we must approach the future with humility and in a mature spirit of testing and learning as we go. Planning theorist John Friedman suggests that the archtypical citizen of the future will be neither the "economic man" whose values are greed and self-aggrandizement, nor the "socialist man," the saint who is always ready to sacrifice himself for the collective good. He will rather be the "learning man," constantly experimenting, practicing, progressing by trial and error in a self-conscious effort to create a better society and a better human being in himself.[9]

Competent economic planning thus requires that we explicitly choose—along with employment levels and housing investment—the *values* we want to affirm. There is no getting around this responsibility. By whatever name we call it, we will have economic planning. Therefore we will have the choice of what values to support, whether we exercise that choice or not. We are responsible for the future; we become what we do, as individuals and as a society. The dying ideology obscures this truth by leaving the cultivation of individual character to the televised merchants of Pac-Man, new cars, and Club Med vacations. Ignoring the relationship between our economic system and our values does not mean that we leave it up to each individual to decide his or her values; *it means that we reinforce the corporate and bureaucratic values of the dominant economic institutions* whose interests are to keep us materialistic, self-absorbed, greedy, and apathetic.

The implicit goals of broker state planning—the concentration of resources on private consumption, and public spending on the military —are also antithetical to expanded participation. Such planning channels our energies into the cultivation of our own private interests, which leaves the world and its fate in the hands of bureaucratic power, which is both despised . . . and obeyed. Asked about the increased participation of American citizens Ronald Reagan promised in his election campaign, presidential aide Ed Meese said: "Yeah, they get to vote for President every four years."[10] This is the death knell for democracy. The psychological alienation of the private individual grows daily; at some point it may be too wide for democracy to cross. The conservative nightmare of bureaucracy gone wild must then surely come to pass.

The self-evident way out is the practice of active citizenship. It is, however, a common observation that Americans do not *want* to take responsibility for their country. Everywhere we look, people seem to have turned away from participation. Even voting, the most minimal act of participation, scarcely brings out half of those eligible in a presidential year, and less for congressional races in off-year elections. Personal careers, television, drugs, spectator sports—almost anything, it seems, is more important than thinking about, much less doing something about, the way our country is run.

Nevertheless, somehow vast numbers of Americans at the same time give themselves to causes outside their own private work world. A Gallup poll in 1981 found that about eighty-four million people—52 percent of the population over eighteen years old—did unpaid volunteer work for community, religious, educational, and similar organizations.[11] As we have seen, increased neighborhood and community participation in civic issues by ordinary people—protesting, giving officials a piece of their mind, proposing *their* ideas—has been a major source of challenge to the existing planning system.

The recent past has also shown that Americans are capable of great national political efforts. In our own lifetimes we have seen a civil rights movement in which black Americans—after two hundred years of slavery, another hundred of oppression and servitude, and repeated prophecies of impossibility—suddenly demanded and achieved equal political rights in the space of a decade. Similarly, forty years after women's suffrage—when the tiny group of feminists had all but given up hope for a renewed fight for equality—American women were suddenly galvanized into an extraordinarily fervent and complex movement dealing not only with political or even economic equality but also with vastly more complex issues of personal and sexual relationships. The ecology movement, the antiwar movement, and the movement for nuclear sanity all brought millions of Americans into political activism, taking responsibility for the future of their community, country, and planet.

The list of efforts to which people have voluntarily dedicated their energies despite expert predictions of sustained apathy suggest that we have consistently underrated the individual's willingness to participate. Such participation is often seen as a disruption to the orderly processes of government and business; it is resisted by political and corporate leadership. Therefore it often becomes disorderly and disruptive. It should be read as people hungry to take responsibility for their community.

Each movement has its own unique history and politics. But the fact is that they occurred despite the lure of television and the assorted distractions of American life—and they have made a difference. We cannot help but ask: If grass-roots movements have risen to challenge successfully the most deeply felt personal attitudes about race and sex, is it too much to imagine that a politics can be fashioned to remove an obsolete and demonstrably unworkable economic ideology that is squandering our material well-being and destroying our experience of real community?

The decade of the 1960s was characterized by political involvement and a reaching out to take responsibility for the world. The 1970s— the time of the "me" generation—was characterized by concern with individual fulfillment and personal liberation. The symbols of *both* the 1960s and the 1970s—the demonstrator and the jogger—represent aspects of the modern American psyche that must be integrated in order to build a political economics of community. Such an integration can occur only if we move beyond abstractions to practical strategies —strategies that neither simply protest nor escape, strategies that *rebuild*.

Who among us will do what must be done? Go down the list: women and minorities, whose drive for equality is stalled by the stagflation strategy of conventional economics; working people, up to their necks in debt, suddenly not knowing where the next paycheck is coming from; small- and medium-sized businesspeople, whose tax cuts are meaningless without customers with money in their pockets; managers, who know the bureaucratic failings of corporate life; environmentalists, who are learning that unemployment, hunger for jobs, and pressures to reduce costs bring ecological disaster; young people, whose dream of owning a home is gone.

A meaningful vision of community is the only way to unite those who are now isolated and bring us all back into citizenship. The metamorphosis of the American economy continues. It is bringing us face to face with our responsibility for the country's future. The market does not choose. *We* choose.

Chapter 1 INTRODUCTION

1. ABC News–Harris Survey (June 2, 1980).
2. *The New York Times* (Oct. 18, 1979).
3. George Lodge, *The New American Ideology* (New York: Alfred A. Knopf, 1979), p. 302.

Chapter 2 THE BROKER STATE

1. *Expenditure Trends in OECD Countries, 1960–1980* (Paris: Organization for Economic Cooperation and Development, 1981); and *Economic Report of the President, 1982*, Council of Economic Advisors (Washington, D.C.: USGPO), pp. 233 and 320. (Hereafter cited as *Economic Report of the President,* [year].)
2. William Simon, *A Time for Truth* (New York: McGraw-Hill, 1978), p. 41.
3. Ibid., pp. 193–95.
4. David Vogel, "Business's 'New Class' Struggle," *The Nation* (December 15, 1979). p. 626.
5. George Gilder, *Wealth and Poverty* (New York: Basic Books, 1980).
6. Ibid., pp. 114–115.
7. *Statistical Abstract of the United States, 1980*, Census Bureau, U.S. Department of Commerce (Washington, D.C.: USGPO), p. 454, (hereafter cited as *Statistical Abstract* [year]); Census Bureau, *Current Population Reports* (July 1983).
8. Malcolm Sawyer, "Income Distribution in OECD Countries," *OECD Economic Outlook, Occasional Studies* (Paris, July 1976).
9. Everett C. Ladd, "What the Voters Really Want," *Fortune* (Dec. 18, 1978).
10. Lloyd Free and Hadley Cantril, *The Political Beliefs of Americans* (New Brunswick, N.J.: Rutgers University Press, 1967), as discussed in Walter Dean Burnham, "American Politics in the 1980s," *Dissent* (Spring 1980), p. 151.
11. *The New York Times* (Mar. 20, 1977).
12. Simon, *A Time for Truth*, p. 196.
13. Ibid., p. 229.
14. Herman E. Krooss, "Presidential Address: Some Random Thoughts on Business and Government," *Business and Economic History: Papers Presented at the 21st Annual Meeting of the Business History Conference, 1972*, pp. 2–3.
15. *Historical Statistics of the United States* (1966 ed.), pp. 712, 139.

16. Lester Thurow, *The Zero-Sum Society* (New York: Basic Books, 1980), p. 156.
17. *Statistical Abstract, 1981,* pp. 354, 878; *World Almanac, 1983;* U.S. Office of Management and Budget, U.S. Budget for Fiscal Year 1984, pp. 5–7, 5–8.
18. Information supplied by U.S. Department of Defense, Public Information Office (Mar. 1981).
19. Richard J. Barnet, *The Economy of Death* (New York: Atheneum, 1970), p. 120.
20. John M. Blair, *Economic Concentration* (New York: Harcourt, Brace, Jovanovich, 1972), pp. 380–85.
21. Gordon Adams and Christopher Paine, "The R&D Slush Fund," *The Nation* (Jan. 26, 1980).
22. *The New York Times* (Sept. 23, 1980).
23. George McGovern, "On the Military Budget," *The New York Times* (June 10, 1980).
24. James Fallows, "America's High-Tech Weaponry," *Atlantic Monthly* (May 1981), p. 29.
25. Ibid., pp. 31–32.
26. John Connally (1971), quoted in *The Defense Monitor,* Center for Defense Information, Vol. VI, No. 7 (Sept.–Oct. 1977), p. 2.
27. *Economic Report of the President, 1982,* pp. 122–25.
28. *Dollars and Sense* (May–June 1980), pp. 14–15; *Special Analyses of U.S. Budget, FY 1982.*
29. See *Moody's Industrial Manual, 1981,* pp. 2165–70.
30. Senator Russell Long in Common Cause, *Gimme Shelter* (Washington, D.C., 1978).
31. Common Cause, *Gimme Shelter.*
32. See the study prepared for Congressman Charles Vanik, *Congressional Record* (June 27, 1980), p. H5823.
33. *Tax Notes* (Washington, D.C., Dec. 14, 1981), pp. 1448–61.
34. John Karl Scholz, "Tax Expenditures, "Appendix C of *Setting National Priorities, the 1984 Budget,* Joseph A. Pechman, ed. (Washington, D.C.: The Brookings Institute, 1983), p. 245.
35. "The Economic and Budget Outlook, an Update," Congressional Budget Office (Sept. 1982), p. 35; see also the statement of Donald T. Regan before the Joint Economic Committee of the U.S. Congress (July 19, 1983), p. 7.
36. Robert Sobel, *The Fallen Colossus* (New York: Weybright and Talley, 1977), p. 335.
37. Testimony of Treasury Secretary John Connally before the Senate Banking Committee in *Emergency Loan Guarantee Legislation,* Hearings Before the Committee on Banking, Housing, and Urban Affairs, U.S. Senate, 92nd Congress, Part I (June 7–16, 1971), pp. 18, 19.
38. *The Wall Street Journal* (Aug. 23, 1974; Apr. 24, 1980; May 30, 1980).

39. *The New York Times* (Apr. 29 and May 29, 1980); *Business Week* (Nov. 23, 1981); *In These Times* (Sept. 23–29, 1981).
40. *Business Week* (Apr. 14, 1980 and May 19, 1980); *Fortune* (June 30, 1980); *Boston Globe* (May 6, 1980).
41. *The New York Times* (October 10, 1979).
42. See, for example, *The New York Times* and *The Wall Street Journal* (Mar. 2, 1983) for U.S. Commerce Department statements.
43. George Will, *Newsweek* (Dec. 12, 1977).

Chapter 3 THE ROAD TO DUNKIRK

1. *Time* (Dec. 31, 1965).
2. Arthur M. Okun, *The Political Economy of Prosperity* (Washington, D.C.: The Brookings Institution, 1970), p. 33.
3. John Maynard Keynes, *The General Theory of Employment, Interest, and Money* (New York: Harcourt, Brace and Company, 1958), p. 129.
4. *The New York Times* (Jan. 7, 1971).
5. Robert Lekachman, *Inflation: The Permanent Problem of Boom and Bust* (New York: Random House, 1973), p. 48.
6. U.S. Department of Commerce, *1977 Census of Manufacturers: Concentration Ratios in Manufacturing* (Washington, D.C.: USGPO, 1981); *Statistical Abstract, 1981*, p. 541; and Federal Trade Commission, Bureau of Economics, *Economic Report on Corporate Mergers, 1969, Appendix A* (Washington, D.C.: USGPO).
7. *Employment and Earnings*, Bureau of Labor Statistics (Dec. 1981), pp. 70–76.
8. John Blair, ed., *Roots of Inflation* (New York: Burt Franklin, 1975), p. vi.
9. Price increases throughout the book are calculated from Bureau of Labor Statistics Consumer Price Index data.
10. *Economic Report of the President, 1983*, p. 196.
11. *Economic Report of the President, 1978*, p. 141.
12. Gar Alperovitz and Jeff Faux, "Symbolist Economics," *Social Policy* (May/June 1980), p. 52.
13. The original Kemp-Roth bill was introduced in Congress on July 14, 1977.
14. "Loopholes Loom Large at Tax Time," *Dollars and Sense* (May–June 1980).
15. Tax Foundation, Inc., *Monthly Tax Features 23* (Oct. 1979), cited in Paul Blumberg, *Inequality in an Age of Decline* (New York: Oxford University Press, 1980), p. 93, and *U.S. Budget in Brief, 1972, 1981*, and *1982*, Office of Management and Budget (Washington, D.C.: USGPO).
16. *People and Taxes*, Washington, D.C. (July 1978), p. 7; *Boston Globe* (Sept. 4, 1979); *Community Jobs*, The Youth Project, Washington, D.C. (Apr. 1980).

17. See chapter 7, pp. 116–117.
18. Jack Kemp and David Stockman, "Avoiding a GOP Dunkirk" (Dec. 1980).
19. Herbert Stein, *The AEI Economist* (Washington, D.C.: The American Enterprise Institute, July 1978), p. 6. See, also, Walter Heller before the Joint Economic Committee (June 28, 1978), repr. in "Leading Economists' Views of Kemp-Roth," Committees on the Budget, U.S. Congress (Aug. 1978), pp. 103–110.
20. *The Wall Street Journal* (Dec. 19, 1980).
21. *Business Conditions Digest* (Jan. 1983), p. 94; *Economic Report of the President, 1982*, p. 268.
22. Donald Regan before the Economic Club of Indianapolis, September 15, 1981, as cited in *Questions and Answers About the Reagan Economic Program* (Washington, D.C.: The COIN Campaign, 1981).
23. William Greider, "The Education of David Stockman," *Atlantic Monthly* (Dec. 1981), p. 51.
24. *The Wall Street Journal* (Dec. 19, 1980).

Chapter 4 THE ECONOMICS OF DECLINE

1. *The Washington Post* (Dec. 13, 1981).
2. *Statistical Abstract, 1981*, pp. 879, 880.
3. George Lodge, *The New American Ideology*, p. 288.
4. Wassily Leontief, quoted in Robert Heilbroner, "The American Plan," *The New York Times Magazine* (Jan. 25, 1976).
5. Robert Roosa, from press release of the Initiative Committee for National Planning (Feb. 27, 1975).
6. Thornton Bradshaw, "My Case for National Planning," *Fortune* (Feb. 1977), pp. 100–104.
7. J. Irwin Miller, quoted in *The Republic* (Columbus, Ind.) (Sept. 23, 1974).
8. Felix Rohatyn, *The New York Times* (Dec. 1, 1974).
9. *Statistical Abstract, 1981*, pp. 396, 781.
10. *Dun's* (Dec. 1973), p. 59.
11. John Kenneth Galbraith, *The New Industrial State* (New York: Mentor/New American Library, 1968), pp. 44–45.
12. *Business Week* (Dec. 18, 1978), p. 62.
13. Daniel Bell, *The Coming of the Post-Industrial Society: A Venture in Social Forecasting* (New York: Basic Books, 1973), p. 284.
14. *Newsweek* (May 4, 1981), p. 30.
15. Karl Frieden, "Government Ownership of Iron and Steel Plants During World War II," memo, National Center for Economic Alternatives (May 3, 1978).

16. *The New York Times* (Dec. 1, 1974).
17. *Business Week* (June 30, 1980), p. 120.
18. *The New York Times* (Oct. 18, 1979).
19. *The New York Times* (Jan. 27, 1981; June 18, 1981; July 1, 1981).
20. "Rebuilding the Road to Opportunity: Turning Point for America's Economy," Special Task Force on Long-Term Economic Policy, Democratic Caucus/U.S. House of Representatives (Sept. 1982).
21. Emma Rothschild, "Reagan and the Real Economy," *New York Review of Books* (Feb. 5, 1981).
22. See Thierry J. Noyelle and Thomas Stanback, Jr., *Cities in Transition.* Conservation of Human Resources Series, Landmark Studies. (Totowa, NJ: Osman, 1982); and Bob Kuttner, "The Declining Middle," *Atlantic Monthly* (July 1983).
23. *The New York Times* (June 27, 1980).
24. *The New York Times,* cited in *Public Opinion* (Mar.–Apr. 1978).
25. *Business Week* (June 30, 1980), p. 145 (emphasis added).
26. *Statistical Abstract, 1980,* pp. 28, 465.
27. Edward Furey, "The Fear, the Numbing Fear," *The New York Times* (Apr. 1, 1975).
28. See *Disorders and Terrorism,* Report of the Task Force on Disorders and Terrorism, National Advisory Committee on Criminal Justice Standards and Goals (Washington, D.C., 1976).
29. Richard Barnet, *Roots of War: The Men and Institutions Behind U.S. Foreign Policy* (New York: Penguin, 1973), pp. 93–94.
30. David Nyhan, "Tough Times Ahead for Class of '82," *Boston Globe* (Feb. 25, 1982).
31. Irving Kristol, *The Wall Street Journal* (Nov. 26, 1979) (emphasis added).

Chapter 5   A COMMUNITY-SUSTAINING ECONOMICS

1. Frank de Leeuw et al., "The High-Employment Budget: New Estimates, 1955–1980," *Survey of Current Business* (Nov. 1980), pp. 13–43.
2. Steven Sheffrin, *The Costs of Continued Unemployment,* Exploratory Project for Economic Alternatives (Washington, D.C., 1977), pp. xii, 9, 10.
3. *Monthly Labor Review* (Mar. 1983).
4. Felix Rohatyn, "The Coming Emergency and What Can Be Done About It," *New York Review of Books* (Dec. 4, 1980), p. 24.
5. Theodore J. Lowi, *The Politics of Disorder* (New York: Basic Books, 1971), p. 5.
6. Ibid., p. 12, emphasis added.
7. James Morrison, *Small Business: New Directions for the 1980s,* National

Center for Economic Alternatives (Washington, D.C., 1980), p. 2, and *The Washington Post* (Aug. 27, 1982).

8. *Statistical Abstract, 1981,* p. 390.
9. Noah Webster, 1787, in People's Bicentennial Commission, *Voices of the American Revolution* (New York: Bantam, 1974), p. 150.
10. Thomas Jefferson, 1785, ibid., p. 160.
11. Peter Drucker, "The Job as Property," *The Wall Street Journal* (Mar. 4, 1980), editorial page.
12. Information supplied by countries' U.S. information offices.
13. H. C. Simon, *Economic Policy for a Free Society* (Chicago: University of Chicago Press, 1948), p. 13.
14. Robert Nisbet, *The Quest for Community* (London: Oxford University Press, 1953 (1971 ed.), p. 246.
15. Ibid., pp. 19, 239, 240.
16. Ibid., pp. xvii, xviii.
17. Martin Buber, *Paths in Utopia* (Boston: Beacon Press, 1970), p. 133.
18. J. W. Forrester, *The Washington Post* (June 8, 1975).
19. Lester Brown, *A Sustainable Society* (New York: W. W. Norton, 1981), pp. 288–90.
20. Bruce Stokes, *Helping Ourselves* (Washington, D.C.: Worldwatch Institute, 1981), p. 14.
21. E. F. Schumacher, *Small Is Beautiful: Economics as If People Mattered* (New York: Perennial/Harper & Row, 1975), pp. 66, 258 (emphasis in original).
22. Alexis de Tocqueville, *Democracy in America*, Vol. 2, Chap. VIII.
23. Schumacher, *Small Is Beautiful,* p. 75.
24. Michael Walzer, *Radical Principles: Reflections of an Unreconstructed Democrat* (New York: Basic Books, 1980), p. 46, emphasis added.

Chapter 6 PRODUCTIVITY AND STABILITY

1. *Economic Report of the President, 1983,* p. 209.
2. "The Productivity Slowdown: Causes and Policy Responses," staff memorandum, Congressional Budget Office, in "Capital Formation and Industrial Policy," Committee on Energy and Commerce, U.S. House of Representatives (July 1981), p. 303.
3. *Economic Report of the President, 1983,* p. 209.
4. *Employment and Earnings* (Mar. 1982), Tables A-1 and B-2.
5. *Handbook of Labor Statistics,* Bureau of Labor Statistics (Dec. 1980), p. 151 (hereafter *Handbook of Labor Statistics*) and *Economic Indicators of the Farm Sector: Production and Efficiency Statistics, 1979,* U.S. Department of Agriculture, Statistical Bulletin No. 65, p. 90.
6. Emma Rothschild, "Reagan and the Real Economy"; and *Employment and Earnings* (Mar. 1981), p. 58.

7. *Handbook of Labor Statistics,* pp. 189, 209, 229.
8. Emma Rothschild, "Reagan and the Real Economy."
9. *Handbook of Labor Statistics,* p. 467, and *Statistical Abstract, 1981,* p. 883.
10. *Statistical Abstract, 1981,* p. 883.
11. *Social Indicators III,* U.S. Bureau of the Census (Dec. 1980), p. 365.
12. Edward F. Denison, "Explanations of Declining Productivity Growth," *Survey of Current Business* (Aug. 1979), p. 9.
13. Ezra Vogel, *Japan as Number One* (Cambridge, Mass.: Harvard University Press, 1979), pp. 82–83.
14. Denison, "Explanations of Declining Productivity Growth," p. 9, and *The New York Times* (Apr. 29 and Aug. 9, 1980).
15. Organization for Economic Co-operation and Development, *Historical Studies, 1960–81* (Paris, 1983), p. 44.
16. U.S. National Science Foundation, *Science Indicators, 1978,* and Jon Halliday, "The Road to Rearmament," *The Nation* (Feb. 13, 1982), pp. 186–88.
17. *Statistical Abstract, 1981,* p. 598.
18. See, for example, Denison, "Explanations of Declining Productivity Growth," pp. 15–17, and Dale Jorgenson, *Challenge* (Nov.–Dec. 1980).
19. Edward F. Denison, "Accounting for Slower Economic Growth" (Washington, D.C.: The Brookings Institution, 1979), p. 14C.
20. Michael Mohr, "The Long-Term Structure of Production, Factor Demand, and Factor Productivity in U.S. Manufacturing Industries," in John Kendrick and Beatrice Vaccara, eds., *New Developments in Productivity Measurement* (Chicago: University of Chicago Press, 1980), p. 187; see also Martin Neil Baily, "Will Productivity Growth Recover? (Has It Done So Already?)," *Brookings Discussion Papers in Economics* (Dec. 1983).
21. Michael Mohr and Paul Christy, "The Industry Composition of Postwar Productivity Growth," U.S. Department of Commerce, Bureau of Industrial Economics (Nov. 1981).
22. "Executives Still Support Reaganomics," *Business Week* (Apr. 26, 1982), p. 20.
23. "The Productivity Slowdown: Causes and Policy Responses," p. 329, emphasis added.
24. Robert H. Hayes and William J. Abernathy, "Managing Our Way to Economic Decline," *Harvard Business Review* (July–Aug. 1980), p. 70.
25. David Vogel, "America's Management Crisis," *The New Republic* (Feb. 7, 1981), p. 22.
26. Hayes and Abernathy, "Managing Our Way to Economic Decline," p. 75.
27. Ibid., p. 71.
28. *The New York Times* (Apr. 26, 1981).
29. Consumer Federation of America, in *Boston Globe* (Apr. 27, 1982).

30. Steve Lohr, "Overhauling America's Business Management," *The New York Times Magazine* (Jan. 4, 1981), p. 88.
31. See in particular Hayes and Abernathy, "Managing Our Way to Business Decline," and David Kraus, "Executive Pay: Ripe for Reform?" *Harvard Business Review* (Sept.–Oct. 1980), pp. 36–38 ff.
32. *The New York Times* (Feb. 27, 1982).
33. Robert D. Hamrin, *Managing Growth in the 1980s: Towards a New Economics* (New York: Praeger, 1981), p. 25.
34. American Center for the Quality of Work Life, "Industrial Democracy in Europe: A 1977 Survey" (Washington, D.C., 1977); and Harry and Joanne Bernstein, "Industrial Democracy in Twelve Nations," U.S. Department of Labor, Bureau of International Labor Affairs monograph, no. 2 (Jan. 1979).
35. *The New Republic* (Sept. 29, 1979), pp. 16–18 ff.
36. "How the Japanese Manage in the U.S.," *Fortune* (June 15, 1981), p. 99.
37. Quoted in Harry and Joanne Bernstein, "Industrial Democracy in Twelve Nations," U.S. Department of Labor, Bureau of International Labor Affairs, Monograph No. 2 (Jan. 1979), pp. 59.
38. Ibid., p. 57.
39. *Statistical Abstract, 1981*, p. 882.
40. Lester Thurow, "Where's America's Old Team Spirit?" *The New York Times* (July 26, 1981), and Steve Sheffrin and Lester Thurow, "Estimating the Costs and Benefits of On-the-Job Training," *Economie Appliquée* 30 (3): 507–19 (1977).
41. "Autos: Studying the Japanese," *The New York Times* (Feb. 27, 1982).
42. Ezra Vogel, *Japan as Number One*, p. xix.
43. James O'Toole, *Making America Work* (New York: Continuum, 1981), p. 61.
44. Paul Bernstein, "Worker-Owned Plywood Firms Steadily Outperform Industry," *World of Work Report* (May 1977), in Karl Frieden, *Workplace Democracy and Productivity* (Washington, D.C.: National Center for Economic Alternatives, 1980), p. 11.
45. Cited in *Workplace Democracy and Productivity*, pp. 22, 21.
46. Ibid.
47. Personal communication to authors.
48. David Jenkins, *Job Power: Blue and White Collar Democracy* (Garden City, N.Y.: Doubleday, 1973), pp. 314–15.
49. *Business Week* (Mar. 28, 1977).
50. Andrew Zimbalist, "The Limits of Work Humanization," *Review of Radical Political Economy* (Summer 1975).
51. Thomas Brooks, quoted in William W. Winpisinger, *AFL-CIO American Federationist* (Feb. 1973), p. 10.
52. Studies by Louis Jacobsen at the Public Research Institute of the Center for Naval Analysis, cited in Barry Bluestone and Bennett Harrison,

Capital and Communities (Washington, D.C.: The Progressive Alliance, 1980), pp. 67–69.

53. O'Toole, *Making America Work*, p. 61.
54. Bureau of Labor Statistics, Handbook of Labor Statistics, pp. 465–66. Even when the Japanese rate is revised to reflect U.S. unemployment measurement standards, it is significantly lower. Also see Koji Taira, "Japan's Low Unemployment: Economic Miracle or Statistical Artifact? *Monthly Labor Review* (July 1983), pp. 3–9.

Chapter 7 A FULL-PRODUCTION ECONOMY

1. Associated Press story in *Portland* (Me.) *Press Herald* (Mar. 21, 1981).
2. *Statistical Abstract, 1981*, p. 393.
3. *Fortune* (Nov. 20, 1978).
4. *UAW Washington Report* (Mar. 6, 1981).
5. *Fortune* (June 15, 1981).
6. George Gilder, *Wealth and Poverty*, p. 157.
7. Gilder misinterpreted a study of nonparticipants in the Massachusetts labor force (including students, the elderly, mothers, and the disabled, many of whom either do not want to or are unable to work) to reach his conclusion that most unemployed have incomes above the national median income. In fact, the reason for the high figure reported in Massachusetts (47.7 percent with incomes over fifteen thousand dollars in their household) can be attributed almost entirely to students over sixteen still living with their parents, and wives who do not work outside the home. See Maryann Bouba and Andrew Sum, "The Extent of Job Desires of Persons Outside of the Labor Force in the United States and Massachusetts: Implications for Targeting CETA-Related Employment and Training Resources," Massachusetts Department of Employment Security, Research Paper No. 11 (Feb. 1979). Data on income for unemployed from *Statistical Abstract, 1981*, pp. 340–41.
8. National Advisory Council on Economic Opportunity, *Annual Report, 1980* (Washington, D.C.: USGPO), pp. 49–63.
9. *Statistical Abstract, 1982*, pp. 318–344. Food stamp income guidelines supplied by Food and Nutrition Service, U.S. Department of Agriculture.
10. Based on 1 percent of Social Security, 3 percent of AFDC, 8 percent of food stamps, and 18 percent of veterans' benefits.
11. Sheldon Danziger, Robert Haveman, and Robert Plotnick, "How Income Transfer Programs Affect Work, Savings and the Income Distribution: A Critical Review," *Journal of Economic Literature* 19 (3) (1981), pp. 975–1028.
12. *Handbook of Labor Statistics*, p. 467.

13. *Statistical Abstract, 1981,* p. 883.
14. This is the total for U.S. Labor Department expenditures for employment and training programs from 1963 through 1981. Information supplied by U.S. Department of Labor (Dec. 1981).
15. George Johnson, *Challenge* (May–June 1979), p. 55.
16. Daniel Moynihan, *On Understanding Poverty* (New York: Basic Books, 1969), pp. 12–13.
17. Over six years, fiscal years 1975–80 inclusive, a total of 5,737,500 public-service jobs were created. Source: telephone call to U.S. Department of Labor (Dec. 1981).
18. *Handbook of Labor Statistics,* pp. 49–52.
19. Economic scenarios prepared for "National Economic Recovery Project" (May 1983), Office of U.S. Representative Richard Ottinger.
20. See, for instance, Pechman's testimony each year before House and Senate committees and the annual publication *Setting National Priorities,* The Brookings Institution, Washington, D.C. For a specific review of revenue possibilities in the individual income tax, see "Comprehensive Income Taxation and Rate Reduction," testimony before the Senate Finance Committee (September 30, 1982) by Joseph A. Pechman and John Karl Scholz. For a review of corporate tax loopholes, see Robert S. McIntyre and Dean C. Tipps, "Inequality and Decline," Center on Budget and Policy Priorities, Washington, D.C., 1983. The $388.4 billion tax expenditure estimate is taken from *Setting National Priorities, The 1984 Budget* (1983), p. 244.
21. David Linowes, "Build Homes and Help the Economy," *The New York Times* (July 1, 1980).
22. John L. Palmer and Isabel V. Sawhill, eds., *The Reagan Experiment* (Washington, D.C.: The Urban Institute Press, 1982), p. 62. (Calculations are for fiscal years, not calendar years.)
23. 1980, 2.1 percent of GNP, based on *Survey of Current Business* (Mar. 1982), Table 3.7B–3.8B, p. 11. The figure excludes military spending for durables, nondurables, and structures, and federal, state, and local spending for nondurables. Historical data are from *National Income and Product Accounts of the U.S. to 1970* and *America in Ruins* (Washington, D.C.: Council of State Planning Agencies, 1980), p. 8.
24. All figures on job creation are based on calculations by NCEA research associates Russell Libby and Patrick Rooney using input-output data supplied by the Bureau of Labor Statistics. The data, "Employment Requirements Table, 1978," Bureau of Labor Statistics, Office of Economic Growth, Charles Bowman, supervisory economist, provide figures on a thousand jobs created per million dollars of new final demand in 1972 dollars, using 1978 productivity levels. Various estimates (cited below) for spending needs in the public sector were converted to 1972 dollars using the GNP implicit price deflator, and the results were

multiplied by the job-creation value for the appropriate BLS category to produce estimates of job creation from various public-spending strategies.

25. Department of Transportation, *Second Annual Report to Congress on Highway and Bridges Replacement and Rehabilitation* (Mar. 1981).
26. National Transportation Policy Study Commission, *National Transportation Policies Through the Year 2000,* final report (June 1979), USGPO. Based on the "Medium Growth Scenario," Chap. 10, pp. 171–205.
27. Ibid.
28. Ibid.
29. Ibid.
30. Council on Environmental Quality, *Environmental Quality, 1979,* pp. 118–19.
31. Ibid., and *America in Ruins,* pp. 2–3.
32. *Dollars and Sense* (Summer 1976) and *The Nation* (Nov. 7, 1981).
33. *America in Ruins,* pp. 2–3.
34. Leonard Rodberg, "More Jobs Under the Sun: Solar Power and Employment," *Social Policy* (May/June 1980), pp. 10–20.
35. See David Linowes, "Build Homes and Help the Economy," for housing estimates.
36. *Business Week* (Oct. 26, 1981), p. 142.
37. See Sheffrin, *The Costs of Continued Unemployment.*
38. Otto Eckstein, "Disinflation," *Inflation: Prospects and Remedies* (Washington, D.C.: Center for National Policy Studies, Oct. 1983), p. 22.
39. *The Wall Street Journal* (Mar. 12, 1980); Michael Gorges, "Non-Tariff Measures That Restrict Trade," Congressional Research Service (May 5, 1983).
40. Jane Jacobs, *The Question of Separation* (New York: Random House, 1980).
41. *Cambridge Economic Policy Review,* No. 5 (Cambridge University, Apr. 1979). Keynes also argued a similar thesis in *The General Theory,* Chap. 23, "Notes on Mercantilism . . . ," p. 333–51.
42. C. Fred Bergsten, "The Dollar, the Yen, and U.S. Trade," testimony before the Subcommittee on Trade of the House Ways and Means Committee (Nov. 30, 1982).
43. *International Economic Indicators* (June 1983), p. 36.
44. Ibid.
45. *Statistical Abstract, 1982,* p. 868. (Great Britain's percentage is an estimate based on 1980 export levels.)

Chapter 8 COMMUNITY FULL EMPLOYMENT

1. *The New York Times* (Jan. 14, 15, 16, Mar. 18, and May 12, 1982). *Economic Report of the President, 1983.*

2. U.S. Senate Committee on Agriculture and Forestry, Subcommittee on Rural Development, "Where Will All The People Go?" (Oct. 23, 1973), pp. 13–18.

3. Gary S. Fields, "Place-to-Place Migration: Some New Evidence," *Review of Economics and Statistics* 61: 21–32 (Feb. 1979).

4. President's Commission for a National Agenda for the Eighties, *Urban America in the Eighties: Perspectives and Prospects* (Washington, D.C.: USGPO, 1980), pp. 13, 100.

5. David Smith with Patrick McGuigan, *Towards a Public Balance Sheet* (Washington, D.C.: National Center for Economic Alternatives, 1979), and *Monthly Labor Review* (May 1981).

6. *The New York Times* (Oct. 16, 1979 and Apr. 15, 1980), and Bluestone and Harrison, p. 99.

7. See "Draining America Dry," *The Progressive* (July 1981), and *Fortune* (Feb. 23, 1981).

8. Jeff Faux and Russell Libby, *Absentee and Local Ownership of Maine Manufacturing* (Washington, D.C.: National Center for Economic Alternatives, 1980), and Jeff Faux, "Colonial New England," *The New Republic* (Nov. 25, 1972), pp. 16–19.

9. Bluestone and Harrison, *Capital and Communities*, p. 91.

10. David Barkely, "Plant Ownership Characteristics and the Locational Stability of Rural Iowa Manufacturers," *Land Economics* (Feb. 1978), p. 99.

11. Bluestone and Harrison, *Capital and Communities*, p. 96.

12. Dr. Willard Mueller, "The Merger's Impact on the Community," *AFL-CIO American Federationist* (June 1971), p. 15.

13. Personal communication to Jeff Faux.

14. For a detailed discussion of the public balance sheet concept and for more details on the accounting for Youngstown, see David Smith with Patrick McGuigan, *Towards a Public Balance Sheet.*

15. The Youngstown plan also comprised research and development efforts, and experimentation with new worker participation strategies; its justification included such public balance sheet benefits. Other factors, including the need for additional steel in a national full-production plan, would be treated in a fully comprehensive accounting. See Chapter Fifteen.

16. Personal communication with authors. The Library Bureau now successfully operates under a revised ownership structure.

17. *Business Week* (Aug. 20, 1979) and *Fortune* (May 3, 1982).

18. Dan Luria and Jack Russell, *Rational Reindustrialization* (Detroit: Widgetripper Press, 1981).

19. The National League of Cities has stated its support for the concept of community full employment.

20. Joint Economic Committee, "Case Studies in Private/Public Cooperation to Revitalize America: Passenger Rail" (Washington, D.C.: USGPO, Nov. 1981).

Chapter 9 THE BASIC NECESSITIES

1. See, for example, *The New York Times* (Sept. 25, 1980), p. 10.
2. *Economic Report of the President, 1982*, pp. 98, 295.
3. Ibid., pp. 320, 233, 295.
4. Ibid., pp. 233, 316–17.
5. Ibid., pp. 102–8, and *The Washington Post* (Dec. 9, 1981).
6. Benjamin M. Friedman, "Time to Reexamine the Monetary Targets Framework," Discussion Paper No. 875 (Cambridge, Mass.: Harvard Institute of Economic Research, Jan. 1982), p. 7.
7. *Economic Report of the President, 1982*, pp. 295, 303.
8. Benjamin M. Friedman, "Time to Reexamine," p. 7.
9. *Economic Report of the President, 1982*, pp. 233, 295, 303.
10. For a good review, see "Monetarism: A Time for Retreat" (Washington, D.C.: National Policy Exchange, Feb. 1982).
11. *Economic Report of the President, 1982*, p. 295.
12. Walter Heller, "Shadow and Substance in Inflation Policy," *Challenge* (Jan.–Feb. 1981), p. 11.
13. *Economic Report of the President, 1982*, p. 291.
14. *Monthly Labor Review* (May 1982), p. 85.
15. *Statistical Abstract, 1981*, pp. 99, 102, 108, 100.
16. Focusing on well-known CPI housing measurement problems, some analysts have argued that inflation in the necessities is less than inflation as measured by the overall Consumer Price Index. But Joseph Bowring, using a variety of experimental housing cost indices and incorporating new data on higher food and energy expenditures of the poor during the 1970s, has shown that necessity-related inflation is higher than measured by the CPI in all instances. Others believe that inflation during the 1970s hurt virtually all income classes "relatively" the same. The argument ignores the obvious distinction between the poor (who are intensely burdened by an equivalent "relative" percentage statistical loss in real income) and the rich. Bowring also shows that low- and moderate-income families suffered a larger relative loss in real incomes when the effects of expenditures on energy and food are accounted for. See Joseph J. Minarik, "A Critique"; Gar Alperovitz and Jeff Faux, "Missing the Point: A Reply"; and Joseph Bowring, "Necessities Inflation and Distributional Impact," *Challenge* (Jan.–Feb. 1981); Joseph Bowring, "How Bad Were the Seventies?" *Challenge* (July–Aug. 1981), pp. 42–50, and letter published in *Challenge* (Nov.–Dec. 1981).
17. An important exception that begins to explore new anti-inflation strategies in connection with food and energy is Barry Bosworth and Robert Z. Lawrence, *Commodity Prices and the New Inflation* (Washington, D.C.: Brookings Institution, 1982). See also the plea by James Tobin and Robert Solow, for work on housing and medical sector issues, "Liberals Have More to Do Than Laugh," *The Washington Post* (Jan. 10, 1982).

18. For an initial statement of the following argument see Gar Alperovitz and Jeff Faux, "An Economic Program for the Coming Decade," *Democratic Review* (Nov. 1975); Gar Alperovitz and Jeff Faux, "Building a Democratic Economy," *The Progressive* (July 1977); and Leslie E. Nulty, *Understanding the New Inflation: The Importance of the Basic Necessities* (Washington, D.C.: Exploratory Project for Economic Alternatives, 1977).
19. Memo to Governor Carter and Bert Lance from Patrick Caddell, "Consumer Confidence" (December 20, 1976).
20. "Inflation and the Working Poor," *Boston Globe* (July 29, 1979).
21. Paul Blumberg, *Inequality in an Age of Decline* (New York: Oxford University Press, 1980), pp. 174–214.
22. Michael Best and William Connally, *The Politicized Economy* (Lexington, MA: Heath, 1972), pp. 80–81.
23. E. Ray Canterbery, "Basic Necessities and the Economic Crisis" (Tallahassee: Florida State University, Apr. 3, 1981), p. 2 (draft).

Chapter 10 ENERGY: STABILITY AND COMMUNITY

1. Walter Levy, "Oil: An Agenda for the 80's," *Foreign Affairs* (Summer 1981), p. 1085.
2. Harvey O'Connor, *The Empire of Oil* (New York: Monthly Review Press, 1955), pp. 66–76.
3. Energy Action, "Cash Flow Sheet" and "Where Have All The Dollars Gone?" (June 21, 1981) in Karl Frieden, "The Impact of Rising Energy Prices on the Poor" (Washington, D.C.: National Center for Economic Alternatives, June 29, 1981) (unpublished report).
4. Federal Trade Commission, *Quarterly Financial Report for Manufacturing, Mining, and Trade Corporations* (first quarter 1981); Democratic Study Group, "Windfall Profit Tax Conference Report," *Fact Sheet No. 96–29* (Mar. 7, 1980); and *Newsweek* (Nov. 30, 1981), p. 80.
5. The windfall profits tax is estimated at 23 percent of the increase in oil company revenues due to decontrol. Democratic Study Group, "Windfall Profits Tax."
6. *Newsweek* (Feb. 9, 1981), p. 65.
7. *Monthly Energy Review* (Aug. 1983), pp. 6, 8, 15.
8. Ibid. (Mar. 1983), p. 22 (based on real dollars).
9. Roger Stobaugh and Daniel Yergin, eds., *Energy Future* (New York: Random House, 1979), p. 157.
10. Thornton Bradshaw, "My Case for National Planning," *Fortune* (Feb. 1977), pp. 100–104.
11. "Has the Persian Gulf Passed Its Prime?" *Washington Post* (December 27, 1981).
12. Cited in Robert Sherrill, "The Case Against the Oil Companies," *The New York Times Magazine* (Oct. 14, 1979), pp. 105, 104.

13. Karl Frieden, "The Perils of Oil Import Dependency," Part IV (Washington, D.C.: National Center for Economic Alternatives, 1980), p. 50 (unpublished report) (emphasis added).
14. Ibid.
15. Solar Energy Research Institute (SERI), *A New Prosperity: Building a Sustainable Energy Future* (Andover, Mass.: Brick House Publishing Company, 1981), p. 1.
16. Ibid., p. 1.
17. Ibid., p. 2.
18. Ibid., p. 3; *The New York Times* (Feb. 1, 1982).
19. *A New Prosperity*, p. 5.
20. Office of Management and Budget, *Major Themes of Additional Budget Details* (Fiscal Year 1983), p. 187.
21. See, for example, *Energy Future: A New Prosperity;* The Ford Foundation Energy Policy Project Staff, *A Time to Choose: America's Energy Future* (Cambridge, Mass.: Ballinger, 1974); Roger Sant, "The Least-Cost Energy Strategy: Minimizing Consumer Costs Through Competition" (Arlington, Va.: The Energy Productivity Center of the Mellon Institute, 1979); and the National Research Council's Committee on Nuclear and Alternative Energy Systems, "U.S. Energy Demand: Some Low Energy Futures," *Science* (Apr. 14, 1978).
22. Committee on the Budget, U.S. House of Representatives, "President Reagan's FY1983 Budget" (Feb. 1982), p. 85.
23. Office of Management and Budget, Appendix to the Budget for Fiscal Year 1984, pp. I-53, -54.
24. Testimony of James Benson before the Joint Economic Committee, "Creating Jobs Through Energy Policy" (Washington, D.C.: USGPO, Mar. 15 and 16, 1978), pp. 27 et seq.
25. For a similar recent analysis, see "A Perspective on Electric Utility Capacity Planning," Report of the Congress: Small Research Service, for the Subcommittee on Energy Conservation and Power, of the Committee on Energy and Commerce. U.S. House of Representatives (Aug. 1983).
26. *The New York Times* (Jan. 13, 1980).
27. *A Nuclear Energy Primer: Issues for Citizens,* League of Women Voters Educational Fund (1982), pp. 12–13.
28. "Exxon's Abrupt Exit from Shale," *Fortune* (May 31, 1982), p. 105.
29. Roger Sant's research has found that in 1978, with existing technologies, the United States could have used 17 percent less energy than it did *and still maintained prevailing living standards.* See Sant, "The Least-Cost Energy Strategy."
30. Marc H. Ross and Robert H. Williams, *Our Energy: Regaining Control* (New York: McGraw-Hill, 1981).
31. Information provided by Kathy Fletcher, Seattle, City Light Company.
32. Ibid.

33. James Ridgeway, *Energy-Efficient Community Planning* (Emmaus, Pa.: JG Press, 1979), p. 50.
34. Ibid., p. 49.
35. Ibid., p. 40.
36. Jan Hamrin, "Energy Saving Homes: Don't Bet on Technology Alone," *Psychology Today* (Apr. 1979), pp. 18, 32–33.
37. "Looking Ahead by Cutting Back," *Time* (Nov. 10, 1980), p. 86.
38. *Energy Consumption in New York City* (New York City Energy Office, 1981), p. 6.
39. *Community Energy Self-Reliance: Proceedings of the First Conference on Community Renewable Energy Systems*, sponsored by the Solar Energy Research Institute, U.S. Department of Energy, University of Colorado at Boulder (Aug. 20–21, 1979) (Washington, D.C.: USGPO, 1980), p. 48.
40. "Looking Ahead by Cutting Back," *Time* (Nov. 10, 1980), p. 86.

Chapter 11 FOOD

1. *Monthly Labor Review* (Feb. 1981), p. 106, (Apr. 1981), p. 94.
2. *Economic Report of the President, 1982*, p. 248.
3. U.S. Department of Agriculture, *A Time to Choose* (Washington, D.C.: USGPO, 1981), pp. 24–25.
4. *The Global 2000 Report to the President, Technical Report* (Washington, D.C.: Council on Environmental Quality, 1980–81), p. 28.
5. Ibid., Vol. 1, p. 12.
6. Frances Moore Lappé, *Diet for a Small Planet* (New York: Ballantine Books, 1975), pp. 9, 10, 14.
7. Dan Morgan, *The Merchants of Grain* (New York: Viking Press, 1979).
8. *The New York Times* (Dec. 5, 1976).
9. *Agricultural Outlook*, U.S. Department of Agriculture (Apr. 1983), p. 1.
10. Anthony Lewis, "The Reagan Record (2)," *The New York Times* (Jan. 16, 1983).
11. U.S. Department of Agriculture, "Economic Indicators of the Farm Sector: Production and Efficiency Statistics," Statistical Bulletin No. 65 (Washington, D.C.: USGPO, 1979), p. 90.
12. Barry Commoner, *The Closing Circle* (New York: Alfred A. Knopf, 1971), pp. 149–50.
13. Office of Management and Budget, *Additional Details of Budget Savings* (Washington, D.C.: USGPO, Apr. 1981), p. 27.
14. *Survey of Current Business* (Nov. 1980), p. S-11.
15. *Statistical Abstract, 1981*, pp. 5, 657.
16. *Statistical Abstract, 1971*, p. 336, and *1981*, p. 463.
17. *Business Week* (Oct. 13, 1980), p. 133 (emphasis added).

18. Jeff Faux, "Reclaiming America," *Working Papers for a New Society* (Summer 1973).
19. *Business Week* (Mar. 22, 1982 and Apr. 5, 1982).
20. *The Washington Post* (Jan. 28 and 30, 1982); *The New York Times* (Jan. 30, 1982).
21. E. Philip LeVeen, "Towards a New Food Policy: A Dissenting Perspective" (Apr. 1981), Berkeley, California (unpublished paper), pp. 49, 51, 52.
22. Schnittker Associates, "Stabilizing Domestic Food Prices by Changes in the Export Marketing System," unpublished report (Washington, D.C.: National Center for Economic Alternatives, Jan. 1979), pp. 16–19.
23. Richard Barnet, *The Lean Years* (New York: Simon & Schuster, 1980), p. 165.
24. Ibid., p. 172.
25. Jim Hightower, *The National Catholic Reporter* (Dec. 1979).
26. *Statistical Abstract 1980*, p. 706; *There Are Alternatives* (Washington, D.C.: The COIN Campaign, 1979).
27. See the Industrial Reorganization Act, 92nd Congress, 2nd Session, Senate Bill 3832.
28. Michael Schaaf, *Cooperatives at the Crossroads* (Washington, D.C.: Exploratory Project for Economic Alternatives, 1977), p. ix.
29. Joe Belden with Gregg Forte, *Toward a National Food Policy* (Washington, D.C.: Exploratory Project for Economic Alternatives, 1976), p. 152.
30. Barry Commoner, "The Need for Renewable Energy: The Transition to Solar," *Current*, June 1979, pp. 8, 9.

Chapter 12 HEALTH AND HOUSING

1. See the hearings before the Subcommittee on Long-Term Care of the Special Committee on Aging, U.S. Senate, "Nursing Home Care in the United States," various volumes (Nov. 1974).
2. *Statistical Abstract, 1981*, pp. 99, 100.
3. *Healthy People: The Surgeon General's Report on Health Promotion and Disease Prevention* (Rockville, Md.: U.S. Public Health Service, 1979), p. 6.
4. Dr. Quentin Young, "The High Cost of Health Care," Committee for a National Health Service (Washington, D.C., 1978).
5. *Statistical Abstract, 1981*, pp. 103, 104.
6. Committee for National Health Insurance, "Health Care for All Americans" (Washington, D.C., 1980), p. 6.
7. U.S. Office of Consumer Affairs, *People Power* (Washington, D.C.: USGPO, 1980), pp. 290–93.

8. *The New York Times* (May 7, 1978).
9. Congressional Quarterly, *Health Policy: The Legislative Agenda* (Washington, D.C., 1980), p. 68.
10. See "The Health Service Act," H.R. 3884, *Congressional Record* (June 11, 1981).
11. American Medical Association study, reported in *The Washington Post* (Oct. 15, 1983).
12. *Health Policy: The Legislative Agenda*, p. 56.
13. It is estimated that the health-*care* system contributes only about 10 percent to the improvement of personal health; the remaining 90 percent depends upon social, economic, and behavioral factors. As the U.S. Surgeon General pointed out: "Nearly all the gains against the once-great killers . . . have come as a result of improvements in sanitation, housing, nutrition, and immunization." *Healthy People*, p. 6.
14. *Federal Reserve Bulletin* (Mar. 1982), p. A50.
15. Calculations based on Bureau of Census, *Annual Housing Survey, 1980*, Part A, pp. 11, 12.
16. *Statistical Abstract, 1980*, p. 787.
17. Calculations based on standard interest-rate tables.
18. *Economic Report of the President, 1982*, p. 284.
19. *AFL-CIO Federationist* (Nov. 1980), p. 23.
20. Federal Home Loan Bank Board, *Journal* (Aug. 1982), p. 72.
21. Phone call to U.S. Census Bureau (May 1981).
22. National Association of Home Builders, in Rick Rybeck, "Housing, Inflation, and the Poor," unpublished report (Washington, D.C: National Center for Economic Alternatives, 1981).
23. Rybeck, "Housing, Inflation, and the Poor," p. 2.
24. *Dollars and Sense* (Oct. 1978); *Shelterforce #15* (May 1979).
25. Cushing Dolbeare, president, National Low Income Housing Coalition, "The Need to Limit Homeowner Deductions," Testimony before the House Committee on Ways and Means, U.S. House of Representatives (Mar. 31, 1981), citing work done by Anthony Downs of the Brookings Institution.
26. *U.S. Budget, Fiscal Years 1976 and 1982*.
27. *Historical Statistics of the United States, 1790–1970*, pp. 641–42.
28. Cushing Dolbeare testimony.
29. David Linowes, "Build Houses, Stimulate the Economy," *The New York Times* (July 1, 1980).
30. National Association of Housing Co-ops (Washington, D.C., May 1981).
31. *People Power*, pp. 129–30, 108–10.
32. *The New York Times* (June 6, 1976).
33. Computer runs from U.S. Department of Housing and Urban Development (Mar. 6, 1981).

34. *Shelterforce* (Spring 1979), p. 9.
35. Robert C. Wood, *The Necessary Majority: Middle America and the Urban Crisis* (New York: Columbia University Press, 1972), pp. 87–88.
36. Robert Lightfoot, "Public Ownership in Europe," unpublished report (Washington, D.C.: Exploratory Project for Economic Alternatives, 1974).
37. American Institute of Architects, *A Plan for Urban Growth: Report of the National Policy Task Force* (Jan. 1972).

Chapter 13 BREAKING THE INFLATION BARRIER

1. *OECD Economic Surveys: Austria* (Fall 1982), p. 222.
2. David D. Driscoll, "Wage and Price Policy in Austria," in "Wage and Price Policies in Australia, Austria, Canada, Japan, the Netherlands, and West Germany," Joint Economic Committee (June 24, 1982), p. 16.
3. Robert A. Gordon, *Economic Instability and Growth: The American Record* (New York: Harper & Row, 1974), p. 14.
4. *The Wall Street Journal* (Jan. 16, 1979); *The New York Times* (Feb. 26, 1979).
5. Arthur Okun and George Perry, eds., "Special Issue: Innovative Policies to Slow Inflation," *Brookings Papers on Economic Activity*, No. 2 (1978).
6. Strictly speaking, TIP proposals also include those offered by Henry Wallich, Lawrence Seidman, and others, which use tax *penalties* rather than incentives to achieve compliance. But the use of legal tax penalties for violations of a given standard (to the extent they are severe enough to work) in fact transforms TIP proposals into a mechanism extremely close to mandatory controls. See Sidney Weintraub and Henry Wallich, "A Tax-Based Incomes Policy," *Journal of Economic Issues* (June 1971), and Lawrence S. Seidman, "Tax-Based Incomes Policies," in Okun and Perry, eds., "Special Issues."
7. Robert F. Lanzillotti et al., "Phase II in Review: The Price Commission Experience" (Washington, D.C.: Brookings Institution, 1975).
8. *Economic Report of the President, 1982*, p. 277.
9. Barry Bosworth in Okun and Perry, "Special Issue," p. 20.
10. On the need for mandatory controls and sectoral policies, particularly in connection with energy and food, see Barry Bosworth, "Policy Choices for Controlling Inflation," in "Controlling Inflation: Studies in Wage/Price Policy" (Washington, D.C.: Center for Democratic Policy, 1981).
11. On administering controls, see Thomas Dougherty, *The New Inflation* (Lexington, Mass.: Lexington Books, 1981).
12. For an overview of related issues involved in such definitions, see Edward S. Herman, *Corporate Control, Corporate Power*, a Twentieth Cen-

tury Fund Study (New York: Cambridge University Press, 1981), pp. 187–94.

13. See Lawrence S. Seidman, "Tax-Based Economic Policies."
14. Malcolm Sawyer, "Income Distribution in OECD Countries," p. 14.
15. Lester Thurow, *The Zero-Sum Society*, pp. 201, 202.
16. Ibid., p. 156.
17. *Statistical Abstract, 1981*, p. 388.
18. Lester Thurow, *The Zero-Sum Society*, p. 172.
19. For a detailed analysis of popular opinion on income distribution, see Lee Rainwater, *What Money Buys: Inequality and the Social Meanings of Income* (New York: Basic Books, 1974), especially Chap. 3. See also Jennifer L. Hochschild, *What's Fair?: American Beliefs About Distributive Justice* (Cambridge, Mass.: Harvard University Press, 1981).
20. *Economic Report of the President, 1982*, p. 317.
21. *The Wall Street Journal* (Feb. 3, 1983).
22. Ronald Muller, *Revitalizing America*, p. 306.
23. Philip Stern, "Reining the Fed," *The New York Times* (Jan. 16, 1981).
24. Frank P. Jones, *Macrofinance* (Cambridge, Mass.: Winthrop Publishers, 1978), p. 80.
25. Lester Thurow, in *Newsweek* (Mar. 1, 1982), p. 29.
26. Leland S. Stauber, "Income Policy: Sources of Success in Austria," 6th Annual Convention of Eastern Economic Association, Montreal, Canada (May 8–10, 1980), pp. 4, 15, 16.

Chapter 14 BEYOND THE BROKER STATE

1. Charles Lindblom, *Politics and Markets* (New York: Basic Books, 1977), p. 356.
2. Ralph Nader, "The Case for Federal Chartering," in R. Nader and Mark Green, eds., *Corporate Power in America* (New York: Grossman Publishers, 1973), pp. 67–93.
3. Edward Herman, *Corporate Power, Corporate Control* (New York: Cambridge University Press, 1981).
4. *Common Cause* (Aug. 1982).
5. Joseph Schumpeter, *Capitalism, Socialism, and Democracy*, 3rd ed. (New York: Harper & Row, 1950), p. 134.
6. H. C. Simons, *Economic Policy for a Free Society* (Chicago: University of Chicago Press, 1948), p. 34.
7. Ibid., pp. 57–60.
8. See the essay "A Positive Program for Laissez Faire," ibid., pp. 40–77.
9. Ibid., pp. 58–59.
10. Henry Fairlie, "Profit Without Honor," *The New Republic* (May 7, 1977).
11. *Publishers Weekly* (Sept. 3, 1982).
12. At the state level, governments have reserved powers that allow them to

operate in any manner not specifically denied to them by the federal Constitution or by their own statutes. These powers have been liberally interpreted, as illustrated by Chief Justice Taft's opinion in a leading case that a state may engage in "almost any private business if the legislature thinks the state's engagement in it will help the general public and is willing to pay the cost of the plant and incur the expense of the operation." See *Wolff Packing Company* v. *Court of Industrial Relations of the State of Kansas,* 262 U.S. 522 (1923); Wolfgang Friedman, ed., *Public and Private Enterprise in Mixed Economies,* Chap. 6 (New York: Columbia University Press, 1974); and Meredith Wright and Gladys Kessler, "Property Rights and Public Enterprise," unpublished manuscript (Washington, D.C.: Exploratory Project for Economic Alternatives, 1975).

13. Annemarie Hauk Walsh, *The Public's Business: The Politics and Practice of Government Corporations* (Cambridge, Mass.: MIT Press, 1978), p. 346.
14. *Public Power,* as reported in *Bangor* (Me.) *Daily News* (Sept. 1, 1982).
15. "Public Power Costs Less," *Public Power* (May–June 1981), pp. 14 16.
16. Ibid., p. 16.
17. *Taking Charge: A New Look at Public Power* (Washington, D.C.: Environmental Action Foundation, 1976), pp. 23, 24.
18. Ibid., p. 33.
19. Charles Lindblom, *Politics and Markets,* p. 114; Chalmers Johnson, *Japan's Public Policy Companies* (Washington, D.C.: American Enterprise Institute, 1978), p. 14; William Keyser and Ralph Windle, eds., *Public Enterprise in the EEC* (Alphen gan den Rijn, Netherlands: Sit Thobb and Woodhoff, International Publishers, 1980).
20. "The State in the Market," *The Economist* (Dec. 20, 1979), p. 51.
21. *The Wall Street Journal* (Sept. 3, 1974 and Aug. 12, 1975).
22. *The Wall Street Journal* (May 23, 1974).
23. *The Wall Street Journal* (Feb. 5, 1975).
24. William A. Robson, *Nationalized Industry and Public Ownership,* 2nd ed. (London: George Allen & Unwin, 1969), p. 440.
25. Richard Pryke, *Public Enterprise in Practice* (New York: St. Martin's Press, 1979), p. 103.
26. Ibid., pp. 442, 444.
27. William Shepherd, *Public Enterprise: Economic Analysis of Theory and Practice* (Lexington, Mass.: Lexington Books, 1976), p. 110.
28. John Kenneth Galbraith, *Economics and the Public Purpose* (Boston: Houghton Mifflin, 1972), p. 242.
29. See Chapter II, "Worker Ownership," in Karl Frieden, *Workplace Democracy and Productivity,* pp. 7–17, and "Turning Workers into Bosses," *Mother Jones* (Nov. 1982).
30 Estimates by William Schweke, program director, Corporation for Enterprise Development, Washington, D.C.

31. See, for example, H. R. 2847, 98th Congress, 1st Session, for a comprehensive federal bill dealing with advance notification of plant closings and permanent layoffs and with retraining for dislocated workers.
32. See *An Evaluation of the Title VII (CDC) Program,* prepared for the Community Services Administration (1981) by the National Center for Economic Alternatives, for details on the program's operations.
33. *Statistical Abstract, 1982,* p. 669.
34. See *The United States Government Manual, 1982/83,* pp. 648–49, for a description of the bank's operations.
35. Quoted in Gordon Chase, "Managing Compared," *The New York Times* (Mar. 14, 1978).

Chapter 15 TOWARD DEMOCRATIC PLANNING

1. Kalman H. Silvert, *The Reason for Democracy* (New York: Viking Press, 1977), excerpted in *Society* (May–June 1977), p. 31.
2. Alfred Eichner, quoted in Ronald Muller, *Revitalizing America* (New York: Simon & Schuster, 1980), p. 303, emphasis added.
3. *The Wall Street Journal* (Aug. 12, 1975).
4. See Clement Bezold, ed., *Anticipatory Democracy: People in the Politics of the Future* (New York: Vintage Books, 1978), esp. pp. 5–35.
5. Felix Rohatyn, "Alternatives to Reaganomics," *The New York Times Magazine* (Dec. 5, 1982), and Senator Edward Kennedy, "The U.S. Needs a NASA to Help Run Its Economy," *Newsday* (Apr. 6, 1983).
6. Advisory Commission on Intergovernmental Relations, "Regional Growth: Interstate Tax Competition" (Washington, D.C.: Mar. 1981), p. 20.

Chapter 16 REBUILDING AMERICA

1. Hannah Arendt, *Between Past and Future: Eight Excercises in Political Thought* (New York: Viking Press, 1954), p. 9.
2. See, for example, the support for wage-price controls noted in *Public Opinion* (Dec./Jan. 1980), p. 21; *The New York Times* (Feb. 11, 1980), and *Fortune* (Mar. 1979); for gas rationing, *The New York Times* (June 12, 1979) and, *The Wall Street Journal* (Feb. 11, 1980); for food price controls and limits on food exports, cited in Joe Belden, *Toward a National Food Policy* (Washington, D.C.: Exploratory Project for Economic Alternatives, 1976), p. 40; for national health insurance and full employment policies, *Fortune* (Mar. 1979).
3. *Statistical Abstract, 1981,* pp. 482, 485.
4. *The New York Times* (Nov. 14, 1982).
5. *Statistical Abstract, 1981,* pp. 40–41, 122; *Time* (Apr. 23, 1979).

6. Daniel Yankelovich, "New Rules in American Life: Searching for Self-Fulfillment in a World Turned Upside Down," *Psychology Today* (Apr. 1981), p. 85.
7. Kevin Phillips, *Post-Conservative America: People, Politics, and Ideology in a Time of Crisis* (New York: Random House, 1982).
8. Raymond Williams, *Culture and Society, 1780–1950* (New York: Harper Torchbooks, Harper and Row, 1958), p. 334.
9. John Friedman, *Retracking America: A Theory of Transactive Planning* (Garden City, N.Y.: Doubleday, 1973), p. 231.
10. *The New York Times* (March 8, 1981).
11. President's Task Force on Private Sector Initiatives, *Volunteers: A Valuable Resource* (1982), pp. 4, 8–10.

Index

About the Authors

Gar Alperovitz and Jeff Faux are codirectors of the National Center for Economic Alternatives, a research organization. Gar Alperovitz, historian and economist, lives in Washington, D.C., and writes and speaks often on national economic affairs. Jeff Faux is a professional economist and participates in politics and economic affairs at all levels. He lives in Maine.